Swings
Hanging from Every Tree

Daily
Inspirations
for Foster
and
Adoptive
Parents

Second Edition

Published by:

Chaddock Press
205 South 24th Street, Quincy, IL 62301
(217)222-0034

2nd Edition © 2012, Chaddock Press., U.S.A.
All rights reserved.

International copyright protection is reserved under Universal Copyright Convention, and bilateral copyright relations of the U.S.A.

No part of this book may be reproduced, stored in a retrieval system, or transmitted in any form or by any means, electronic, mechanical, photo-copying, recording or otherwise, without express written permission of the author or publisher. If you would like to use written excerpts in a newsletter or other printed material, please reference your source (e.g., Swings Hanging from Every Tree, ©2012, Chaddock Press).

Chaddock Press has made an honest effort to insure the accuracy of all quotations and stories referenced or presented in this book. Any mis-attributed or otherwise incorrect quotes are unintentional errors. Any similarity between persons or places presented in this text and those of any particular reader are purely coincidental.

Cover and interior design by Kim Rokusek, Chaddock Press
Cover photo by Shutterstock
Interior pictures by Shutterstock, iStockphoto, Chaddock staff and students.

We are pleased to feature photos including some of our Chaddock children, staff and friends within this publication. The photos included are not reflective of or the actual subject of the story presented on the page. In no way are the photos connected to any stories that are included within "Swings Hanging from Every Tree".

ISBN # 0-9859696-0-8

Acknowledgments

"Swings Hanging from Every Tree" was first published in 2001 by Wood 'n Barnes Publishing. Spend 5 minutes with this book and you will know that "Swings" was a labor of love for the team at Wood 'n Barnes. What they have created in this book is inspiration, love, understanding, and support all bound together in a neat little package for foster and adoptive parents. The lovely and unexpected surprise is that anyone who loves a child can find inspiration between the covers of "Swings."

It is with great appreciation that we thank the original team that gave the gift of "Swings Hanging from Every Tree" to readers from across the world:

David Wood, Wood 'n Barnes Publishing

Ramona Cunningham, Wood 'n Barnes Vice President, Editor, and Parent

Susan Stone, Writer, Foster/Adoptive Parent, Administrator, and Case Worker

Dargie Arwood, Contributor, Foster/Adoptive/Biological Mother and Grandmother

Canela Winstead, Assistant Editor

When Chaddock was approached by David Wood about purchasing the rights to "Swings Hanging from Every Tree" our team jumped at the opportunity without hesitation. By providing understanding and inspiration to readers, "Swings" reflects our mission of providing hope and healing to children and families. It is a perfect fit for Chaddock.

Our goal with the second publication has been to improve a good thing and ensure that more copies are available to parents who can benefit from the daily inspiration it provides. We have achieved that goal but it wouldn't have been possible without the Chaddock Press team and supporters.

Debbie Reed, Chaddock President/CEO

Contents

January

		Page
1	Aging Out / Pat	2
2	Bumblebee / Susan	3
3	Make a List / Dargie	4
4	Profound Comfort / Bobbi	5
5	Smudged Fingerprints / Dargie	6
6	One at a Time / Robin	7
7	Pizza / Dargie	8
8	Advice from an Adopted Child / Jackie	9
9	Children Are Our Future / Sarah	10
10	Courageous Living / Susan	11
11	New Habits / Dargie	12
12	Being Family / Debi	13
13	Finding Your Place / Susan	14
14	With Care from God / Jerry	15
15	Dessert Anyone? / Dargie	16
16	Not Quite Grown / Susan	17
17	Little Guests / Dargie	18
18	Memories / Jean	19
19	Keep on Sliding / Susan	20
20	Mr. Swirly / Rick	21
21	The Boy On My Porch / Carolyn	22
22	The Mind You Save Could Be Your Own / Susan	23
23	Super Bowl / Lesa	24
24	Circle of Healing / Susan	25
25	Joy & Sorrow / Sheila	26
26	Open Heart / Dargie	27
27	Native Tongue / Susan	28
28	Delayed Gratification / Sally	29
29	A Lot of Good / Debi	30
30	Laugh / Dargie	31
31	Logical Consequences / Susan	32

February

		Page
1	Parenting is a Job / Susan	33
2	The Hunger / Bob	34
3	What the Future Holds / Pat & Susan	35
4	Behind the Scenes / Dargie	36
5	The Memory She Needed / Mony	37
6	Taking a Break / Susan	38
7	Black & White / Valerie	39
8	Creativity / Lesa	40
9	The Visit / Susan	41
10	How Long is Forever? / Twana	42
11	I Love You / Dargie	43
12	Family Portrait / Dargie	44
13	Warriors / Shirley	45
14	Love is All There Is / Susan	46
15	Feeling Safe / Dargie	47
16	Handprint / Susan	48
17	Mommy is a "Relative" Word / Karen	49
18	Keep Your Feet Off the Table / Jan	50
19	A Brief List / Gina	51
20	Are We Too Old for This? / Kate	52
21	I'm Gonna Tell You the Truth / Susan	53
22	Free Day Sunday / Susan	54
23	My Legacy / Robin	55
24	Paperwork / Dargie	56
25	Helping a Child Be a Child / Jan	57
26	A Long Way to Where He Is / Susan	58
27	Dad's Hat / Carolyn	59
28	You Could Get Buried Alive / Dargie	60
29	No Apparent Reason / Darryl & Milissa	61

March

		Page
1	Building a Foundation / Bob	62
2	Recipe for a Foster Home / Dargie	63
3	My Little Man / Karen	64
4	Making Time / Tish	65
5	Angry Girl / Susan	66
6	Belonging / Nancy	67
7	Different Paths / Susan	68
8	Walk on the Clouds / Dargie	69
9	Letter to My (Foster) Parents / Sharon	70
10	Gotya Day / Teresa & Susan	71
11	Developing Values / Susan	72
12	Green-Eyed Monster / Dargie	73
13	More to the World / Marie	74
14	Silver Lining / Shirley	75
15	Falling Apart / Dargie	76
16	What Do They Know? / Bonnie	77
17	St Patrick's Day Blessing / Susan	78
18	The Moon & the Stars / Susan	79
19	Things to Do / Dargie	80
20	Net Growth / Renee	82
21	These Boots / Nancy	83
22	Hitting the Jackpot / Susan	84
23	The Big Picture / Dargie	85
24	Pedaling Along / Rick	86
25	Sunday School Offering / Dargie	87
26	The Longing / Pam & Susan	88
27	Missing in Action / Bob	89
28	Some Stay / Donna	90
29	Perfect Little Angel / Jan	91
30	Sowing Seeds / Tonya Jo	92
31	Gone, But Never Forgotten / Trish	93

Contents

April

		Page
1	Building a Nest / Dargie	94
2	Progress / Susan	95
3	Easter Miracle / Bobbi	96
4	Good Enough? / Susan	97
5	Will You? / Charlene	98
6	Spring / Dargie	99
7	Forever Mommy / Robin	100
8	Hugs / Dargie	101
9	Everyday Is a New Day / Julie	102
10	Teach a Boy to Garden / Tonya	103
11	I Read the Book / Dargie	104
12	Making Changes / Susan	105
13	To My Precious Son / Leigh	106
14	I Changed the Program / Susan	107
15	The Most Valuable of All Things / Robin	108
16	Robot / Dargie	109
17	The Adventure / Sheila	110
18	Wit & Wisdom / Debi	111
19	Becoming A Woman / Dargie	112
20	Possibilities / Susan	113
21	Surprised By Kindness / Dargie	114
22	How Can We Win? / Deena	115
23	Successful Moments / Susan	116
24	Do We Care Enough? / Jim	117
25	How to Hope / Rick	118
26	Breakthroughs / Jan	119
27	Close to My Son / Kate	120
28	Meetings / Dargie	121
29	My Bunny / Bob	122
30	Out of the Mouths of Babes / Valerie	123

May

		Page
1	Quarantine / Dargie	124
2	Families Like Ours / Teresa	125
3	Advice to Myself / Steve	126
4	Baby Holders / Dargie	127
5	The Observation Room / Susan	128
6	Material Possessions / Robin	129
7	The Quilt / Susan	130
8	Weed Eater / Dargie	131
9	Simplify / Judy	132
10	Is It Worth It? / Marjie	133
11	Mommy, I Love You / Pat	134
12	A Rainbow of Children / Carolyn	135
13	Mother's Day / Patty	136
14	Mother By Choice / Susan	137
15	The Towel / Susan	138
16	Making A Difference / Susan	139
17	Purple / Anonymous	140
18	Birth Parents / Joanne	141
19	One Hour Speed Clean / Dargie	142
20	Group Homes / Wendy	143
21	It's a Scream / Dargie	144
22	Hellos & Goodbyes / Susan	145
23	Believe in Yourself / Albeta	146
24	Love with A Pure Heart / Dargie	147
25	Our Kids / Shirley & Tom	148
26	What Makes a Family? / Susan	149
27	Never Too Old / Dargie	150
28	Summer Job / Robin	151
29	Advice About Advice Giving / Rick	152
30	How Many Kids Do I Have? / Bob	153
31	Child's Play / Susan	154

June

		Page
1	Typical Siblings / Valerie	155
2	When the Student is Ready / Susan	156
3	Laundry / Dargie	157
4	Positive Addiction / Marjie	158
5	From Russia With Love / Troy	159
6	I'm Not the Enemy / Dargie	160
7	Fighting the Good Fight / Nancy	161
8	The Day We All Got Married / Dargie	162
9	Persistence / Susan	163
10	Trust / Tonya	164
11	Empty Nest? / Dargie	165
12	The Long Road / Lesa	166
13	Wrapped in Safe Arms / Darlene & Susan	167
14	Because You Loved Me / Stephanie	168
15	Birdseed Blunder / Dargie	169
16	Feed My Lambs / Lesa	170
17	Daddy's Home / Dargie	171
18	His, Mine & Theirs / Cathy	172
19	The Treasure Chest / "C" & Susan	173
20	Satisfying the Hunger / Carolyn	174
21	What it Takes / Matthew	176
22	What's It Really Like? / Tonya	177
23	Respite / Deena & Susan	178
24	Patience / Trish	179
25	Mommy, Don't Leave Us! / Dargie	180
26	My Dream for The Children / Sharon	181
27	All They Need Is Love? / Susan	182
28	To Adopt or Not to Adopt / Dargie	183
29	A Time & A Season / Cathy	184
30	To Go Up In a Swing / Robert Lewis Stevenson / Susan	185

v

Contents

July — Page
1. Life Book / Susan — 186
2. Insta-Party / Dargie — 187
3. Macaroni & Cheese / Nancy — 188
4. Missingmomitis / Susan — 189
5. Just for Today / Cheryl — 190
6. A Simple Blessing / Dargie — 191
7. Fresh Perspective / Cynthia — 192
8. Instant Know-How / Susan — 193
9. False Allegations / Liza — 194
10. Reality Check / Allen — 195
11. Laughter / Dargie — 196
12. Angels & Witches / Robin — 197
13. In the Greenhouse / Susan — 198
14. What Mountains? / Dargie — 199
15. Surprising Therapeutic Moments / Lesa — 200
16. Finding the Inner Child / Susan — 201
17. A True Miracle / Jennifer — 202
18. Watch What You Say / Dargie — 203
19. After They Leave / Marjie — 204
20. My Angel / Willie — 205
21. Unnecessary Moves / Wendy & Susan — 206
22. Shooting Bullets / Rick — 207
23. Perfect / Dargie — 208
24. Focus On The Positive / Trish — 209
25. Group Outing / Susan — 210
26. Creativity Abounds / Carolyn — 211
27. Passing Time / Dargie — 212
28. A Mouse in The House / Susan — 213
29. Chosen / Margaret — 214
30. Love Only Multiplies / Dargie — 215
31. Grace / Lesa — 216

August — Page
1. A Special Family / Dargie — 217
2. Stability / Stacey & Susan — 218
3. The Rewards of Fostering / Dianne — 219
4. Hurt Feelings / Dargie — 220
5. Right Time, Right Placement / Bobbi — 221
6. A Special School / Susan — 222
7. Little Skater / Dargie — 223
8. Roles / Jim — 224
9. Family of Choice / Sharon — 225
10. Sisters / Papa Duane — 226
11. Foster Parent Pledge / Karen/ Susan — 227
12. The Need to Nurture / Susan — 228
13. Jamie / Judy — 229
14. I Just Like Surprises / Dargie — 230
15. Alphabet Soup / Susan — 231
16. Raising Boys / Carolyn — 232
17. Does it Ever Get Easier? / Kathy — 233
18. The Highchair / Dargie — 234
19. Taking Time / Susan — 235
20. The Perfect Match / Marie — 236
21. Comparisons / Susan — 237
22. Up in the Air / Tish — 238
23. Keeping Promises / Dargie — 239
24. Sea Monkeys / Susan — 240
25. Christmas in August / Caroline & Dargie — 241
26. Borrowed Child / Dargie — 242
27. Powerful Words / Susan — 243
28. From the Heart of Kids / Gina — 244
29. Family Tree / Susan — 245
30. May You Have / Stephen — 246
31. My Butterfly / Margaret — 247

September — Page
1. Tea Party / Deena & Susan — 248
2. Family Meetings / Dargie — 249
3. The Phone Call / Robin — 250
4. Saving Grace / Donna — 251
5. For the Money? / Susan — 252
6. Serving Up Spaghetti / Dargie — 253
7. No Fame, Fortune, Glamour / Sandi — 254
8. Opening Every Door / Robin — 255
9. To Medicate or Not to Medicate / Dargie — 256
10. Time to Leave / Susan — 257
11. Willing to Risk / Lesa — 258
12. The Music of Living / Mony — 259
13. A Place for Everyone / Dargie — 260
14. Moving In / Stacey & Susan — 261
15. Guilt / Rick — 262
16. Rare Moments / Unknown — 263
17. The Unpacked Ornament / Robin — 264
18. Adjusting the Focus / Dargie — 265
19. Seeing Below the Surface / Susan — 266
20. Did Anyone Ever Tell You…? / Lesa — 267
21. Children Learn What They Live / Dargie — 268
22. Losing Mother / Carolyn — 269
23. Peer Pressure / Susan — 271
24. The Right Reason / Carolyn — 272
25. Like Everyone Else's Kids / Deena — 273
26. My Child Would Never Do That / Dargie — 274
27. What Every Kid Needs / Linda — 275
28. We Care / Kathy & Susan — 276
29. Egg Drop / Dargie — 277
30. Great Expectations / Sally — 278

Contents

October
		Page
1	Roller Coaster / Canela	279
2	Leaves / Dargie	280
3	I'm in the Way / Jen	281
4	Fantasy Date / Susan	282
5	Our First / JC & Neva	283
6	Don't Come with Me to the Bus / Dargie	284
7	Concurrent Planning / Deborah	285
8	The Lifestyle / Linda	286
9	Baggage / Dargie	287
10	The Circle of Giving / Jim & Susan	288
11	Investing in Humanity / Cathy	289
12	Visual Identity / Carolyn	290
13	Can Cows Jump Over the Moon? / Dargie	291
14	Until I Die / Susan	292
15	Freedom Walk / Robin	293
16	Survivor / Lesa	294
17	Adoption Announcements / Dargie	295
18	Whatever Works / Susan	296
19	Five More Minutes / Dargie	297
20	Saying Goodbye / Susan	298
21	Surprises / Dargie	299
22	Just One Kid / Liza	300
23	Let Us Eat Cake / Susan	301
24	Weighing The Balance / Bonnie & Susan	302
25	Through The Eyes of a Chid / Dargie	303
26	Loud & Clear / Susan	304
27	Should We Coddle the Children? / Deena	305
28	Grief / Dargie	306
29	Allegations of Abuse / Cathy	307
30	Adventure Walk / Susan	308
31	The Halloween Costume / Robin	309

November
		Page
1	Suggestions From a Foster Child / Marcy	310
2	Goal: Reunification / Dargie	311
3	Nurturing Males / Susan	312
4	Dress-Up Girl / JC & Neva	313
5	Visions & Dreams / Susan	314
6	Time for Yourself / Dargie	315
7	The Best Interest of the Child / Susan	316
8	Owning The Road / Dargie	317
9	Runaways / Robin	318
10	Teenagers / Dargie	319
11	Do You Work? / Linda	320
12	Dress-Up / Dargie	321
13	Holidays / Jim	322
14	Intermittent Reinforcement / Trish	323
15	Do It Your Way / Dargie	324
16	Compassionate Understanding / Steve	325
17	Letting Go / Susan	326
18	Landmarks / Dargie	327
19	Bunk Beds / Rick	328
20	The Fine Line / Susan	329
21	Little Helper / Dargie	330
22	What is Family? / Donna	331
23	"Thank You" / Dargie	332
24	Impact / Cathy	333
25	Magnificent Obsession / Susan	334
26	Willing To Give / Dargie	335
27	Roots / S.I.	336
28	From Their Heart To Yours / Gina	337
29	I Never Taught You To Breathe / Susan	338
30	Believe the Impossible /F.M.K.	339

December
		Page
	Thinking of Fostering? / Susan	340
1	A Good Christmas / Susan	341
2	School Meetings / Dargie	342
3	The One We Kept / JC & Neva	343
4	The Choice / Wendy & Susan	344
5	Christmas Love / Wendy	345
6	All Kinds of Love / Valerie & Susan	346
7	The Runaway / Dargie	347
8	Foreign Worlds / Susan	348
9	Experience / Dargie	349
10	Power Struggles / Carolyn	350
11	Role Reversal / Dargie	351
12	Coping With the System / Susan	352
13	Learning / Dargie	353
14	Someday / Deena	354
15	The Mother & Child Necklace / Susan	355
16	Leaving Too Soon / Dargie	356
17	Unspoken Messages / Susan	357
18	Giving Back / Donna	358
19	Never Give Up / F.M.K.	359
20	Overwhelmed / Dargie	360
21	Finding One's Magic / Susan	362
22	Christmas Memories / Stacey	363
23	Odd Lots / Pat/Susan	364
24	Wish List For Foster Parents / Susan	365
25	The Joy of Christmas / Tonya Jo	366
26	Heroes / Dargie	367
27	Courage / Anonymous	368
28	New Year's Eve Reflections / Dargie	369
29	Prayer for Our Foster Children / Dargie	370
30	Old Mommy / Susan	371
31	Endings / Susan	372

Introduction

When we discovered this book, we knew that we wanted to be a part of sharing it with even more foster and adoptive parents who truly are "angels on assignment" to the children who turn to them for love and support. The job is hard, and messy, and at times heartbreaking… and foster and adoptive parents gladly walk this path to give a precious child the chance for a better life. It is our hope that this book will help remind you that you are not alone. Whether it's a smile of recognition at a common experience reflected here, or an insight needed at just that moment, it is our hope that the daily stories shared here will help either lighten the load, or give a bit of extra strength to your back, to help you journey through another day.

Our thanks and blessings to you!
Debbie Reed, President/CEO of Chaddock School

This book was designed to be read on a daily basis. We realize that not all of us fit into the same daily pattern. Knowing this, we have included a couple of helpful features for those times when you need to hear or offer words of encouragement about a specific concern. The stories have been placed seasonally and a topical index is provided in the back of the book. We invite you to share the stories and quotes from this book with others. If you would like to use written excerpts in a newsletter or other printed material, please reference your source (e.g., Swings Hanging from Every Tree, ©2012, Chaddock Press).

Swings
Hanging from Every Tree

January 1

Aging Out

*"I'm not more than a wisp of smoke to the world,
but to God I am a flame of hope
and promise in a darkened room."*

Joan Noeldechen

In a day and age when many young people stay in their parents' home well into their twenties the child welfare system continues to emancipate foster children at the age of eighteen in most cases. Where do they go? Who do they turn to when they need help?

"It is when the checks stop coming that we really need to reexamine why we are doing this. I am a single parent; I have very little for my retirement. I do own a five bedroom house and an overgrown farmhouse. I am sixty years old and will probably have to work until I am seventy. I have some pretty things, a car that runs, a small IRA and a smaller savings account; but, more importantly I have over thirty grown kids who call from time to time to find out how I am. I also have about twenty who call me "Mom" and come to visit every few weeks. Would I have more money, a more secure future on this earth if I hadn't kept kids past their emancipation date, hadn't helped with college, bought shoes for the baby, paid for a week of daycare when the kids ran short, paid a gas or electric bill? Of course. But I believe there is another life where money doesn't matter, where my God will be pleased that I helped a child rather than saved a dollar."

Pat, foster parent for over 30 years to almost 100 children.

Bumblebee

2 January

"Aerodynamically, the bumblebee shouldn't be able to fly, but the bumblebee doesn't know it, so it goes on flying anyway."
Mary Kay Ash

He was barely eight, and very adult-like for his age. This boy thought he could do anything, and he tried whatever crossed his mind. It never really occurred to him that he might not be able to succeed at a task until he was in the middle of it and overwhelmed. At that point, he would solicit help from anyone within earshot.

His mother had been abused and neglected by her birth parents, spent several years in foster care, gone through one failed adoption, and was finally adopted as a teenager. Needless to say, she had difficulty with attachment. In her own way she learned it was important for her son to be attached to people, so she made sure he had the opportunity.

I was spending some time with him one evening when he decided to drag out a box containing the pieces for a wooden shelf. I was in the other room; he was watching television and trying to assemble this four-foot shelf. After realizing he was unable to complete it without help, he recruited me. At one point, I smashed my finger and he immediately jumped to my side and said, "I'll kiss it for you." I looked at him and clearly saw an attached child - a child who put himself in my place, related to the pain I felt, and offered to help me make it better. In that moment my heart smiled and I was hopeful.

Susan, foster and adoptive parent, grandparent, and former foster family recruiter and trainer.

January 3 — Make a List

"Each day, and the living of it, has to be a conscious creation in which discipline and order are relieved with some play and some pure foolishness."

May Sarton

I have doctor appointments, school meetings, various therapy sessions, not to mention a house to clean, and cabinets to stock. I cannot do it all in one day. I have to pace myself so I don't get overwhelmed.

Making a "to do" list helps me in many ways. First of all, I don't forget things… as long as I remember the list. Also, it gives me great pleasure and a sense of accomplishment to check things off.

A very wise lady once told me to prioritize my list. When I did she then said, "Now, scratch off everything past number ten."

I responded, "But, but…"

She said, "If you take on too much, you set yourself up for failure or burnout." She was right. Besides, kids aren't the only ones who need to succeed.

Why not make a list today that allows you to succeed. And then enjoy checking off your accomplishments!

Dargie, mother and grandmother of many step, birth, foster, and adopted children.

Profound Comfort

4 January

"Kind words can be short and easy to speak, but their echoes are truly endless."
Mother Teresa

We'd had our foster care license for a month when the social worker asked if I could meet her to pick up a one-day-old baby girl. I quickly grabbed some things and headed across town to the hospital where she filled me in… healthy baby… no known problems.

I could hear muffled voices and crying while the social worker was inside the room. The wait outside that room seemed like an eternity. I talked to the baby's nurse and another woman. I found out later that the other woman was the mother's counselor. I nearly panicked when the social worker came out without the baby and said I should go in and get the baby now.

As I entered the room, I prayed, "Please God, give me Your words to say to this new mother." As I stood there, she dressed the baby in the soft yellow outfit she had brought for the trip home. I waited as she wrapped her baby in the handmade quilt she had decorated so beautifully with fine embroidery work that included the baby's name. She finally looked up; I met her fearful gaze and said, "I'll take good care of your baby."

Weeks later she told me how much those simple words had meant to her and the peace she felt about releasing her baby into my care. God doesn't always give us the gift of profound eloquence. Sometimes God just gives us simple words of profound comfort.

Bobbi, birth, foster, and guardianship mom.

January 5 — Smudged Fingerprints

"Life is God's novel, so let him write it."
Isaac Bashevis Singer

We are in the long process of adopting a sixteen-year-old orphan we've had with us for almost two years. He made the decision to be adopted because he wants a forever family. I have learned that you cannot rush an adoption - even if nobody opposes.

Recently, after going to give my fingerprints, which is mandatory to adopt in our state, I got a call. The prints were smudged and must be redone, so it will be another six months or so for them to process. It will be close to his 18th birthday when we enter the judges chambers to sign for him to be our child.

When I think of criminals who leave perfect prints by accident and the thousands of prints I've cleaned from windows and doors, it amazes me that a forty-year-old mom cannot purposefully make a clean print! I must remember, though, that all of this is in God's hands, and He makes no mistakes. After all, He created all of our fingerprints uniquely. I guess it makes sense that it may take some time to create this uniquely wonderful family too.

Dargie, mother and grandmother of many step, birth, foster, and adopted children.

One at a Time

*"We are all better than we know;
if only we can be brought to realize this,
we may never be prepared to settle for anything less."*
                                                Kurt Hahn

I have often fostered orphaned kittens from a local animal rescue agency. These kittens require around-the-clock care, similar to that of an infant.

Once I had two separate litters of kittens, and at the same time I was fostering a self-centered, sometimes cruel, teenage girl who had little empathy for anyone. She immediately picked out her favorite kitten and would care for only that one. She ignored, scoffed at, and criticized the other kittens. One day, she coldly told her foster sister, "I hope your kitten dies!"

The next afternoon, I asked her about it as I picked up the kitten and let it walk across the table. I told her she had behaved as if she didn't care but I thought that was probably a defense from all the pain she had known. She turned her head away and a tear fell softly down her cheek. She cried and apologized to her foster sister. I put my hand on her shoulder and told her I appreciated her apology and that she could help care for the kittens because I knew she loved them. She did help care for them, always picking out one over the rest, loving it completely until finally only one remained.

Her love was never given freely. It came at a cost from deep inside. She could only risk it one person or one animal at a time.

Robin, foster parent to over 30 children, 3 children in pre-adoptive placement.

January 7 — Pizza

"Nothin' says lovin' like somethin' from the oven."
Pillsbury advertising slogan

Dough   1 pkg. dry yeast
2 cups hot water (not too hot)
dash or two of salt
1 t. sugar (to feed the yeast)
flour (enough to make the dough not sticky)

Mix yeast with water, salt, and sugar. Stir in flour a little at a time until ball forms. Let rise for about 15 minutes. Section and pat out onto an oiled pan sprinkled with corn meal. Top with tomato sauce, your choice of ingredients… and, of course, lots of cheese. Bake at 425° for about 15 - 20 minutes. It should be brown on top and bottom. Lift with spatula to check.

I have made homemade pizzas with almost every child that has passed through my home. I let them pat out the dough, top it, watch it bake, and eat it. It is a FUN experience, a little messy, but worth the effort. It gives the children a wonderful memory to take with them when they leave. Remember, there is no right way to make it, and the process is way more important than the product.

It is my hope that in the process of making pizzas the kids come to know that the same is true for people. We are all in process of becoming something more than we have been. And, even though we all roughly have the same basic ingredients, each of us is unique. As they enjoy their "imperfect" pizzas, I pray that they will come to know how wondrous they truly are.

Dargie, mother and grandmother of many step, birth, foster, and adopted children.

Advice from an Adopted Child

8 January

*"The purpose of life, after all, is to live it,
to taste experience to the utmost, to reach out eagerly
and without fear for newer and richer experiences."*
Eleanor Roosevelt

I would like to share some things I have learned from my own experience, as well as from the experiences of others I have talked to, about being an adopted child. Here is my quick list of advice:

1. Bonding begins at birth. Just because a baby is adopted doesn't mean you can't breast feed or hold your baby skin-to-skin on your breast while you feed him a bottle.
2. Get as much information on the birth family as you can and keep it in a special place. It is a nice feeling to see that your adoptive parents took the time to place your history in a nice book or box.
3. If you have a fertility issue, grieve the loss of the child you will never have. If you carry that baggage around, it will rear its ugly head over and over again.
4. Do not blame the birth family if your child has problems, especially not in front of your child.
5. Be as supportive as possible if your child wants to search for her birth parents. This is an opportunity to bring you closer together.
6. Accept your child for who s/he is. Unconditional love means a lot more than biology. Everything in life happens exactly the way it is supposed to happen. Your adopted child is the child you were meant to have.

Jackie, adopted at six-days-old, searched for and found her birth parents, currently works with emotionally disturbed children and is beginning her life as a mother.

January 9 — Children Are Our Future

"Things which matter most should never be at the mercy of things which matter least."
Goethe

I foster for a very simple reason. Children are our future. If I can make a difference in a child's life and help that life be better, more productive, happier, safer, then I think I have made the world a better place - one child at a time.

It's interesting to me that when I get frustrated or close to throwing in the towel, I happen to spend a bit of time with some former foster children who lived with me for years before being adopted by a wonderful family in my church. They come back and regale me with memories of the things we did together, just being a family.

They remember the little things, the time we made those special brownies or the human pyramid in the back yard. They remember the kitten, my silly songs, and the marigolds we planted. They remember the vacations too but not as much as the seemingly unimportant, everyday moments.

I am confident that the security and love I offered made a difference in their ability to successfully attach to that forever family. Despite the barriers in the system, loving and caring for a child is the easy part. It is also the part that makes a difference.

Sarah, single, foster and adoptive mom.

Courageous Living

10 January

"Have courage for the great sorrows of life and patience for the small ones. And when you have... accomplished your daily task, go to sleep in peace. God is awake."

Victor Hugo

I knew a boy who was about ten years old and in foster care for the first time. The plan was for him to go back home as soon as his mother and new stepfather completed the required tasks. He was doing okay in the foster home and enjoying visits with his parents.

As time went on, his mother decided she was not able to do what was required of her to get her son back. She made the decision to voluntarily relinquish her parental rights.

This boy, who had planned to return home, was now faced with losing his parent permanently. I wondered how a ten-year-old could possibly fathom this situation. I watched him come in to his therapy visits, and I heard of his very normal behavior within the loving foster family. He just went on living. I'm not sure I could have done that when I was ten.

Today, when I'm faced with a difficult task, I try to remember how hard it must have been for him to just get up and go on every day. I trust that his courage will serve him well, and I bless the family that helps him heal.

Susan, foster and adoptive parent, grandparent, and former foster family recruiter and trainer.

January 11 — New Habits

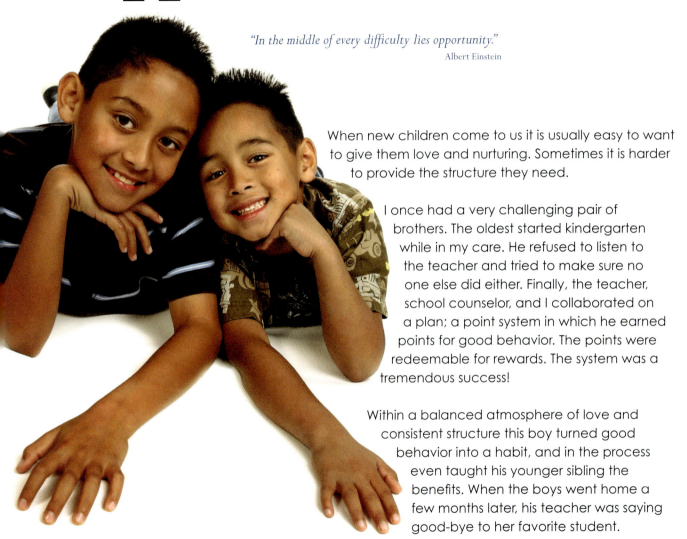

"In the middle of every difficulty lies opportunity."
Albert Einstein

When new children come to us it is usually easy to want to give them love and nurturing. Sometimes it is harder to provide the structure they need.

I once had a very challenging pair of brothers. The oldest started kindergarten while in my care. He refused to listen to the teacher and tried to make sure no one else did either. Finally, the teacher, school counselor, and I collaborated on a plan; a point system in which he earned points for good behavior. The points were redeemable for rewards. The system was a tremendous success!

Within a balanced atmosphere of love and consistent structure this boy turned good behavior into a habit, and in the process even taught his younger sibling the benefits. When the boys went home a few months later, his teacher was saying good-bye to her favorite student.

Dargie, mother and grandmother of many step, birth, foster, and adopted children.

Being Family

"We all enter the world with fairly simple needs: to be protected, to be nurtured, to be loved unconditionally, and to belong."
— Louise Hart

We have always tried to make every child who comes to our home feel that he or she is part of our family and that they belong, no matter how long they stay.

One day my four-year-old African American son was standing with me at the kitchen sink as we washed dishes. Outside the window was a tree and there were two squirrels playing as we watched. He watched them for a few minutes and then told me they were a mom and her little boy squirrel.

"How do you know that?" I asked.

He explained how they looked alike but said that one was smaller. Then he looked up at me, gave me a big hug and said, "And I look just like you Mom!"

With some surprise I asked why he thought that. He reached his little hand up and patted the dimple on my cheek and said, "'Cause we both gots a hole in our cheeks."

Debi, birth and adoptive parent, foster parent to over 30 children in the past 12 years.

January 13 — Finding Your Place

"Far away, there in the sunshine, are my highest aspirations. I may not reach them, but I can look up and see their beauty, believe in them, and try to follow where they lead."

— Louisa May Alcott

I always hoped for a role as a wife and mother. I imagined I would work to help make ends meet, but my focus would be on my family. I guess God had other plans.

At mid-life, I find myself single and never having given birth; but I have found many ways to have my dream anyway. I have cared for the children of my relatives as well as, kids who were total strangers to me at first. I have loved them all, and I have been blessed by each of them in return. And I have had to let many of them go.

It is not the life I imagined; but maybe it is the life I am really good at, maybe it is the life that makes God smile. If you have not yet found your niche, your place in the world, keep looking. Maybe you will find you are already living it. Maybe it just looks different than you imagined and you're living it anyway. It is amazing how life works that way sometimes.

Susan, foster and adoptive parent, grandparent, and former foster family recruiter and trainer.

With Care from God

14 January

"A family is a 'gallery of memories' to those who have been blessed by the presence of children."
— James Dobson

Our lives were empty, incomplete without a child.
We sent our prayers; in answer, God smiled.
Not knowing the plans that God had in store,
We opened our house to the kids at the door.

They came here with problems, issues and fears.
Unknown expectations, their eyes filled with tears.
They were away from their families, their mom and their dad.
Only carrying the memories of the times they have had,
Remembering the sad times, but especially the good,
Hoping to go home, yes wishing they could.

We opened our hearts and gave them our love,
Knowing in our hearts they were gifts from above.
To them we were strangers, new town, and new home,
New set of rules, new limits to roam,
Would we know what they liked, their hopes and their dreams?
Would we be there to hug them through pain and extremes?

As days went by, we adapted to the change
We all become family, it was no longer so strange.
The children got help, some birth parents too.
Back to their families, the dreams had come true.
Again life is empty, incomplete for a child.
Our prayers we sent and again God smiled.

Jerry, foster parent to 5 children in the year he has been fostering with his wife, Sharon.

January 15 — Dessert Anyone?

"Happiness is not a state to arrive at, but a manner of traveling."
Margaret Lee Runbeck

In their sometimes world of abuse, neglect, and constant change it is good to have funny moments for the foster kids to recall. It is especially good if it involves a person they trust and look up to. An example might be when that person makes a mistake and they get tickled instead of upset and everyone starts laughing together about it.

One Sunday before church, I had plenty of time to make a dessert for us to enjoy. I proceeded to put the ingredients into the blender and turn it on. Liquid flew all over the room and there I stood covered with the sticky sweetness. After the initial shock, I couldn't help but laugh. Dessert was dripping from my hair, clothes, and even my eyelashes. As I walked to the shower to clean up, the kids saw me.

That was one dessert that was enjoyed by all with no calories! They enjoyed seeing me covered with goo. Actually, it was hilarious. Cleanup was pretty extreme, but they have a fun memory. And even though I was the only one to actually get a taste, it made life a little sweeter for us all.

Dargie, mother and grandmother of many step, birth, foster, and adopted children.

Not Quite Grown

16 January

"It will help us and our children if we can laugh at our faults. It will help us tolerate our shortcomings, and it will help our children see that the goal is to be a human, not perfect."

Neil Kurshan

For those of us who adopt teenage children time is a strange concept. We come into these relationships with our hearts spilling over with all this love we have stored up to give. They come to us suspicious of that love and developmentally at a stage where it is their job to begin pulling away from parental influence.

At times they practically want to sit in our laps because the child inside them still craves parental love and attention. At other times they feel the stirrings of emerging independence that cause them to look at us as though we do not have a clue about the world. This is a normal phenomenon of adolescence, but for these children who have experienced so much inconsistency in their lives it can be extreme.

Parents are rarely ready for this impending separation, and adoptive parents, who have had so little time to teach all the lessons they believe are important, have the greatest challenge of all. While it seems we are being asked to give our four-year-olds the keys to the family car, they are not really four. We need to adjust our thinking to allow them to be nearly grown in the few short years we have them. We must focus on the things they have learned and how far they have come. We need to trust what we taught them, and we need to leave space for them to return to us throughout their lives; because, especially with these children, the learning will take place over a lifetime.

Susan, foster and adoptive parent, grandparent, and former foster family recruiter and trainer.

January 17 — Little Guests

"Misery is when grown-ups don't realize how miserable kids can feel."
Suzanne Heller

When I have kids for only a few days, I try my best to make it like a vacation. I have rules, of course, but I am not too rigid about them. I know that the child(ren) will soon be going to another place with another set of rules, and I want them to make the transition as painlessly as possible.

So, we snuggle (if they will) and read books (if age appropriate), watch movies, and talk. I fix their favorite foods, which are usually the easiest to cook anyway, and I do my best to make them feel like my pampered guests.

I have had several little "guests" leave us with arms reaching for me – partly because they liked it at my house but mainly for fear of the unknown. And, when I think of what it must be like to move from one place to another, with different people and different rules, I don't blame them a bit.

Dargie, mother and grandmother of many step, birth, foster, and adopted children.

Memories

18 January

"One thing I know: the only ones among you who are really happy are those who have sought and found how to serve."
— Albert Schweitzer

My last foster child is scheduled to leave soon because I have decided to stop fostering. I haven't seen many changes in the system over the years, but helping children has been very rewarding.

I have pictures of all the children, the day they arrived and the day they left. I learned that saying good-bye never gets easy, you only hope and pray they will be safe.

I have memories to comfort me. Memories of taking a child to the beach for the very first time and watching him run through the waves screaming with joy. I remember watching them dig into a banana split, or play on a playground. I loved the look on their faces when they got brand new clothes and shoes. It made me feel good to watch them parade around feeling good about themselves.

I am very grateful for a loving husband and family that have supported me for nine years. They have all been there through cries of a newborn waking for a feeding in the middle of the night, sick pre-schoolers, doctor visits, foster sibling rivalry, and sharing—lots of sharing. Sharing Mom and Dad, uncles and aunts, and grandparents with children they had never met.

That part of my life is over, and I will miss it. I will move on to do other wonderful things, but I will always have a special place in my heart for foster children.

Jean, birth, foster, and adoptive mom.

January 19 — Keep on Sliding

"Don't threaten a child: either punish him or forgive him."
Talmud

New foster and adoptive parents are often surprised by the things their charges do not know. One foster mother reported that her first foster child, a six-year-old boy, was unfamiliar with bathing. Her own six-year-old son had been in charge of his bath for sometime so it did not occur to her that her foster son would not be sure how things might work.

For his first bath she gave her foster son clean clothes, a washcloth, a towel, and a bottle of bubble bath. She told him to call her if he needed anything. Several minutes later she heard squealing coming from the bathroom and found both boys slipping and sliding on bubbles which had overflowed from the tub and were now covering the tile floor. She was informed that the foster child thought he was supposed to use the whole bottle of bubble bath instead of the capful her son knew to use.

At this point, several things could have happened, but she kept it light and assumed innocence. She told the boys, who were having a great time, that they could keep sliding until the bubbles were gone, and she stayed and watched to make sure they were safe. Later, she instructed her foster son in the proper way to use bubble bath.

A lighthearted approach and the presumption of innocence made what might have been a painful childhood memory into a happy time of learning and connection.

Susan, foster and adoptive parent, grandparent, and former foster family recruiter and trainer.

Mr. Swirly

"If the only solution tool you have is a hammer, then you tend to see every problem as a nail."
                                        Abraham Maslow

A fourteen-year-old, autistic, foster child had an interesting compulsion. He loved to watch things swirl round and round in the toilet bowl. He would hide clothing and towels under his shirt, sneak into the bathroom, throw an article in the bowl, and flush them away one at a time. He delighted in watching the articles swirling around the toilet before they disappeared.

You can imagine the sewage problem this caused (for the entire neighborhood). However, rather than punish Mr. Swirly, it was decided to prescribe periods of swirling with some important modifications. Several times each day he was allowed to swirl clothing and wash rags with a stick in the bathroom sink. Gradually, the location of swirling was changed from the sink to a bucket that was eventually moved to the laundry room. Once there, he was taught to wash and dry clothing. With the ultimate swirling experience of the clothing spinning in the washing machine and dryer, he found himself in "swirling heaven."

In many problems, we find the seeds of solution. Rather than attempting a wholesale expunging of a problem behavior, we may find more success in gently shaping troublesome activity into more appropriate actions. In many situations it is helpful to "meet the child where he is." If we restrain the urge to expect immediate change and to normalize the child, we often find a more gradual pace for change which the child will not sandbag, or for that matter, flush down the toilet.

Rick, clinical psychologist, trainer, and consultant who has worked with foster and adoptive children and their parents over the past 20 years.

January 21 — The Boy on My Porch

"Success seems to be largely a matter of hanging on after others have let go."

William Feather

I went home one day and found a neighbor boy sitting on my porch. He explained that he and his mother had a fight and when he left she clapped as he walked away.

I took him to the social services agency where I worked and let the supervisors handle the situation. He was in several placements over the next year or so and he was eventually thrown out of them because of his behavior. I was his worker for awhile, and I told a judge he needed the freedom to do some things on his own.

He went to a few more placements and then the agency asked him what he wanted. He said he wanted to come live with me because I was the only one who understood him. So, I became a foster parent, and he lived with me until he graduated from high school.

When he was of age, he was awarded custody of his little brother and a couple of years later he also got custody of his sister. He and the woman he has loved for many years now also have a child of their own.

Sometimes this boy would make me so upset I would break into a sweat and my bangs would stand straight in the air! Now when I think of him, I smile and I am grateful to have been able to provide what he needed.

Carolyn, social worker and foster parent to teen boys.

The Mind You Save Could Be Your Own

22 January

*"I'd rather see a lesson than hear one any day.
I'd rather you walk with me than merely show me the way."*
Unknown

Foster children often punish their foster parents for the wrongs done to them in the past. Of course, this is not a conscious decision; but as foster parents we feel the brunt of their pain and frustration.

Traditional parenting tells us we must be strong, increase structure, and let them know who the parent is. However, one of the basic problems for foster parents is that the birth parents are incapable for some reason of assuming that role at this point in time. How confusing this must be for these children.

Their reaction to being in a foster home can seem outrageously unbalanced with anger. We find ourselves thinking things we never thought we would. Like, "You ungrateful little brat!" or "If you want to see stubborn, I'll just show you!"

Often the solutions we used with our birth children do not work. And we cannot necessarily generalize parenting strategies from one foster child to the next. Each case is different and we have to be open to learning what each particular child needs. It helps to talk to other foster parents and get some ideas. Nothing can sound sweeter than a new idea from an experienced foster parent after you've tried everything you know to try. Take time to seek out other foster parents through your local association or in an on-line support group. The mind you save could be your own!

Susan, foster and adoptive parent, grandparent, and former foster family recruiter and trainer.

January 23 — Super Bowl

"Happiness is the sense that one matters."
Samuel Shoemaker

The foster parents of two boys, ages ten and twelve, were excited about getting to share their Super Bowl Party tradition. The party always included great food, fun game-related activities, and lots of cheering. The foster parents promoted the party enthusiastically, assuring the boys that it would be great fun. However, each time the subject arose, the boys acted bored or shrugged it off.

Finally, the foster dad expressed his disappointment at their lack of interest. "I thought you guys would really like this party, but you act like you don't even want to be there." The boys eyes grew wide. "You mean we can come to the party? We don't have to stay in our room?" Light bulbs turned on in everyone's minds.

The boys' history of Super Bowl Parties was that the adults had a great time, and the kids had to stay out of sight in their room or get physically punished. They thought the foster parents were rubbing in what a good time the adults would have. The foster parents never dreamed of hosting a non-child-friendly event and didn't realize they needed to clearly indicate that the boys were involved.

When the boys were still there a year later, they began to anticipate the next Super Bowl Party. They asked questions like, "Will we have another party?" Will you make that dip again?" Can I invite my friend?" Family traditions have an incredible way of healing old hurts.

Lesa, therapeutic foster parent and trainer of foster parents.

Circle of Healing

"Children are the message we send into a time we will never see."
Neva Everett

Last week we had a panel discussion for our foster parents in training. This particular group was small with only three people on the panel: two foster parents and a former foster child.

The training participants were riveted to their seats while the foster parents described the joys and surprises of fostering. However, the room filled with emotion as the other guest spoke. She spoke of her time in foster care and her chin quivered as she described the school counselor who picked her up from her foster home every morning at 6 a.m. so she wouldn't have to change schools and leave her friends. She told how much she wishes she could contact those foster parents now to thank them. She described how her gestures and table manners are specific bits of learning she picked up in the homes of strangers who cared for her years ago. And, she tells them all they can make a difference in the life of a child, even if it doesn't seem so at the time.

I can see she is healing as she thanks this room full of people who are getting ready to step into the shoes of those foster parents she still loves. I have to believe that her genuine gift of thanks reaches the spirit of those people who taught her not to lick her fingers at the table so many years ago.

Susan, foster and adoptive parent, grandparent, and former foster family recruiter and trainer.

January 25 — Joy & Sorrow

"She said she usually cried at least once each day not because she was sad, but because the world was so beautiful and life was so short."

Brian Andreas

Tonight, all my kids and I went bowling. We had such a great time and the kids were so happy. We do a lot of family activities together, and we love each others' company. Foster parenting has given me many opportunities. I have been given the privilege of meeting two incredible boys who have changed my outlook on many issues. I smiled when I saw my foster son hold my new baby and had tears in my eyes when she smiled at him. I have been to "boy" activities like basketball games and had the honor of cheering for my oldest boy as he won the All City Cross Country meet for his team. It was wonderful at Christmas when the boys bought gifts for others instead of just receiving. And watching them grow as individuals has been cosmic. My younger foster son has taught me lessons in tolerance, but he has also taught me how to really laugh at things.

My foster children are leaving me in about two weeks after a year of being together; and yes, it hurts. But I thank God every day, and recently even more so, for giving me the opportunity to grow in myself and to help children grow and expand their vision for the future. I would not trade all the tears that I have shed for the joy that has been brought to me each and every day.

Sheila, single mom to 5 smiling kids.

Open Heart

"If someone listens or stretches out a hand or whispers a kind word of encouragement or attempts to understand, extraordinary things begin to happen."
                                            Loretta Girzartis

When I was first approached about doing foster care, I didn't think I was qualified. However, I finally made the call when I heard about a juvenile diabetic that nobody would take because they were afraid to be responsible for his shots and diet.

It broke my heart to think that this child had no place to go "home" upon leaving the hospital. I couldn't help that little fellow, but he opened my heart. I decided to make myself available for the next hard-to-place, medically-fragile child who needed a home.

As a foster parent, I have had to learn to open my heart and leave the rest in God's hands. I have learned that, with His help, I can do more than I ever imagined possible.

Dargie, mother and grandmother of many step, birth, foster and adopted children.

January 27 — Native Tongue

"…we must recognize the whole gamut of human potentialities, and so weave a less arbitrary social fabric, one in which each diverse human gift will find a place."

Margaret Mead

God gives some people children so they can remember how to love.

You have loved your sons far beyond your childhood experience of being loved

And I, your second mother, who was not included when you bought your first prom dress, watch in amazement

As you offer me a bouquet of flowers with the tiny hands of your little boy

And for the first time I understand the language of love you speak.

We adopted our daughter when she was 15 and we expected to have a wonderful, happy life filled with love. We were unprepared for the lack of trust and the difficulty she had joining our family. It has been several years now since she first became "my child," and I am just now learning the subtle ways she shows her affection for me. I have learned how important it is to allow children who have been hurt to develop their own ways of caring. And most importantly I have learned to let go of my expectations about how things "should" be, and in doing so I have discovered the wonders of how things actually are.

Susan, foster and adoptive parent, grandparent, and former foster family recruiter and trainer.

Delayed Gratification

"We must have infinite faith in each other."
Henry David Thoreau

The biggest rewards when working with children who have Reactive Attachment Disorder come only through delayed gratification. They come in those amazing moments when all the fighting and biting fade away and you can see the child as a whole child.

The rewards are a long time coming, but when they do come, hold onto your socks because they will be knocked off!

Sally, foster care professional.

January 29 — A Lot of Good

"We can preach and lecture all we want, but to our children, our life really is our message."
Sandra Burt & Linda Perlis

Some people ask me, "How can you care for these children who come to your home bruised and battered, what messages are you giving your biological children?" When I think of this I see six children who have grown with compassion, kindness, and love. They are not quick to judge, instead they try to look past behavior to better understand.

When my daughter was in fifth grade she noticed a girl who was often teased by the other girls. One day my daughter had to go back to the locker room to get her towel, and as she turned the corner there sat the girl with her shirt removed, her back covered with bruises. My daughter walked out of the gym class with her new friend in tow and demanded to see the nurse and the principal. Her friend shared with school officials that she was beaten by a family member, and she was placed into care for a short time while the family got the help they needed.

So, when I have my days of doubt about whether I'm doing the right thing for my children, I remember how they handle these situations, how they are learning from them. And I take comfort in the words of my friend who says, "there is a lot of good that comes out of your house." And I know deep in my soul that what we are doing was meant to be.

Debi, birth and adoptive parent, foster parent to over 30 children in the past 12 years.

Laugh

"I thank God for this most amazing day;
for the leaping greenly spirits of trees
and a blue true dream of sky;
and for everything
which is natural which is infinite
which is yes"

       ee cumings

Don't be afraid to laugh. Laugh when you make a mistake...let the kids know you're human. Laugh when your kids are funny...even if you're in a bad mood.

It seems that I set the mood at home, and when I'm not happy it affects everybody. That's a big responsibility, so it's important to learn to laugh.

Looking back, I think I do take life too seriously sometimes. What would you rather your children remember? Days when they had to hide (for fear of getting yelled at) or days when you laughed and enjoyed each other.

I want all my kids to think of me with a smile on their lips, and a warm feeling in their hearts.

Dargie, mother and grandmother of many step, birth, foster, and adopted children.

January 31 — Logical Consequences

> *"This is one of the miracles of love: it gives a power of seeing through its own enchantments and yet not being disenchanted."*
>
> C.S. Lewis

I should have known when my middle-school-age foster sons asked me if I had any pins and thread they could use that trouble was brewing. I didn't, however. (I'll fall back on the excuse that I was new at the job.) I even rounded up exactly what they asked for - then I forgot all about it, until the principal called.

Seems the boys were making blow darts, wrapping thread around the head of the pin and then shooting them at people through straws. First, I was horrified, then rather amazed and secretly proud of them. They had a whole little business going. They were making the things and selling them as fast as they brought them into school. The principal said that when word got out that the staff had caught on to the latest instrument of torture, the trash cans were filled with the things by the end of the day.

They got the natural consequence of being expelled, but I was not satisfied that they understood why this behavior was harmful. So, I charted out a cross-stitch pattern for them and for an hour each evening they sewed with a very sharp needle, rather than the regular ballpoint cross-stitch needle, so they would "get the point." They did and I still have those bloodstained samplers today. Every time I look at them I smile and remember how hard it is sometimes to praise the ingenuity without praising the inappropriate behavior.

Susan, foster and adoptive parent, grandparent, and former foster family recruiter and trainer.

Parenting Is a Job

1 February

"Loving is giving and it has nothing to do with what you receive."
                                    Wayne W. Dyer

Fostering and other parenting is a balance of loving and providing structure for kids to be able to learn. When we love our own birth children, they tend to love us back. Foster children are not always able to do that. In those times, with those children, we call upon our courage.

Courageous parenting is done by those who go on loving and dealing directly with behaviors no matter what the child is able to give in return. A courageous foster or adoptive parent can allow a child to not love them if that is what the child needs. The goal is to provide a better life for the child, not to satisfy our need for connection.

And if we are lucky, some day we may find that some of those children are able to express a connection to us that we did not require. At that point it is just like a sweet, unexpected dessert.

Susan, foster and adoptive parent, grandparent, and former foster family recruiter and trainer.

February 2 — The Hunger

*"It would all be so beautiful if people were just kind…
what is more wise than to be kind?
And what is more kind than to understand?"*

— Thomas Tryon

I was always worried about getting enough to eat in the foster homes where I lived. I figured my latest home would be no different. When I arrived in late July, I was shown around the farm. The first thing I looked for was where they hid the food. My new foster mom told the other kids to take me out to play. Before I went out, I stole a half-gallon of ice cream and hid it in my bed.

It was about 85° outside, and we played until bedtime. When I jumped into my bed, I hit the chocolate ice cream—what a mess! My new mom heard the noise and said we should send the "noisemaker" downstairs. She met me on the stairs and saw the chocolate mess on my underwear.

I told her I had an accident, and she didn't yell at me. Instead she cleaned me up, sat me on the kitchen counter, and told me she knew why I had taken the food. Then she did the most remarkable thing. She made me a lunch to take to bed with me and said she would refill the bag whenever it was empty. What a smart lady! The next morning I told her I didn't think I would need the bag filled again. I stayed in her home for thirteen years and that was the last time I took food; her kindness and understanding satisfied my hunger.

Bob, adoptive parent of 6 children, biological parent to 6 more, and foster parent to over 125 children in the past 22 years.

What the Future Holds

"To know the road ahead, ask those coming back."
Chinese Proverb

Only those people who come to believe that what they do as foster parents makes a difference can continue to do the job. It is very difficult sometimes to hold on to that belief and that is why being connected to someone who has done it longer than you can be so helpful. With years of experience, comes a different sort of understanding of what we are doing and the many, many ways we help even when we don't see the direct results.

"Since I have been fostering for so long I have seen many of my 'kids' grow into productive adults. It is hard when kids come and go, and we see some children so damaged and so few children turn around. We can't look into the future five or ten years and see what is going to happen in their lives. Having young men and women come 'home' to show me their families and call with their accomplishments is great encouragement for me. I remember thinking some of those kids would be in jail before they hit 20. The real joy is that in almost one hundred kids only two that I know of have spent time in jail. I feel horrible about those two, but I know that there were so many more that could have ended up that way and didn't."

Pat, foster parent for over thirty years to almost one hundred children.

Susan, foster and adoptive parent, grandparent, and former foster family recruiter and trainer.

February 4 — Behind the Scenes

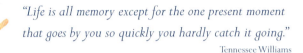

"Life is all memory except for the one present moment that goes by you so quickly you hardly catch it going."
— Tennessee Williams

Those of us who have become used to dealing with hyperactive children often overestimate the knowledge of the rest of the world as to how to deal with the kids. When we took our two-year-old hyperactive, adopted son to a portrait studio, I quickly became aware that the lady there had never worked with anyone quite like him.

She kept saying, "Take your hand away when you feel comfortable." I kept saying, "You don't have that much time." I finally suggested that we cover my arm with the blanket they used for tiny babies so that I could anchor his bottom to the seat and he couldn't dive off the table. It worked, we ended up with great pictures, and I was a thankful mom.

I hope that woman was kidding when she said she thought she might have a heart attack. However, it did remind me how much the parents of hyperactive kids deal with on a daily basis. We must constantly be on our toes, watching and anticipating their next move, and since they move pretty quickly that's a lot of work. I guess what I did for the picture is what we do in life… we give them normal experiences and hold on to them from behind the scene the best we can.

Dargie, mother and grandmother of many step, birth, foster, and adopted children.

The Memory She Needed

5 February

"He (God) does not let His knowledge of the big picture wipe His tears away."

Don Hudson

I watched as she wrapped her beautiful, two-day-old baby in the quilt we had made for him while she was pregnant. We had spent every moment we could with the baby—holding, rocking, singing, talking, filling him with our love. She wrote in her diary, we took picture after picture and tried to soak up every possible memory. For a couple of days we ignored the outside world, let go of all the surrounding circumstances and were the mother and grandmother of a precious baby boy. But, now it was time to face reality.

We drove directly to the lawyer's office, where the adoptive parents were anxiously waiting. Although she felt confident she had made the best possible choice, doubts flooded over her. Would they unconditionally love and protect him? Would they fill his life with the goodness, kindness, and happiness he deserved?

Overwhelmed with what was happening, tears began streaming down her face. She carefully placed her new baby into his adoptive mother's arms. It was done, she had to leave before she broke down completely or grabbed her baby and ran. She looked up to see her tears reflected in the adoptive mother's eyes and on her face. She watched as the adoptive mother immediately turned, gave the baby to her husband, then turned back to embrace her. She felt the obvious love and concern in that hug, saw eyes filled with deep gratitude and quiet joy, heard words of reassurance that they would always love and protect him, and she knew she had the answers she needed, the memory she needed to take with her.

Mony, birth grandparent.

February 6 — Taking a Break

"Drag your thoughts away from your troubles... by the ears, by the heels, or any other way you can manage it."
— Mark Twain

Sometimes when I'm having a hard day emotionally, I need to take a break from what's going on in my head or from those things I can't change or fix. As an adult who has been through this many, many times, I know I can't escape forever; even so, I still look for a healthy way to distance myself and possibly get a better perspective or frame of mind before reality hits again.

I may take a short nap, go for a walk, turn on television, play solitaire, or go to a movie to help me balance out my life. Much of the work we do with children is a matter of helping them find balance. Many have experienced emotional or physical pain and have learned to survive through various avenues of escape. One of the most useful things we can do is help them broaden their vision of healthy possibilities.

Finding a healthy activity in which to become involved will not change their painful life situation; they will be faced with the pain again. However, constructive time away from the direct assault of that pain can help the child rest and rejuvenate.

Life has a way of bringing the pain back whether we are prepared to deal with it or not. As foster and adoptive parents we work to ensure that the next time the wave comes the child will be stronger because he took an afternoon to play in the sprinkler, paint a picture, or compete in the family silly faces contest.

Susan, foster and adoptive parent, grandparent, and former foster family recruiter and trainer.

Black & White

7 February

"The first problem for all of us, men and women, is not to learn, but to unlearn."
— Gloria Steinem

After eyeing my African-American foster baby and my very fair complexion quite seriously for a while, a grocery store clerk finally stated, "Um, your husband must be quite dark."

My sort of offhanded response was, "Oh, I'm not married."

Her eyes widened, her mouth dropped open, and she suddenly became very busy with the cash drawer. Then she said, "Well, I meant the baby's father must be dark."

She just couldn't leave it alone, could she? Well, neither could I.

My response was, "Oh, I wouldn't know. I don't know who the father is." Then I pushed my cart away and left her standing there with her mouth open, speechless.

Valerie, adoptive parent and foster parent for medically fragile children for 10 years.

February 8 — Creativity

"Against the ruin of the world, there is only one defense - the creative act."

Kenneth Rexroth

When the foster father of one of our more creative foster children remarked that he had never heard the song she was playing on the piano, she replied, "Of course not, I'm playing in Japanese."

However, her foster dad was equally creative. When she came home from school saying her teacher had yelled and cursed at her in front of the whole class, the foster dad listened and responded with sympathy. "Why, we can't have teachers doing that! I'm going to the principal. Give me the names of other students in your class that I can say witnessed this behavior."

"Well, I can't do that. I mean none of them heard her. I mean she even burst my ear drum."

"She yelled and no one heard her?"

"Well, she didn't exactly yell. She just moved her lips."

And so the story continued until the child finally acknowledged that her teacher had not yelled or cursed or burst her ear drum. She was simply angry with her teacher for giving her homework. This creative foster dad was able to get the real story without creating an angry scene where it seemed he did not trust his foster daughter. Sometimes foster parents have to be at least as creative as their charges!

Lesa, therapeutic foster parent and trainer of foster parents.

The Visit

*"Loving a child doesn't mean giving into all his whims:
to love him is to bring out the best in him,
to teach him to love what is difficult."*

Nadia Boulanger

I am a strong advocate for family visits. Recently a child in my care went home for a visit with his mom. When he came back later that day his first words were, "My mom got me a bird!" I knew I was in trouble.

For the rest of that evening he would not listen to anything I said and basically demanded to go home so he could play with his bird. Frankly, I felt for him. If I'd been given a bird and then taken away from it, I'd be mad too.

I kept thinking, "Doesn't his mother understand kids at all?" I finally came to the realization that she just wanted her kids to have the things she never had. Her timing might be off a little, but she was trying to do good.

So, I called and suggested she not buy him anything wonderful unless she gave it to him at the beginning of the visit or let him bring it back with him. She quickly asked me if I wanted the bird at my house…not exactly what I had in mind.

We have come to an understanding; we both love this child and want him to have the world. We are both learning that the most wonderful world for him is one in which he is secure in the love we all have for him, and that doesn't require expensive gifts or colorful birds.

Susan, foster and adoptive parent, grandparent, and former foster family recruiter and trainer.

February 10

How Long Is Forever?

"Words are, of course, the most powerful drug used by mankind."
Rudyard Kipling

We had been fostering medically fragile kids for a couple of years when we received a call about a four-year-old with AIDS. We said no because we had lost a baby to this disease six months before. Then we got a second request, but we already had three biological teenagers, two two-year-olds, and a one-year-old, so we again said no. The third time we had to admit he had been on our minds. He moved into our home the next day.

We were told he had six to twelve months to live. We arranged for him to get his wish of going to Disneyland granted. Then, we set about helping him have a fairly normal life.

He is now seven, and during his most recent hospitalization I sat beside his bed praying for strength. He was not conscious and I cried, telling him softly how I had loved having him, thanking him for staying as long as he had, and assuring him that he would forever be a part of us. He never moved, never blinked an eye, just slept.

He improved slowly and after twenty-one days he walked out. When the nurse asked what made him so tough, he said, "I saw my mama cry and I had to get better. She loves me for always." We are in the process of adopting him now. Every kid needs a forever home, who is to say how long forever is?

Twana, foster mom to medically fragile and severe special needs children for over 4 years.

I Love You

11 February

"My assumption is that the story of anyone of us is in some measure the story of us all."
  Frederick Buechner

We were driving down the street of the small town I used to live in, when my fifteen-year-old foster son began fantasizing about living there. "I want a house just like that, we'll have cookouts with steak and crab salad, if I can afford crab," he began to share.

"May I come too?" I asked.

"Yes, and my wife and kids will be there."

"Can they call me Grandma?"

"Yes!" He went on to describe the events of the day as we listened.

When we arrived at my brother's house, the kids piled out of the van and he turned to say "I love you," for the first time during his thirteen-month-stay in our home. Who would have guessed that a trip down **my** memory lane would pull at **his** heart strings?

I guess sometimes it takes getting out of our comfort zone and getting a new perspective to get in touch with feelings. Perhaps our reason for the visit (my dad's illness) helped him see that I have also been a child worried about a parent and not always "the mom." We often try to hide our vulnerability, but I want all my kids to know that I am human, too.

Dargie, mother and grandmother of many step, birth, foster, and adopted children.

February 12 — Family Portrait

"Treasure each other in the recognition that we do not know how long we shall have each other."

Joshua Loth Liebman

The word "family" can mean many different things. The makeup of a foster or adoptive family can change from the time you schedule a portrait to the day of the appointment. In a family like ours you could make yourself crazy trying to get a family portrait with these constant changes.

We decided a long time ago that family was whoever was with us at the moment. So, we gave up the idea of one photo capturing our family and we are making a family portrait album, with plenty of room for additions.

Dargie, mother and grandmother of many step, birth, foster, and adopted children.

Warriors

"One more day to serve
One more hour to love
One more minute to praise
For this day I am grateful."
　　　　　　Mary Lou Kownacki

My husband and I consider ourselves true warriors for our kids and for fostering in general. This job is not easy, but it is the most rewarding job I've ever had.

It is true that we have had our problems; some kids just could not conform to the necessary rules and guidelines. But even when they leave, we always tell them that just because they are going home or wherever doesn't mean we are through with them. We reassure them that we will always be there for them if they need us.

If we move, they are the first to get our new address and phone number. They know if they call, we will be there as fast as we can. God surely gave us life so we could help kids who have no one. What a blessing we have been given!

Shirley, biological, adoptive, and therapeutic foster parent.

February 14 — Love Is All There Is

"Extravagant love allows no one to remain unchanged."
Sharon Hersh

At one time I thought it was critical for all children to do their homework when they first got home from school, go to the dentist for regular checkups, be part of some team or club, and get the best grade possible at school. That was back before I ever fostered or had children of my own. Over the years my priorities have changed tremendously.

Now I value honesty and kindness above nearly everything else. If I have a child who cheats on a test and admits he did it, I feel joyous. When one of my kids is able to stay in his regular class at school for a whole day, I'm delirious. When a child learns the difference between "to," "too," and "two" I'm on Cloud Nine.

The specifics of my desire for the children I love have changed, but the goal has not. The goal was always for them to have the best life possible, for them to find happiness and contentment. At one time I thought this would come from getting a good education and being socially connected. The children have taught me that, in this life, real love is all there is.

Now my wish for them is to feel genuine love, to be loved and to love in return. I hope to give them just a taste of that while they are with me and I pray it will take root and grow.

Susan, foster and adoptive parent, grandparent, and former foster family recruiter and trainer.

Feeling Safe

15 February

"Kindness is giving others territory in which to be safe."
James Houston

One foster mom reported telling her latest foster child that the exterminator was in the house for his regular appointment. Apparently the child was not awake enough to understand what was going on and, consequently she came running out of her room yelling that there was a strange man in the house. This girl had never known if she could trust her own family to love her and keep her safe.

Many of our foster or adoptive children have lived in homes with very loose boundaries. Some kids did not have a specific bed to sleep in and they may have had to deal with strangers coming in and out of their homes. This creates in these children a sort of hypervigalence to their surroundings.

When she realized who the "stranger" was, a protector in a sense, she and her foster mom laughed about the incident. And it made them both aware of how important it would be to go the extra mile to help this girl feel safe.

Dargie, mother and grandmother of many step, birth, foster, and adopted children.

February 16 — Handprint

"…today well lived makes every yesterday a dream of happiness and every tomorrow a vision of hope."

from the Sanskrit

He is gone now, went back home to his mom. He used to cry for her when I wouldn't let him do something he wanted, like eat ice cream just before dinner. At barely three years of age he would sit very still with tears streaming down his round cheeks and moan quietly, "I want my mom." They are back together now, and I am very happy for both of them. I believe they will do well together. And I go on with my life, feeling only joy for the part I played in this happy ending.

Then one day as I am getting out of the shower, I reach for a towel and see his tiny handprint on the mirror that is otherwise covered with steam and I begin to cry. I am flooded with memories. The memory of him standing there at the sink learning to brush his teeth, the way he smiled and leaned forward to examine his work when he was done. The joy I felt seeing him so happy.

I am overwhelmed and I cry and smile and talk out loud to the little boy who is no longer here, but will always be in my heart. As I finish dressing and prepare to leave the bathroom, I look at the handprint again as it is beginning to fade away and I decide to leave it for now. Someday soon I'm sure I will wipe it away, but for today it stays.

Susan, foster and adoptive parent, grandparent, and former foster family recruiter and trainer.

Mommy Is a "Relative" Word

"Parenthood teaches you that there is more than one answer to every question in life."

Richard Delaney

Our first foster child was a two-year-old boy. After about one week, he called me "Mommy." After listening to the trainers at foster parent class, I knew that I had to support his birth mom, talk nicely about her, and encourage reunification. So, in two-year-old terms, I explained to him that I was not his mommy, that he sees his mommy on Tuesday mornings. I told him that his mommy loves him and that I am taking care of him until she gets better.

The second time he called me mommy, I told him the same thing, only I was not as detailed. The third time he called me mommy, I went about what I was doing and asked him to call me by my name. He came up to me later that day and pulled on my pant leg. He said, "Mommy?"

I said, "What do you need, honey?"

He smiled and said, "Come, Mommy."

I followed him and helped him with his game. I then thought to myself that I was messing up. I was not listening to what they said in the classes. I am not his mommy. He just NEEDS to call me mommy and it is okay. His mommy is someone he sees for two hours once a week. Mommy is a "relative" word.

Karen and her husband are birth and foster parents.

February 18 — Keep Your Feet Off the Table

"Some people regard discipline as a chore.
For me, it is a kind of order that sets me free to fly."
Julie Andrews

When our foster daughter arrived last year she had very few social skills and no manners at all. Table manners were one of the areas we tackled early on and, after some rebellion, she quickly picked up some of the basics.

In order to get in some practice, we would go out to eat. One night after she lived with us for a few months, we were out to dinner in a nice restaurant and we noticed her look of astonishment as she gazed around the dining room. She leaned forward and whispered to us, "Look, everyone is copying us - they all have their napkins on their laps too!"

Trying not to laugh, we explained that it wasn't just our family that placed napkins on their laps during meals. Apparently she hadn't noticed the behavior of other diners in other places we'd eaten.

A few weeks later, one of her brothers came to visit us for a few days and we overheard her warning him, "We put our napkins on our laps here, and keep your feet off the table." I guess our lessons were sinking in.

Jan, foster parent.

A Brief List

 February

"Our entire life…consists ultimately in accepting ourselves as we are."

Jean Anouilh

In my daily practice as a counselor I encounter kids from all walks of life. In many instances these kids come from less than ideal circumstances. The greatest common denominator among these at-risk kids and their frequent behavioral problems is a low self-concept. It is imperative that these kids learn a sense of accomplishment, respect and confidence. They deserve to feel good about themselves so they will, in turn, view others with respect, dignity and empathy. I have been mindful in my experiences with children to "hear" what they say they need from those of us they look to for direction.

The following brief list is gleaned from the thoughts shared by those children. These ideas come from the heart of kids, prompting us as caregivers to keep in mind what is important to them, and of what is truly important in life.

- Encourage me to accomplish the impossible.
- Reward me whenever you can.
- Believe in me.
- Respect kids as individuals.
- Never call me stupid.
- Let me help make choices.
- Help me to see that I am special.
- Ask my opinion, listen to my reply.
- Don't embarrass me in front of others.

Gina, counselor, mentor, mother, and author of "For the Kids."

February 20 — Are We Too Old for This?

"The entry of a child into any situation changes the whole situation."

Iris Murdoch

When we started fostering, my husband said he felt guilty that he could not love the foster kids in the same way he loves our biological children. When we were asked to adopt our foster son it was a major decision. We had to consider our age, the fact that we had nearly finished raising our biological children, and face fears about finances and health. When we spoke to other foster parents about it we only got "guarded support."

Today our adopted son is two and my husband has rediscovered fatherhood in a whole new way. Our adopted son gets more of his father than any of our biological children did. The transformation has been wonderful and my husband even looks younger!

Adopting has filled a need for us we didn't even know we had. My birth children are overwhelmed sometimes with the crazy, unexplainable, all-encompassing love they feel for their brother. Our family will never be the same, and all I can say is thank you to the powers that be for giving us the courage to accept this wonder gift.

Kate, birth, step and adoptive parent.

I'm Gonna Tell You the Truth

21 February

"It is a risk to love. What if it doesn't work out? Ah, but what if it does?"

Peter McWilliams

Recently, I observed a conversation between one of the foster parents for our agency and one of her friends. He asked her, "What is the hardest thing about being a foster parent?"

When I heard the question, I tensed up because I knew this foster parent had just had a child leave her home after repeatedly trying to work out problems which included verbal and physical aggression. My fear, as a foster parent recruiter, was that a potential foster parent might bolt if she told him what she had experienced.

She looked him straight in the eye and said, "I'm gonna tell you the truth. The hardest part of being a foster parent is that you will fall in love with these kids." And I knew that, for her, that really was the hardest part. It was not the difficulty of the child's behavior or the names she had been called, or even the physical attacks she had suffered. Rather, it was loving a child because she is a loving person, and then being willing to let that child go.

It is my hope that all foster parents know that the time they spend with their foster children will give those children possibilities they did not have before. The glimpse into healthy family life, no matter how short, gives these children a choice. They may not be able to act on it for years, and we may never know what they choose, but we are helping them have a choice.

Susan, foster and adoptive parent, grandparent, and former foster family recruiter and trainer.

February 22 — Free Day Sunday

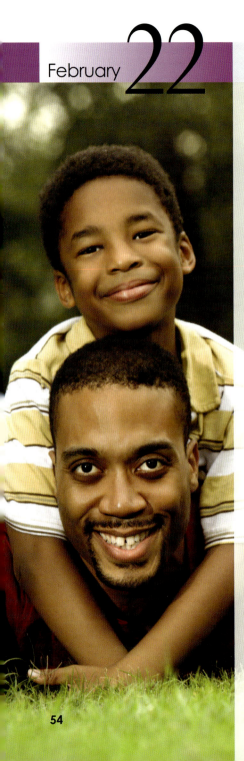

"Now and then it is good to pause in our pursuit of happiness and just be happy."

Guillame Apollinaire

Sometimes I forget how much the small things mean to kids. Recently, we had a huge city-wide festival and one of their money making ventures was to sell lapel pins. When you purchased the pins there were a few coupons included. Our family had amassed about ten of the coupons for a variety of small, free items and I had promised the eight-year-old we would drive around and pick up all the freebies on Sunday after church. He quickly dubbed the adventure "free day Sunday."

When the day arrived we spent about an hour driving around redeeming coupons for bottles of tea, fruit juice and even a pair of earplugs and a key chain. He was thrilled with each new store and each tiny treasure we accumulated. He even decided to wash out his ears when we got home so he wouldn't get the earplugs dirty!

We are often pressured by television, peer interactions and even our own guilt to provide expensive gifts for our children. That day I was reminded of the great joy kids can find in small things, especially when they have an adult who loves them along for company.

Susan, foster and adoptive parent, grandparent, and former foster family recruiter and trainer.

My Legacy

"God alone knows the secret plan of the things he will do for the world using my hands."

Toyohiko Kagawa

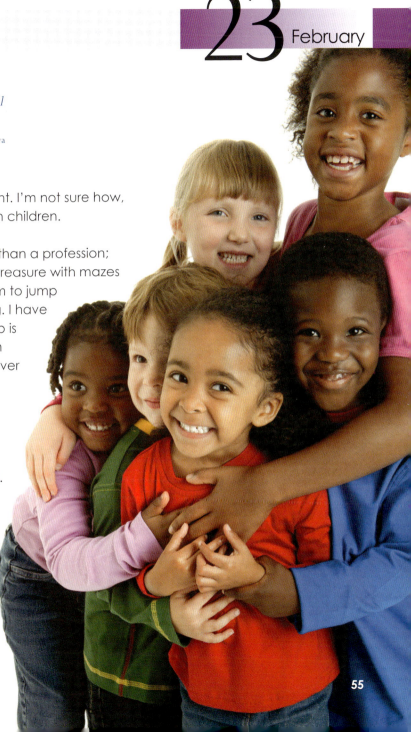

23 February

I have always wanted to be a foster parent. I'm not sure how, but I knew I was not destined to have birth children.

I am a treatment foster parent. It is more than a profession; it is a gift I give myself. Each child is like a treasure with mazes of barriers and obstacles that I teach them to jump through and over. I don't push, pull, or tug. I have learned that doesn't work and that my job is to take their hand, support and hold them up while they reach higher despite whatever dream or nightmare may come.

I am thankful each day for the treasures I have been given. When I flip through my book of memories I may cry, laugh, feel sentimental, or sad, but I never feel regret. I know that when I am a old and gray I will not leave a "little me" behind, but I will leave something just as wonderful. I will leave a little bit of memory in someone's heart of a person who was there for them when they needed it most.

Robin, foster parent to over 30 children in the last 5 years.

February 24 — Paperwork

"I was never good at hide and seek because I'd always make enough noise so my friends would be sure to find me. I don't have anyone to play those games with any more, but now and then I make enough noise just in case someone is still looking and hasn't found me yet."

Brian Andreas

I must get my paperwork done-
    medicine logs, allowance logs, clothing logs, journals,
        adoption papers, fingerprints,
            my life story full of incidents…

Bills to pay,
  checks to write,
      next month I need to book a flight.

Taxes,
    school work,
        IEP's,
          doesn't leave much time for these.

In the bathroom I go to hide,
    close the door, pretend I died,
        and finally when I am done
           I'm ready for some family fun…

I have stories to read,
    and pages to color,
        my life I would trade for no other.

Dargie, mother and grandmother of many step, birth, foster, and adopted children.

Helping a Child Be a Child

25 February

"What is necessary to change a person is to change his awareness of himself."
Abraham Maslow

So many foster children have become parentified in order to keep their family together. Our foster daughter had been the "mom" in her family, very often responsible for cleaning the house and making sure the smaller children were fed and changed. She was also in charge of catering to her parents who were often drunk or sleeping off the effects of their addiction.

It was very hard for her to stop being the parent and let someone else be the mom so she could be the kid. When she moved into foster care she lost not only her family, but her family role and the control that went with it.

Each of her siblings also had their role in the family and they also had problems adjusting to their new situations because their roles changed so dramatically. When one of her siblings came to our home for a visit she often slipped back into being the "mom." I had to gently remind her that, while they were visiting, I was their mom and her job was to be their sister and have fun with them.

I watched them shape their new relationship. She was at first furious with her younger brother because he wouldn't listen to her anymore. Then she began to recognize a healthy sister role and acknowledged he was growing up and he didn't need her to baby him. It's always wonderful to know you have played a part in helping a child be a child.

Jan, foster parent.

February 26 — A Long Way to Where He Is

*"They who give have all things,
they who withhold have nothing."*
Hindu Proverb

When the little boy overheard the message that his father had been found, he automatically assumed it meant his father would be coming to see him. I knew it meant nothing of the sort. This father had not made a move to support his child in the eight years he had known about him.

This child, who had never seen his dad, talked of him often, telling the kids at school about the work he did or about the things they did together. His teacher told me it broke her heart to hear him describe all the things he was wishing to be true.

We finally discussed his excitement over the phone message, and I asked him if he had any questions. He spoke clearly as he said, "I know it is a long way to where he is, but if he can't come here, would you take me to see him?"

How do you tell a child that his father may not want him, may deny paternity, may run away again? I told him much of this would be up to his daddy and that we would have to wait and see what his daddy wanted. I held him tight and reassured him of my love and put him to bed. Then I prayed for his father, a long prayer that whatever goodness he had inside to create this child might grow in him so that he could now have the courage to be the father this child deserved.

Susan, foster and adoptive parent, grandparent, and former foster family recruiter and trainer.

Dad's Hat

27 February

"People don't care how much you know until they know that you care."
Unknown

One time a boy of about eleven came from a situation of serious neglect to live with me. I remember watching him in his bedroom unpacking his suitcase. The articles came out one by one without much ceremony until he got to a raggedy, old, greasy hat.

Standing in the middle of his belongings he took hold of the hat and brought it to his nose, his eyes closed, and breathed in the scent with a passion you could see on his face. Then he hugged the hat, carefully, like a delicate flower.

When I asked him what he was doing he looked at me and said, "This is my dad's hat. I just love it; it smells just like him." I learned a great lesson from those words. Not once in all the years with this boy did I make a negative comment about his father.

The one thing I teach over and over to new foster parents is to honor the child's biological parents just because they are his parents. This can be difficult when you are in total disagreement with their behavior, but it will be worth the effort. When we make the mistake of saying something negative about a parent, the child takes it straight to his heart and absorbs it and somehow feels responsible for the inadequacies he perceives. Acknowledging whatever is good and positive can help the child to absorb that part of the parents they so dearly love.

Carolyn, social worker and foster parent to teen boys.

February 28 — You Could Get Buried Alive

*"Who I am is what I have to give.
Quite simply I must remember that's enough."*
Ann Wilson Schaef

One thing I had to give up when I became a parent was the feeling that everything had to be perfect. I learned that perseverance is the key.

I am a morning person. I can get a lot done in the mornings, but once I leave the house it seems like I don't get much done upon my return.

I have learned that I can do little jobs during small blocks of time throughout the day that save time in the long run. While the kids are in the tub, I lay out clothes for the next day. While waiting for the bus, I might sweep off the carport or porch. Before leaving the house in the morning, I start some laundry. I wipe down the bathroom as I prepare for a shower.

Let's face it, with a houseful of kids, it can't always be clean. On the other hand if you don't stay (somewhat) on top of it, you could get buried alive!

Dargie, mother and grandmother of many step, birth, foster and adopted children.

No Apparent Reason

29 February

"Would you know your Lord's meaning in this?
Learn it well.
Love was His meaning."

       Julian of Norwich

About two months after we married, and for no apparent reason, we decided to take sign language classes. We knew no deaf people, but decided it was something we would enjoy. We went faithfully for almost a year, and we learned how to sign fairly well.

We were unable to adopt or foster because we had not been married long enough to meet the requirements and yet, we felt heartbroken for the children who were spending Christmas in shelters and other institutions. We were not sure what to do because international adoption can be very expensive, and we were not eligible to adopt domestically. But not to be beaten, we began to explore the Internet and found our daughter on a website! She was beautiful, she was Romanian...and she was deaf. We knew we had prepared for her entry into our lives without even knowing we were doing it.

After many complications and lots of red tape, she was finally put into her new daddy's arms where she won his heart forever. Later that night she met her new family, and we can only imagine what she must have been thinking in those first few days. We do know that now she has blossomed into a very happy, settled, smart and content little lady who loves her Mom and Daddy very much. And we thank God every day for the joy this child has brought us.

Darryl & Milissa, adoptive parents.

March 1 — Building a Foundation

"A man or woman with many children has many homes."
Lakota saying

People always ask us why we do what we do. I was raised in foster care, so I am repaying a debt to the foster parents who made a difference in my life.

I asked my foster mom why she took us in knowing that someday we would leave her. She told me that it didn't matter how long a child lived with her because she knew that she would add a piece to the foundation that all kids need to grow and be productive.

I thought about that as I got older and realized that foster parents are like home builders adding one brick at a time to a child's life - helping them establish a foundation on which they can build someday. As foster parents, our lives will still be effective long after we are gone. We leave little pieces of ourselves in the foundation of each child we touch.

Bob, adoptive parent to 6 children, biological parent to 6 more, and foster parent to over 125 children in the past 22 years.

Recipe for a Foster Home

2 March

"Prayer is the mortar that holds our house together."
Mother Teresa

- 1 large house (easily rearranged to meet needs as they arise)
- 1 large yard (if space is limited, a nearby park will do)
- 1 medium-size family (willing to share EVERYTHING)
- rules (not too rigid, adjustable with age/ability)
- unconditional LOVE (cannot add too much)
- sturdy furniture (need not be new)
- 1 large vehicle (kept in good repair)
- clothes (assorted sizes)
- a few toys (don't worry, they will multiply with little effort)
- strong church family (optional, but I have seen recipe fail without it)
- good professional help (not optional, to keep asking until needs are met)
- extended family (optional, but very desirable)
- joy
- laughter
- patience

Add foster child, marinate in LOVE and give ample time to adjust. Heart may become tender. If so, feel sense of accomplishment. Enjoy for the duration, however long.

Dargie, mother and grandmother of many step, birth, foster, and adopted children.

March 3

My Little Man

"Love comforteth like sunshine after rain."
William Shakespeare

The day finally came for him to go home. He was so excited. As soon as he woke up he said, "I'm going to Mary's today."

His things were sitting in the middle of the floor, two year's worth of clothes and toys, and two year's worth of growing up. He came to us a toddler and was leaving a "little man." He came barely talking and now had many words to share with the world. He came sitting in a high chair and was leaving able to sit in a big boy seat.

That morning was cloudy. He looked out the window for his worker to appear. He checked his bags and made sure everything was there. When she arrived it started to rain. As she was putting all his things in the car, I was snapping his red rain coat. He was so excited he could hardly stay still for me to put up his hood.

The worker came back into the house after she had loaded his things and he said, "Let's go to Mary's." He took her hand and I watched his little body in the bright red coat walk away. He had grown up so much. He no longer cried when he met new people, no longer screamed when he had to leave our house. He was a happy little boy and he was leaving me. Then he turned, waved and said, "Bye, Mommy."

Karen and her husband are birth and foster parents.

Making Time...

"I am sitting here in the sun
Watching the kittens playing
And the children playing
And I am convinced
There is nothing worth doing more."
    Susan Fromberg Schaeffer

When I get upset because of all the work that has to be done, I take time to sit down with a good cup of coffee and watch the children play. We can learn a lot from them. Some other things that help when it all starts getting to you:

Write about your day. Writing it out helps you relax.

Sometimes it's best to just turn on the music and dance, dance!

If it's your little ones that are getting you down, call someone with teenagers! Compare notes. You'll both feel better.

Let your kids know you need a hug.

Go outside and run in the water or roll in the leaves or build a snowman with the kids. It's great! What it does for them (and for you) is life changing.

Lay in bed with them and be silly and laugh a lot.

Say "yes" three times for every "no" you say to your kids.

Life is short–live it to the fullest, like there is no tomorrow.

Tish, foster parent to approximately 25 children in the past 3 years, biological parent, adoptive parent, and grandmother of 5.

March 5 — Angry Girl

*"I held her close for only a short time, but after she was gone,
I'd see her smile on the face of a perfect stranger and
I knew she would be there with me all the rest of my days."*
— Brian Andreas

As a foster parent recruiter and trainer, I observe from a distance the emotional roller coaster our foster parents often ride when they take in and love a child with an attachment disorder. The following poem was written as a celebration of the depth of love these wonderful families show, as well as a lament for the troubled children who feel a need to push us away.

> Angry girl, whose eyes do you see when you strike back at life building thick walls with words and deeds others dare not approach?
>
> And so, you win, no one gets close enough to hurt you and you lose because you do not know when love is offered.
>
> But, how is an angry girl to know who is safe, who brings love and who can help dismantle the tangled fortress in which she lives?
>
> We reach out in love and later bandage the wounds we receive as you, the wounded child, try to control a world that makes no sense.
>
> And when you move on we are left wondering what more we could have done to ease your suffering, to help you find peace.
>
> And we are left hoping that you saw in us, even if just for a moment, adults who can be trusted, children who accept you as you are, and love big enough to heal your heart.
>
> And we know you will always be in our hearts where we will love you deeply whether you love us back or not.

Susan, foster and adoptive parent, grandparent, and former foster family recruiter and trainer.

Belonging

"Tact is the intelligence of the heart."
Unknown

As foster parents, we are constantly balancing telling the truth with guarding the confidential information of our children. Once as I was checking out of a big, super store, the clerk said, "What a pretty granddaughter you have." I smiled and agreed. Outside, the little girl said, "I'm glad you didn't tell them I was a foster kid."

It is sometimes challenging to let an inaccurate comment go uncorrected but, in this case, the clerk really did not have a "need to know" my true relationship to the child. So, I let her believe what she thought was true, and I felt as though I had protected a little bit of my foster daughter's self esteem in the process.

Nancy, a foster parent for special needs children.

March 7 — Different Paths

"Even in the midst of the unbearable agonies…, there are those who choose to help—to give others: bread, shoes, comfort, whatever. These acts of compassion are the shining, diamond-tough confirmations of human dignity. This is keeping our affairs in order at the highest level."
Robert Fulghum

Some foster parents approach the task of fostering or adoption boldly, knowing from the beginning that is what they are meant to do. Others slip in quietly to see how things work and check out the territory. Then there are the ones who struggle mightily with the decision.

Several people I have worked with over the years have gone back and forth with the "rightness" of the path for them. Some of these people go on to become great foster or adoptive parents while others decide to help children in some other way. Each of us has a different path, just as each of us has a different life purpose. There is no one way that is better than another. It is important to support each family as they go down whatever road takes them to the place where they can do what is possible for them to support the children of our world.

Susan, foster and adoptive parent, grandparent, and former foster family recruiter and trainer.

Walk on the Clouds

8 March

"Faith walks simply, childlike, between the darkness of human life and the hope of what is to come."
Catherine De Hueck Doherty

When my niece was about three, we were driving along when she asked, "Can I get out and walk on those clouds?" Of course I explained (as best I could) how far away those clouds were and that they weren't solid.

Traveling that same stretch of road recently, that memory came back to me. My niece is an adult now, and since that time I have had many new nieces and my own children ask similar questions.

I have also had many foster children through my home; but, I've never had the foster children ask me questions quite like that. Their fantasies are filled more with fear and anxiety. When foster children come to me, I try my best to let them be kids - to give them the freedom to "walk on the clouds" instead of worrying about their families, their safety or their future.

Dargie, mother and grandmother of many step, birth, foster, and adopted children.

March 9 — Letter to My (Foster) Parents

"I've learned that sometimes all a person needs is a hand to hold and a heart to understand."
— Andy Rooney

Dear Mom and Dad,

Thank you for taking us in when you did... you already had 6 children of your own, but somehow you found room for 2 more.

Thank you for NOT sending us away when our original 6 months were up.

Thank you for letting us call you Mom and Dad when we thought that our biological parents were not coming back.

Thank you for hanging in there when the going got tough; it would have been easier to send us back.

Thank you for handling all the tough questions that were asked pertaining to us as foster children and coming to our defense when others would make fun of us or think less of us for being foster children.

Thank you for taking in other foster children even though I know when each child left they took a special piece of your heart.

Most of all, thank you for allowing us to be children in a sometimes crazy world.

Sharon, former foster child.

Gotya Day

10 March

"The only difference between stumbling blocks and stepping stones is the manner by which we choose to see and use them."

Sipri Cuthbert

Adoptive parents come to be in many ways. Some of us were unable to give birth to natural children while others may have chosen to adopt rather than have a natural child. Other parents may adopt in addition to the biological children they already have at home. No matter how we come to be adoptive parents we all have one thing in common. We have been gifted with a child who was born to someone else and we have to come to terms with that fact.

While we may sometimes be tempted to forget the parents who physically created the child we now love, there nearly always comes a day when we must make peace with those biological parents in some way. Some people have a wonderful way of doing that from the very beginning.

"We adopted a drug-exposed infant when he was almost seven-months-old and he was a very small baby. He is nearly a teenager now and every year he has two special days, his birthday and his "Gotya Day." On that day we celebrate the day we got him and usually take him out for the dinner of his choice, and on that day we also say a prayer for the woman who gave birth to him."

Teresa, foster and adoptive parent.

Susan, foster and adoptive parent, grandparent, and former foster family recruiter and trainer.

March 11 — Developing Values

"I'm more involved in unlearning than learning. I'm having to unlearn all the garbage that people have laid on me."

Leo Buscaglia

It's easy for us to see how our choices are influenced by significant people in our lives. Hopefully, at some point we reach a place where we are making choices based on our own internal sense of right and wrong.

I try to imagine what it must be like to have had several sets of "parents" like a lot of teenage foster children have experienced. How many sets of values and beliefs do they carry around inside? How do they know which ones to embrace, which ones to discard or rebel against? How long does it take to process each of these examples and come to the place of developing a personal set of values?

Becoming an individual is never easy, and for our adolescent foster children it is an even more complex task. It takes an enormous amount of patience on our part as they test and try on the variety of values and beliefs they have seen. They need time to move through the process of determining who they will choose to become. Most days, as they exhibit some traits we cherish and some we abhor, we can only stand back, set limits as long as they are in our home, and do a lot of praying.

Susan, foster and adoptive parent, grandparent, and former foster family recruiter and trainer.

Green-Eyed Monster

12 March

"What we love to do we find time to do."
John Lancaster Spalding

It doesn't take a lot of planning and preparation to spend some time, one-on-one with each child in the family. I have found that letting one have the fudge left in the bottom of the pan, taking only one with me to the store to buy soap, helping one with homework, or letting one help make dinner can become a special time. When I'm with that child, s/he gets my full attention; I listen to what the child wants to say.

It is not uncommon for jealousy to appear; the green-eyed monster does occasionally rear its ugly head. However jealousy can be tamed if all the children can count on their own special time alone with the adult who cares for them. We all need to feel special and be heard.

Dargie, mother and grandmother of many step, birth, foster, and adopted children.

March 13 — More to the World

*"What you are is God's gift to you;
what you make of it is your gift to God."*
Anthony Dalla Villa

I have always taken any of the babies they asked me to. When they called me at 4 a.m. to take a little, three-month-old boy with Fetal Alcohol Syndrome I did not hesitate. He cried all the time and only rested about twenty minutes out of the day. There were times I was ready to pull my hair out. I would walk, pat, rock, feed, burp, and I even tried some old wives remedies.

I was about ready for the nut house, when at about nine months of age he just quit crying and became a very happy baby. Later, he was adopted by a single mother who loves him dearly.

I have had kids who were with me for a short while and then went home, many of them were back in foster care within a few weeks or months. It doesn't matter to me how long they are here. I take my children not only into my home, but also into my heart. Even if it is just for a short while, I show them there is someone who loves them, and they are more to the world than pain.

Marie, adoptive parent and foster parent for over 20 years to more than 50 children, many of whom were handicapped.

Silver Lining

14 March

"The Chinese word (symbol) for crisis is written with two brush strokes. The first is for danger and the second for opportunity."
Unknown

Sometimes during a crisis we are able to see a different side of our children. Earlier this year I suffered two mild strokes and was hospitalized. Shortly thereafter, I was diagnosed with Graves Disease.

While I was in the hospital my adopted and foster kids (mostly teen boys), wrote me letters and cards. I was so touched! After I got back home they were protective and doting; they made sure I had everything I needed. They even called me from school every day to make sure I was okay. During that time they started saying "I love you" without me saying it first.

My first night back home and every night since they come to me and want "quality time" before going to bed. They are quick to ask me how my day was, and I feel so blessed to have them in my life. This was a rough time for me and words cannot express how much I love each and every one of these kids. This crisis in our family brought us all closer together.

Shirley, biological, adoptive and therapeutic foster parent.

March 15 — Falling Apart

"Worry often gives a small thing a big shadow."
Swedish proverb

When I explained to my adopted, six-year-old son he would soon begin loosing his teeth he became pretty upset that he was starting to "fall apart." He eventually calmed down, until the day he finally did lose the first tooth.

That day we were all busy getting the house in order when I heard this thunderous stampede on the stairs. All of my children came running toward me in such a rush I was sure someone was bleeding to death. They gathered around the six-year-old's little face, proudly pulling down his bottom lip and holding his tiny tooth next to it. I don't know who was more excited. His little chest was swollen with pride and the rest of us took his picture for the photo album.

By the time the second tooth was lost, the excitement had dwindled to say the least. He wasn't even sure when or where he lost it. I was just so happy that his family was able to help him move from a place of fear to a place of joy regarding this monumental sign of growth. And I'm so glad we continue to be reminded of the wonder of being human as we delight in each of his transitions.

Dargie, mother and grandmother of many step, birth, foster, and adopted children.

What Do They Know?

16 March

"Love cures people, the ones who receive love and the ones who give it, too."

Karl A. Menninger

When I took him in for a neurological consultation, the physician strongly discouraged my thoughts regarding adopting him if he was released for adoption. The doctor predicted that, due to drug exposure in utero and exposure to extreme cold at birth, he would never be able to accomplish any degree of independent abilities. He told me that this child would likely never feed himself, talk, or do much of anything. At the time, the child's little body was rigid and straight as a stick and I had no reason to disbelieve the doctor. I took the doctor's negative prognosis into consideration and then I decided I would not allow it to keep me from fighting for this child. Today, I am smiling as I watch our adopted son, at age seven, entertaining a crowded restaurant with his self-designed dancing maneuvers. He has no shyness whatsoever! He is currently one of the top readers in his class, receives very good grades in math, and is one of the most active children I know.

Bonnie, birth parent, adoptive parent, and foster parent to more than 40 children over the last 8 years.

March 17 — St. Patrick's Day Blessing

*"Although the world is full of suffering,
it is also full of overcoming it."*

Helen Keller

Wouldn't it be grand if we could be a little like St. Patrick who, according to legend, drove the snakes out of Ireland? It would be great to just get rid of the things that frightened or threatened us in some way. Unfortunately, it isn't that easy.

If it were up to me I would leave the snakes alone, but I'd drive away the pain of the children I see every day. Just send it away so that they could play like other kids and feel safe in their world. And, in a way, that is what foster and adoptive parents do. At the very least we give them some goodness and love to balance out the pain. We cannot take the pain away, but we can open up their view of the world and their options. And until the pain becomes manageable for them we can offer them this blessing:

May the pain rise up and leave you
May there always be a person who loves you at your back
May you feel the warmth of human kindness
And feel safe enough to let your goodness shine.

Susan, foster and adoptive parent, grandparent, and former foster family recruiter and trainer.

The Moon & the Stars

18 March

"There is only one happiness in life, to love and be loved."
George Sand

Once I cared for a small boy who was afraid of the dark. The use of a night light didn't help him because it created shadows he imagined to be evidence of something out to hurt him. Leaving the light on in the room proved to be too distracting, because he wanted to get up and play with everything in sight. As I explored options for providing some measure of comfort for him I landed on the idea of glow-in-the-dark stars.

We affixed the moon and several stars to the ceiling and walls of his room and left the light on for awhile before he went to bed. When he did go to bed the stars glowed all around him, he was thrilled. He would tell me stories of what he imagined, dreams of going up there and flying through space. He would fall asleep and the light of the stars would gently fade until the next night.

When he left to go home he took his stars with him. Well, he took all but one. I kept that one and I hung it on my wall near my bed and each night when I turn out the light to go to sleep I see it, and I see him in my mind. I wish him well and go to sleep knowing I gave at least one child the moon and stars.

Susan, foster and adoptive parent, grandparent, and former foster family recruiter and trainer.

March 19 — Things to Do

*"The garden loves the rain and, yes, this is love.
But the love I want for you—the love I want to give you—
is the love the rain gives the garden. Loving is giving freedom."*
Peter McWilliams

*"Life is a song—sing it. Life is a game—play it.
Life is a challenge—meet it. Life is a dream—realize it.
Life is a sacrifice—offer it. Life is a love—enjoy it."*
Sai Baba

On a rainy day:
Read a book.
Make cookies.
Watch home movies.
Tell stories from your childhood.
Help the kids learn to cook dinner.
Clean out a closet together.
Play a game.
Go bowling.
Go to the library.
Go to the mall and look around.

On a sunny day:
Go to the park.
Go on a photo shoot.
Go for a walk.
Wash your vehicle.
Clean up the yard.
Have a picnic.
Build a fort.
Go for a bike ride.
Play outside.
Cook out on the grill.

Dargie, mother and grandmother of many step, birth, foster, and adopted children.

Spring

How do you like to go up in a swing,
Up in the air so blue?

March 20 — New Growth

"Spring is a wondrous necessity."
Vera & Bill Cleaver, Where the Lilies Bloom

Last year was the roughest year we have ever had in the seventeen years we've worked with special needs kids. It was only by the grace of God, many prayers, and the support of others that we made it. Would we do it again? Absolutely!

We took a six-week-old boy whose father had shaken him, thrown him against a wall and then suffocated him. He cried constantly and could not lay in his crib for more than 5 minutes at a time. Eventually his ability to stay in the crib for longer periods of time increased and he began sitting in the baby swing. In spite of needing constant care, he still brought such joy into our lives. Even the intrusion of the nurses turned into opportunities to develop friendships. We had this little angel for one year and now he is with his maternal grandparents who worked very hard to learn about his intensive needs.

It is spring now and as I cleared away the dead plants to make way for new growth, I thought about what we hope to accomplish with each child who comes to our home. We work very hard to clear away the painful memories. We use adaptive equipment, therapies, medications and lots of love to encourage new growth in broken little bodies. We try to give each of them a new start—much like spring after winter.

Renee, loving mom to many.

These Boots

21 March

"Victory is not won in miles, but in inches. Win a little now, hold your ground and later win a little more."

Louis L'Amour

My four foster girls all wanted cowboy boots. I was trying to think of a way to get the boots and also teach them that good behavior pays off. I made up a chart with dates and their names for a month. Whoever did their chores and stayed out of trouble received a star by her name. When they had a good, full two weeks, they would get their boots.

My granddaughter came to me and told me she also wanted boots. I said, "We will buy you a pair." But no, she wanted her name on the chart, too. Her name was added and in about two weeks she and one foster child got to buy their boots.

In a few weeks the rest of the girls got to buy their boots, too. This turned out to be an effective way to reward them for good behavior. And it taught me how hard children will work for something they really want.

Nancy, a foster parent for special needs children.

March 22

Hitting the Jackpot

"Cultivate your sense of humor. Laughter hides in strange places."
Linda Allison-Lewis

I have found the thing that irritates me the most in working with children… silliness. Now why does that bother me? I mean shouldn't I be happy that the child is happy? The thing is this is probably normal nine-year-old behavior but it drives me nuts!

Studying spelling words he has to sing them to me and giggle between each letter. He goes to put on his socks and ends up lying on the bed, feet in the air doing a play with his toes. Eating dinner he laughs hysterically at the way the broccoli is lying on his plate next to the meat.

And just when I'm about to blow my top, expressing my impatience with his sense of timing, he turns to me with a smile and hugs me. Then he whispers in my ear, "I hit the jackpot." When I question this statement he says, "When they asked me which grandma I wanted I looked all through the box and I picked you and I hit the jackpot!"

Okay, maybe I'll live through the nine-year-old silliness because, when it comes down to the bottom line, I know we both hit the jackpot the day we came into one another's lives.

Susan, foster and adoptive parent, grandparent, and former foster family recruiter and trainer.

The Big Picture

"You must be the change you wish to see in the world."
Mahatma Ghandi

As a new foster parent, already part of the system, I had no idea how great the need was for people to love these kids. It wasn't until I attended my first Fall Conference that I saw the big picture. There were literally hundreds of people there—all representing at least one child who at one point or another had been in need of a home. At first the thought overwhelmed and saddened me. I almost sat down and cried.

I drank in the workshops, the luncheon speech, and chatted with seasoned foster parents. All the while I took mental as well as, physical notes. Looking around the room… began to pray and thank God for these people willing to open up their homes and their hearts to children who (more than likely) would say premature good-byes. I was struck by the importance of realizing we are not alone and thankful that I am but one frame in the big picture.

Dargie, mother and grandmother of many step, birth, foster, and adopted children.

March 24 — Pedaling Along

*"Each day, and the living of it,
has to be a conscious creation in which discipline and order
are relieved with some play and some pure foolishness."*

— May Sarton

Foster and adoptive parents claim that a good sense of humor is essential to surviving and thriving with troubled children. This doesn't mean to act like Seinfeld, Robin Williams, or Groucho Marx. Actually, along with a sense of humor, one needs a sense of irony and the ability to detect the humor in a wide range of situations.

When a ten-year-old foster child fell off her bike, she stomped away from the home she was staying in and kept going. The foster mother watched the girl march farther and farther away, wondering how she might intervene without getting into a chase with the child. She spotted the child's small bike and got an idea. Positioning her rather large frame onto the petite bike, the foster mother pedaled after the child but did not attempt to stop her. Without saying a word the foster mother, dwarfing the bike, drove in circles around the child. Eventually the child stopped walking, gave up, turned around and marched back home with the foster mother silently pedaling along side.

Humor can defuse volatile situations and loosen the rigid defenses of a child who is on edge. It can also infuse the ridiculous into encounters that otherwise could be scary or contentious for the child. Using levity during the above crisis allowed the foster mother to sidestep being drawn into the child's misbehavior. The sight of the foster mother on the bike took the edge off the seriousness and turned the child around, figuratively and literally.

Rick, clinical psychologist, trainer and consultant who has worked with foster and adoptive children and their parents over the past 20 years.

Sunday School Offering

25 March

"Every human being is intended to have a character of his own; to be what no other is, and to do what no other can do."
William Channing

I believe all children can be responsible for something and that it makes them proud to do a good job. The worse their behavior, the more they need positive reinforcers. We have tried this theory several times, and always the child was blessed and so were we.

My little, adopted son has a lot of issues. He is in therapy and takes medication for inappropriate behaviors. School is great because it's very structured and he knows exactly what to do and when to do it. Sunday School, however, is a different story. It is very relaxed and less structured, and he has a hard time in there... until it is time for the offering.

His daddy walks down the aisle and passes the collection plate during church, and in Sunday School he gets to be like Daddy. That is his job, and he takes it very seriously. It is a precious thing to watch him do his job so well. He helps the smaller kids and waits patiently for others to dig change from their pockets.

This shows me that he can deal with responsibility, he actually craves it. And, if this little guy does, don't they all?

Dargie, mother and grandmother of many step, birth, foster, and adopted children.

March 26 — The Longing

"Faith is what lies on the other side of reason. Faith is what makes life bearable, with all its tragedies and sudden, startling joys."
            Madeleine L'Engle

Many people come to fostering or adoption because they have not been able to have children of their own or because their childbearing was cut short for some reason. These mothers and fathers live with questions about why they were not able to conceive when women and men who are not capable of caring for their children have babies every day. This internal longing for a child who never comes in the expected way creates a huge love for children and it also creates a parent who is willing to go to all lengths to see that existing children have what they need.

"Maybe we are not able to have children because God knew that He would need mothers like us to help children like the ones we now cherish. In this way, that little baby you have wanted may very well come to you."

Pam, biological parent of 3, adoptive parent of 2, and foster parent of 7.

Susan, foster and adoptive parent, grandparent, and former foster family recruiter and trainer.

Missing in Action

27 March

"The most wasted of all our days are those in which we have not laughed."
Nicolas-Sebastien de Chamfort

One of our foster children left after living with us for 15 months. It was hard on everyone, but I assured the other kids that it wouldn't be long before we had a new baby. The next day the agency called to ask us to take a three-year-old for the weekend. Then we got another call to take a two-year-old boy for a few days. During that time my two-year-old grandson came and we had a total of four kids in diapers.

My wife went out for the evening but told me she would set out pajamas for all the little ones. When I got the kids ready for bed I put pajamas on everyone that was there and I still had one pair left. After checking all the little ones I went and searched the house for the kid with no pj's. I looked in every room in the house and still couldn't find the missing child. Finally, I called my wife on her cell phone and asked her if she had the missing child. She said, "No, who is missing?" I told her I didn't know but I had five pairs of pajamas and only four kids.

My wife enjoyed her night out and she had a good laugh at me. Luckily she had miscounted when she laid out the pajamas and I hadn't lost a child.

Bob, adoptive parent of 6 children, biological parent to 6 more, and foster parent to over 125 children in the last 22 years.

March 28 — Some Stay

"The fragrance of what you give away stays with you."
                                                    Earl Allen

There once was a child who came with a need
A sad story, few clothes, and tears on her sleeve.

We opened our home and invited her in
At first she was distant, then she began to grin.

We could see she was scared with pain deep in her soul
A little life threatened before growing very old.

We gave her a room with a soft, comfortable bed
A place to feel safe, a place to lay her head.

At first she didn't want to sleep, she was too afraid
And when we gave her food she would eat only the bread.

We accepted her for all she was and for all she would be
By showing her kindness and allowing her to be free

We gave, not to take from her, but to add hope to her life
And perhaps give her a standard to carry her through life.

So if she should stay or if she should go away
We know she can survive and be glad she came our way.

Donna

Perfect Little Angel

29 March

"The man with insight enough to admit his limitations comes nearest to perfection."
— Johann Von Goethe

When our nine-year-old foster daughter came here we quickly realized she needed lots of help with her social interactions. The first night at dinner she looked at us sweetly and said in a sad voice, "My mommy always told me not to talk to strangers and now I have to live with them."

Well, as you might imagine our hearts broke right then and there. We tried to comfort her as best we could and we explained the subtle difference between strangers you would meet on the street and foster parents. This girl had been in multiple foster homes and three different schools in the previous four months.

She was a perfect little angel for the first few weeks and we were hooked. Then the honeymoon was over and she became "hell on wheels" for much of the next six months. Later we found out she had used that strangers line on all the foster families she had been placed with and always found it a great sympathy getter. She had learned manipulation as a survival skill and she never hesitated to use it. My hope is that we have learned consistency and providing a nurturing structure as well as she learned manipulation.

Jan, foster parent.

March 30 — Sowing Seeds

"A smile is the beginning of love."
Mother Teresa of Calcutta

Don't give up, even when being a foster parent seems like a thankless job. When you see a child in your care smile for the first time, you will know that somehow, someway, you have given them a promise of hope for the future.

You have made a difference in that child's life, no matter how minute it may seem. With each new smile, know that you have planted yet another seed of hope.

Tonya Jo, foster parent for 120 children over the last 21 years.

Gone, But Never Forgotten

31 March

*"When I hear someone sigh, 'Life is hard,'
I am always tempted to ask, 'Compared to what?'"*
                                            Sydney J. Harris

Each child who has been placed with us holds a special place in our hearts and in our lives. While they are in our home they each select, and we purchase, something for our yard. If it is winter, it would be ornamental in nature—like a bird bath or a ceramic frog. For other seasons we plant trees, shrubs, rose bushes, tulip bulbs, or something like that. We name each plant or ornament after the child, and those items become concrete representations of how each child has become a part of our life.

If a tree or plant isn't weathering well, fear sets in; but, with new spring growth we are overjoyed. Some of our bushes are fifteen years old, and we still know their names. Bulbs bloom and roses flourish and we hold the hope in our hearts that the same is happening for their namesakes.

Trish, birth parent to 3 children, foster parent to nearly 600 children in the last 20 years, and grandparent to biological and foster grandchildren.

April 1 — Building a Nest

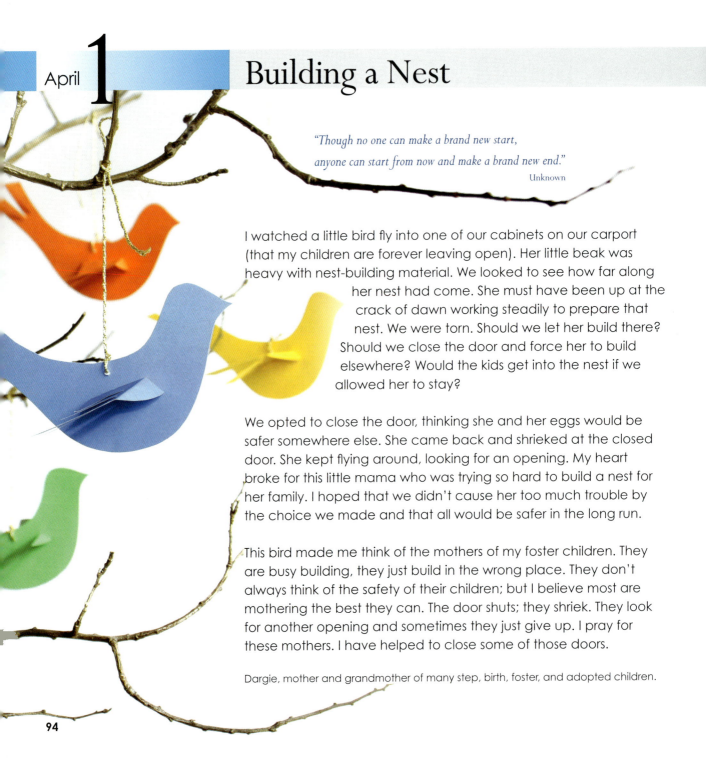

"Though no one can make a brand new start, anyone can start from now and make a brand new end."
Unknown

I watched a little bird fly into one of our cabinets on our carport (that my children are forever leaving open). Her little beak was heavy with nest-building material. We looked to see how far along her nest had come. She must have been up at the crack of dawn working steadily to prepare that nest. We were torn. Should we let her build there? Should we close the door and force her to build elsewhere? Would the kids get into the nest if we allowed her to stay?

We opted to close the door, thinking she and her eggs would be safer somewhere else. She came back and shrieked at the closed door. She kept flying around, looking for an opening. My heart broke for this little mama who was trying so hard to build a nest for her family. I hoped that we didn't cause her too much trouble by the choice we made and that all would be safer in the long run.

This bird made me think of the mothers of my foster children. They are busy building, they just build in the wrong place. They don't always think of the safety of their children; but I believe most are mothering the best they can. The door shuts; they shriek. They look for another opening and sometimes they just give up. I pray for these mothers. I have helped to close some of those doors.

Dargie, mother and grandmother of many step, birth, foster, and adopted children.

Progress

2 April

"We must be willing to get rid of the life we've planned, so as to have the life that is waiting for us."
Joseph Campbell

Recently, I took a few hours of time out of the middle of a busy day and went to read a story to my grandson's second grade class. I sat down in the small chair to read and looked around at the little faces looking up at me. They listened to every word, laughed at things they found funny, and made comments about the story.

After reading we went to lunch together and they all wanted to sit beside me at the table. I watched them trade food and make ketchup sandwiches. I listened as they explained how horrible it was to be sent to the "time out" table. I smiled as I watched them interact with one another and nearly burst with joy when I saw that my grandson had friends. It was great!

My daughter, his mother, was adopted when she was fifteen and things were much different than we had imagined after she came into our family. We had some rough times; but, she is now mom to two boys and, although they sometimes struggle, they are doing well.

When I left the school to drive back to my job where I would be dealing with telephone technicians, plumbing problems and a ton of volunteers, I just kept thinking, "This is what life is really all about." It is really about these kids, creating family and wholeness, and watching progress even in very small steps.

Susan, foster and adoptive parent, grandparent, and former foster family recruiter and trainer.

April 3 — Easter Miracle

"A very good thing about God is that he fits in your heart."
Sarah Gendron, age 5 as quoted by Dandi Daley Mackall in *Why I Believe in God*

We watched the parent visit through a two-way mirror. Our four-year-old foster son played with his Gramma while his mom took the compact from her purse and checked her makeup. He went over to her a few times, but she was in her own little world, too spaced out to notice him. How could he ever get through to her, I wondered?

Easter was coming and our other foster children, four siblings, wanted to invite their parents to our Easter service. Our foster son smiled, "Can I ask my mommy too?"

I told them I'd check with their social workers. It seemed that God had a plan because permission was granted. Easter came and we picked up their parents. Our church had rented a classic old theater to accommodate every one. The music was great, the drama touching, and the message clear and compelling. From that day on their parents came to church with us every Sunday until the children were returned to them.

That was 2 years ago and we still see him and his loving mom almost every Sunday at church, and he still greets my husband with a smiling, "Hi, Daddy."

Bobbi, birth, foster, and guardianship mom.

Good Enough?

"I came to understand that it was all right to do things for people as long as I did it for the sake of doing it… the value being more in the act than the result."

Joanna Field

When I first became a mother, I had ideas about how to do the job RIGHT. I thought children who were raised correctly would naturally grow up to make the choices I felt were appropriate. Life had a lot to teach me. Being a mother for awhile taught me to humbly accept the limitations of the role.

I learned to set limits and consequences that reflect the real world as much as possible so that my children would get a "safe" experience of what was in store for them. I had to let them decide for themselves if a consequence was too high for them to pay. I believed their sense of values and worth would be at least similar to my own. Wrong again.

As our children grow we come to recognize that they are separate from us and that they think, feel, and believe what is inside them, not what is inside us. It is a hard realization.

As parents we must stand strong in what we know to be true and we must be willing to bend with the waves of (sometimes) painful knowledge as we watch our children follow their own path. We do not know their life journey, but if we can lay down at night and know their life has been a little sweeter because we were in it, we are good enough.

Susan, foster and adoptive parent, grandparent, and former foster family recruiter and trainer.

April 5 — Will You?

"Death is not the greatest loss in life.
The greatest loss is what dies inside us while we live."
— Norman Cousins

Child it must be sad, when they take you away,
From the family you have loved from the very first day.

The grief, the anger, and the loneliness you feel,
No wonder you seem to have a cold heart of steel.

Will you give us a chance to show you we care?
Will you give us a small part of your life we can share?

Will you let us get close to you, and help you succeed?
Show you the kind of life we know you can lead?

Don't be afraid child, beside you we will stand,
And always be there to lend you a hand.

And when days look gloomy, and things don't seem bright,
Hold onto the thought that everything will be all right.

Charlene, biological parent of 4, a foster parent for 20 girls in the past 10 years, in the process of adopting an eight-year-old.

Spring

6 April

"Piglet was so excited at the idea of being useful that he forgot to be frightened any more."
Winnie-the-Pooh, A.A. Milne

When told that Spring was just around the corner, the little boy said, "But, I live right around the corner, and Spring isn't there."

Spring comes… every year, eventually. When it comes we get to shed those heavy coats. There is such a sense of freedom, a new beginning. Flowers pop up, trees bloom and grass turns green. The wonders of nature are in full swing.

I have smelled a little Spring in the air, so the kids and I will clean out the storage room this weekend. That's another benefit of Spring—Spring cleaning. The kids may not be too enthusiastic at first, but they get excited when they find hidden treasures (which they always do). It gives us a chance to take the new kids down memory lane as we dig through boxes accumulated throughout our years as a family. We can plan a beach trip while we look through summer stuff and relive Christmas as we put our decorations away properly.

Best of all, it doesn't cost anything and we do it as a family.

Dargie, mother and grandmother of many step, birth, foster, and adopted children.

April 7 — Forever Mommy

*"Parenting is a two-way street.
As you take them by the hand,
they will take you by the heart."*
— Judy Ford

My six-year-old foster daughter was watching me change her two-year-old sister on my huge king size bed. She was folding the blanket her sister lay on over and over between her fingers. She had been chitchatting with me, her big eyes framed by her corn silk, shoulder-length hair.

Their mother had died and their father was incarcerated. They had been taken to the agency and left by their overextended, exhausted foster mother, and they had been in my home for about one week. During a lull in the conversation, she looked up at me and asked, "Will you be my forever Mommy?"

I looked in those expressive eyes and said something about how I may not be her forever Mommy, but I would be her forever friend. She was HIV positive and so was her sister. I wondered how many mommies they would have to have. After they left my home, I lost track of them, and when I saw their siblings a few years later I was too scared to ask about them.

I often think of that day, it is one of many that replays in my mind over and over. I see those eyes and those little hands reaching toward me. When I think of her I pray she got a "forever Mommy." I know she got a forever friend.

Robin, foster mom to 30 children over 5 years.

Hugs

"God has no other hands than ours."
   Dorothee Solle

Human beings crave touch. For the little ones, a story or cuddle time is a great way to meet this need. But what do we do for the older kids and the children who have become frightened of touching. They need hugs too sometimes.

At first touching may be too strange or uncomfortable for these children so it is important to be sensitive and start with small touches like a pat on the back. It's hard to imagine going through life with no hugs but, for some kids, they may need to be brief in the beginning.

By giving genuine and respectful birthday hugs, congratulation hugs, great report card hugs, and thank you hugs, before you know it, they'll be hugging you.

Dargie, mother and grandmother of many step, birth, foster, and adopted children.

April 9 — Everyday Is a New Day

"The sun is new each day."
Heraclitus

One of the most important things that I stress in my home is that everyday is a new day. I try to sit and drink my tea and read my newspaper each morning while watching the sun come up before the children come downstairs.

This allows me to center myself and clean out any leftover negative feelings that I may have toward my children.

I believe that each day is a gift and I try to work hard with the children in a respectful and loving way. Even after a difficult day with a child, when I put them to bed I always say, "Tomorrow is a new day, and it will be a good day to start over."

Julie, biological parent, foster parent for about 6 years specializing in working with children with learning disabilities, ODD, and ADHD.

Teach a Boy to Garden

10 April

"Have a heart that never hardens, a touch that never hurts, a temper that never tires."

Sara Teasdale

One evening, I discovered my two-year-old foster grandson shoveling the contents of the raccoon's litter box onto the floor with a child's spade I had purchased for him. When asked what he was doing, he looked up and said, "Digger, planting, see Nana, digging."

At first I was angry and then I thought, "How can I get mad at that? I'm the one who taught him how to dig." Even before he could walk, I would take him outside with me to work in my hummingbird, butterfly garden. Eventually, I bought him a set of baby garden tools so he could dig and play alongside me.

As we worked, I told him how to dig the hole and plant the new plants, which plants to water and how much water they needed. By the end of the summer, with supervision, he was able to water them himself. As we sat very quietly in the swing, listening to the waterfall and watching the birds and butterflies, he would say "good" and "pretty." When winter came he cried to go to the garden, missing the peace and beauty we both experienced there.

As he shoveled the litter back into the box, I felt sure that he loved the time we spend in the garden together as much as I did. I also had the satisfaction of knowing I had taught him that peace and beauty can be created with the tiniest of hands.

Tonya, foster parent for over 120 children in the past 20 years.

April 11 — I Read the Book

"What it takes to succeed as a foster parent is a deep faith in God and a sense of humor."
Foster Cline

With six teenagers in the house, driving is a hot topic. We have two adolescent girls that are afraid to drive, two boys that can't wait, one that has been driving for almost two years, and one that doesn't care.

I had suggested that the seventeen-year-old girl get a book and start studying for her driver's test when the sixteen-year-old boy said, "She can have my book, I know how to drive."

With surprise in my voice, I asked, "Really?"

He confidently replied, "Yes, I read the book."

Wouldn't it be nice if we could all learn what we need to know in life by "reading the book"? Just think of all the parenting struggles that would save us. Unfortunately, that isn't how it works because real life is not as constant as a book. And besides, the best people to write the book are all too busy raising kids!

Dargie, mother and grandmother of many step, birth, foster, and adopted children.

Making Changes

12 April

"Parenting is a mirror that forces you to look at yourself."
Jon Kabat-Zinn

Most human behavior can be seen as a way to experience pleasure or avoid pain. Even the behaviors we see as destructive and dysfunctional were most likely created out of a desire to be in a place that is better than the one where we began.

It is often confusing for us as adults to observe the behaviors of our foster or adoptive children. We see the futility of the tantrum or the negative social consequences of incessant lying. And, we wonder, why don't they just stop? Can't they see this is harmful to them?

When those thoughts cross my mind, I have a plan. I go to my refrigerator, open the door, and survey all the things I continue to eat that I shouldn't. Knowing how hard I struggle with making changes in my diet that I KNOW are in my best interest helps me understand. I imagine how hard it must be for children to give up the behaviors that have created a place of emotional safety for them. That's got to be much harder than giving up chocolate cheesecake, and I haven't accomplished that yet.

Susan, foster and adoptive parent, grandparent, and former foster family recruiter and trainer.

April 13 — To My Precious Son

*"Not flesh of my flesh, nor bone of my bone,
But still miraculously my own. Never forget for a single
minute you didn't grow under my heart, but in it."*
                                                    Fleur Conkling Heyliger

Let me tell you about the happiest day of my life. It all began with a phone call. A very special woman, your birth-mother, told me she was having labor pains and needed to go to the hospital. Your dad and I rushed to pick her up and get us all there as quickly as possible. The remainder of the day, long into the evening, we sat, walked and slept the time away with your birth-mother. We all anxiously awaited your arrival.

The afternoon of the following day, the doctor was called. One of God's miracles was about to unfold. Watching your birth was proof of such miracles. Your birth-mother, on that day, gave me the greatest gift any adoptive parent could receive. That gift was the opportunity to see the birth of my child and to be the first to hold you.

I am grateful to God for sending you to earth, and to your birth-mother for giving me the opportunity to be your "mom-mom."

Love you always, Mom
  p.s. Did I tell you today, how much I love you?

Leigh, adoptive parent and former foster child.

I Changed the Program

14 April

*"There comes that mysterious meeting in life
when someone acknowledges who we are and what we can be,
igniting the circuits of our highest potential."*

Rusty Berkus

When I worked in a group home with foster children we often received tokens of support from the community in the form of movie passes, complimentary tickets to the bowling alley, and gift certificates for restaurants. I noticed an attitude about these gifts which was something like, "People owe this to me because I'm in foster care." The kids would actually be irritated if something they wanted wasn't available. I began to wonder if we were doing these children more harm than good by giving them something others had to work for. So, I changed the program.

From that point on each item we received for their use was placed in a community store and they had to do volunteer work someplace in the community to barter for the tickets. The children were not happy about this but over time the grumbling lessened. They raked leaves, hauled old newspapers, helped clean a local church and tackled many other projects.

My consistent message to them was, "You are fully capable of earning money like other people; you are not pitiful; you do not have to be dependent on the good will of others to get what you want." This program was successful while I was there and I have to believe those children, who are now adults, carry at least part of that lesson with them.

Susan, foster and adoptive parent, grandparent, and former foster family recruiter and trainer.

April 15 — The Most Valuable of All Things

"It is not enough to feel love for your child, you must be able to express your love through your actions."

Judy Ford

When my children, especially the teenagers, do not understand why I have said no to something they want to do, I tell them the following:

Imagine someone said to you, "Here is the most expensive shiny sports car in the world and I want you to take care of it." Your job would be to wash it and keep it clean, drive it occasionally, take it to the mechanic when it needs a tune-up, keep it safe from thieves and vandals, ensure it had a nice clean place to park and keep it safe from the elements. You would want to fill it with only the best quality gasoline and treat it with care. Now, if someone came to you with that responsibility you'd probably think, "Wow, they really trust me and I have to do my best to take care of this car as if it's my own."

Well, my children are a billion times more valuable to me than a car. My job is to make sure they are safe, protected and cared for in the best possible way. So I would say I have the most important job in the world because I'm taking care of the most valuable of all things… a child.

Robin, foster mom to 30 children over 5 years.

Robot

16 April

"So, learning rather than accomplishment is the issue of parenthood."
Polly Berrien Berends

Last week my husband and I had to take our six-year-old for an EKG and blood work. Every other time we had been in for testing had been a nightmare, and I was anxious just thinking about going. My husband said, "I'll go and help, it will be fine."

We went in after giving our son a brief explanation of what would happen because it had been some time since his last blood test and EKG. We also promised him lunch any place he wanted to go.

My husband lay with him on the bed as he was hooked up for the EKG. We told him to pretend he was a robot. It worked, and we were out of the hospital with both tests finished in half an hour. We ate lunch and enjoyed the rest of the day. We were so proud of his maturity since the last tests.

He woke up the next morning and said, "I don't want to be a robot any more."

"You aren't a robot," I responded.

He raised his shirt and said, "Yes, I am. Look!" I remembered the test and smiled. It took some explaining to help him understand that he only pretended to be still like a robot for the test. It helped me understand how seriously our children take the things we say and, hopefully, I will be more careful the next time.

Dargie, mother and grandmother of many step, birth, foster, and adopted children.

April 17 — The Adventure

"So many things are possible just as long as you don't know they're impossible."
— Norton Juster

For those people considering the adventure, or for those new to foster parenting I will say that it is a challenge. I will also tell you that there is nothing greater, nothing more special, and nothing that I wouldn't do to get to do it all over again.

My family had a great many doubts and concerns about me fostering. I heard everything from "you're crazy" to "your own children will be at great risk." I followed my heart though, and kept pressing on toward the license and the privilege of working with these special children.

Now, that same family grieves with me over the loss of two very special children. My parents are losing their only grandsons as they return to their birth family and it is heavy in their hearts. My sisters also feel a great loss and have expressed their sorrow, but never has anybody said they wished it hadn't happened. Everyone in my life has been touched by these boys and has individually come to me and told me they were glad I went ahead to foster.

There is a good side to fostering, a very rewarding, meaningful, heart enlightening good side. I am sure most foster parents would agree that there is nothing like it in the whole wide world, and that they would do it again despite the good, the bad, and the ugly.

Sheila, single mom to 5 smiling kids.

Wit & Wisdom

18 April

"You only live once, but if you work it right, once is enough."

Joe E. Lewis

Sometimes wit is the saving grace for our foster and adopted children. One Sunday my nine-year-old foster (soon to be adopted) daughter was attending an activity at our church. Another little girl had brought a friend along and was introducing her to the other children.

When they reached my daughter, the little girl introduced her friend and then, turning to the girl explained that my daughter was a "foster kid." Well, without missing a beat, my daughter simply said, "No, I'm a Williams' kid. I don't know anyone named Foster!"

Debi, birth and adoptive parent, foster parent to over 30 children in the past 12 years.

April 19 — Becoming a Woman

"When we are in the presence of another person, we are on holy ground; God is at work in that person, too."
Eugene Peterson

Puberty is not easy. Can you imagine how hard it must be to enter puberty in foster care? All the changes and new emotions are confusing for the most stable child, but who do you talk to when you have just moved into a new foster home and you start your menstrual cycle?

We had a preteen foster daughter once who had just started her journey into womanhood with no one to confide in. As soon as she began to feel comfortable with me she told me what had happened.

My teen age daughter, and my daughter-in-law were there and we all joined in a discussion where she was free to ask every question that was on her mind. They spoke openly about how everything works and why. Combining biology, laughter, love and a sense of connectedness, they explained the art of being a woman.

I am so thankful we could be there for her that week. Even though her stay was brief, we were blessed to have been part of such a special milestone in her life. With the help of women who cared, something mysterious and scary was transformed into something understandable and wonderful.

Dargie, mother and grandmother of many step, birth, foster, and adopted children.

Possibilities

20 April

"Every child, every living person, longs to be able to communicate his thoughts, his feelings, his capabilities, to put his thumbprint on the world and to say, I'm here."

Fredelle Maynard, author of Raisins & Apples

There is an image I hold in my mind which has become the symbol of possibilities for me. It is an image of a thin, attractive teenage boy, ruddy complexion, his long straight hair falling across his face as he gently holds a tiny infant in his arms.

This boy was committed to the department of corrections for his past behaviors. When his probation officer visited my home the last time he was removed, he apologized for ever having placed him there. The probation officer deemed him a "bad kid" with no hope for rehabilitation. I laughed and then I felt like crying and I knew the system had failed this boy.

I had seen him hold and nurture a child with such tenderness that it took my breath away. I watched him soothe the baby's fears and sing tunes most often heard on MTV in a sort of lullaby rhythm. He only exhibited this deeply protected, vulnerable part of himself for a few moments in time, but I never forgot it. And it is that image I hold in my mind when I keep going day after day trying to make the world just a little bit better place for all the other kids out there who are sometimes considered "bad." And I wonder how we can do a better job of seeing and bringing out their goodness.

Susan, foster and adoptive parent, grandparent, and former foster family recruiter and trainer.

April 21 — Surprised by Kindness

"God tells us to burden Him with whatever burdens us."
Unknown

When natural or adoptive parents have a child facing surgery they want to be with the child as long as possible. As a foster parent, I was concerned I wouldn't be allowed to stay with my eight-month-old foster child who was having surgery.

As it turned out, my fears were unnecessary. The nurses and doctors were wonderful, and they let me stay with him up until time to go to the operating room. Afterward the doctor came and took me to my foster son. When he was ready to leave the recovery room, I was allowed to carry him back up to his room. He was up and drinking juice within an hour and we were home in time to meet the other children as they got off the bus.

It was quite a day, but one I remember with warm feelings and a smile. I was thankful for the kindness of the hospital staff and that they were able to recognize that, even though I was a temporary parent for this child, I was certainly still his psychological parent in this situation.

Dargie, mother and grandmother of many step, birth, foster, and adopted children.

How Can We Win?

*"Everything we do seeds the future.
No action is an empty one."*
Joan Chittister

Possibly one of the biggest problems in foster care these days is that workers are inadequately trained. Often they have had no children and very little life experience. Now that doesn't always make a bad worker but, let's face it, some things you just cannot learn from a book, no matter what your profession.

In a social worker's case it isn't a matter of a lost contract when a mistake is made, it's an actual child that suffers and they suffer forever.

They often treat children as numbers in a file with no emotions, no thought to what they might do to their lives. There are a few good workers who care enough to stand up to the system and do right by the kids but they are few and far between and, unfortunately, the system often beats them down too.

We are told to advocate for the kids in our care and yet when we do this we are often reprimanded and condemned for stepping over our bounds. When we don't advocate we are neglectful and are told the kids needs would be better met somewhere else. How can we win in a system like that? How can the kids win? If we don't stand up for the kids and the worker doesn't even know them well enough to stand up for them… who will? Is it any wonder we have such angry kids these days? In fact, is it any wonder we have such angry foster parents these days?

Deena, foster, birth, and adoptive mom to a great bunch of kids.

April 23 — Successful Moments

"I try to tell people to keep having hope. It's always what you don't know and don't expect that's gonna be so great."
Roseanne Barr

It was a rainy, indoor afternoon when the eight-year-old boy walked past me as he was going to plug a video into the VCR. He casually glanced at me and demanded, "Get me a popsicle." I said nothing for a moment and he walked toward the TV and then he stopped abruptly.

He turned and looked at me and said, "Wait a minute. I'm sorry. You're not my slave. I guess I can get it for myself." He then proceeded to go to the kitchen and get his own treat.

He did not understand the full meaning of his statement, but I was smiling from ear to ear! He had heard some of the things I had been saying over the last five weeks. He had actually taken responsibility for something, and he had apologized for being rude.

We can work long and hard with children to teach them appropriate behavior and sometimes they get it and sometimes they don't. Having a clear moment when you can see that something you said, some rule you have in place, some effort you made to teach a skill was successfully adapted: well, that can make your day! Knowing we have accomplished even the tiniest thing often gives us the momentum to keep on going.

Susan, foster and adoptive parent, grandparent, and former foster family recruiter and trainer.

Do We Care Enough?

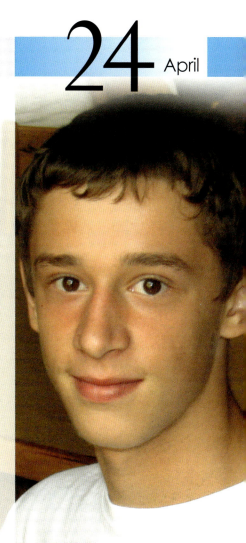

24 April

"Love builds highways out of dead ends."
Louis Gittner

Most of us think of foster families taking care of small children, but Nathan was 16 when his mother abandoned him. He'd never known his dad and had nowhere to turn. Nathan's situation moved one family to compassion and out of their comfort zone. The couple had small children of their own and didn't know the first thing about raising a teenager. But with zero experience and a little bit of faith, the family invited Nathan into their home.

There were many adjustments including new financial and emotional demands. Everyone had to give a little more, take a little less; sacrifices had to be made. But inch, by step, by yard the family and Nathan made those adjustments and melded into a functioning family unit.

Nathan stayed with his foster family until he went away to college. He stays in touch and says that he learned about family from the years he spent with them. Both Nathan and his late-found family are glad they crossed paths.

Most children needing a foster home are not as old as Nathan and not all children needing a foster home stay as long as he did. But whether their situation is like Nathan's or not, their need for family is the same. And you, like Nathan's foster family, can meet that need.

Jim, from his "Family Talk" column in *The Daily Oklahoman*.

April 25

How to Hope

"Let us not look back in anger, nor forward in fear, but around us in awareness."

James Thurber

She was a sixteen-year-old foster child without a wishbone. Although not clinically depressed, she lacked enthusiasm, vision or even chutzpah. Sadly, her past had soured her, and in effect had obliterated her sense of future.

Her stepmother, an enthusiastic, bustling woman with energy to spare, was initially puzzled and incredulous about her stepdaughter's lack of future. She decided something had to be done about it. She coached her stepdaughter on how to hope and daydream out loud with her. She would say, "Let's plan what we'll do this evening… this weekend… this summer… where should we go on our summer car trip?… what are you going to be when you grow up?

Kids need to learn that tomorrows don't need to be rehashed versions of their yesterdays. We should encourage them to plan, to expect, to hope, and to dream. More basically, we need to teach them how to think ahead, not just so they are more plan-full and less impulsive and rash, but so they can derive pleasure from the future.

Rick, clinical psychologist, trainer, and consultant who has worked with foster and adoptive children and their parents over the past 20 years.

Breakthroughs

*"None of us has the power to make someone else love us.
But we all have the power to give away love, to love other people.
And if we do so, we change the kind of person we are,
and we change the kind of world we live in."*

Rabbi Harold Kushner

Our foster daughter came from a family where men treated women very poorly. They abused the females, even the children. Needless to say she has had a great deal of difficulty interacting with my husband. Once she even admitted she was trying to break us up so she and I could live happily ever after without him.

The therapists told my husband not to take it personally, but that wasn't easy to do when she would leave the room when he entered and referred to him as, "him." This very manipulative girl found his buttons quickly and stomped on them every chance she got.

We tried family meetings to discuss the problem. We talked to the therapist about it and we discussed it one on one with the child. She said she was not afraid of my husband, trusted him and knew he would keep her safe and never hurt her.

We have taken a few steps forward and many steps back in her willingness to interact with my husband in a positive manner. Lately, she has appeared more willing to get along with him. She has even hugged him and allowed him to hug her back. I know we will have some backsliding, but the tears glistening in my husband's eyes at their "breakthrough" were worth millions.

Jan, foster parent.

April 27 — Close to My Son

"We must move from asking God to take care of things that are breaking our hearts, to praying about the things that are breaking His heart."
— Margaret Gibb

I had a great job, a new relationship, a new home, and two beautiful kids—life was good! Then my six-year-old son had his tonsils removed. After the surgery the bleeding was not stopping as it should, and I took him back to the doctor several times. A week after surgery when I gave him his nighttime medication, he said, "I love you, Mom," and headed for bed. He died that night.

A year later I was suicidal, but my supportive family dragged me off to a Bereaved Parents Meeting where I saw other parents who were not able to go on with their lives. I realized they had surviving children and those kids were hurting because their parents could not heal and move on. I knew I could not let that happen to my beautiful, innocent daughter.

I went on to have twin girls and my son became an angel in my life, and when I heard of a hurting child I would ask him to give that child comfort. Finally it occurred to me that I didn't have to always send my son because I was able to make a difference here on earth. That realization led me to foster care.

I have not regretted one day since, not even an hour of what we do as a family. It keeps me close to my children, close to that feeling of pure purpose and, as always, close to my son.

Kate, birth, step, and adoptive parent.

Meetings

"Sometimes we focus so hard on all the things we're suppose to do that we forget to enjoy. And children are only with us for a very short time."

Judy Ford

We all have meetings… therapy, doctors, M-teams, workshops, etc. Our area tried to start a support group last year. I appreciate that, but if I add one more meeting to my calendar, it may fall from the weight.

I decided this past Fall to add FUN things like piano and guitar lessons, tumbling, and sports. I want the kids to be busy and have something to build their self esteem. Perhaps that is the support **they** need.

As for myself… I may buy those tai chi tapes. When I get the hang of it and don't look silly any more, I'll invite the kids to join me. It looks like a great stress reliever.

Dargie, mother and grandmother of many step, birth, foster, and adopted children.

April 29 — My Bunny

"Sometimes when I'm unhappy, God tickles me."
Beaux Martin, age 5 as quoted in *Why I Believe in God* by Dandi Daley Mackall

When I was about eight years old and living in a foster home my parents used to come and visit me on holidays. One Easter my parents brought me a solid chocolate, three pound Easter Bunny. I was so excited!

Then my foster mom told me that I had to share the bunny with the other thirteen foster children. I was shocked and decided to hide my big chocolate bunny somewhere no one could find it. I looked around the big farm house and decided to hide it in the basement in a big round furnace. When I opened the door I saw a perfect spot, a ledge right in the middle of the furnace. I put my bunny on the ledge and closed the furnace door.

For several days I would sneak down to the furnace and eat pieces of my bunny. Then one night it got cold. We were all in the front room watching television when my foster dad said, "Something stinks." My foster mom added, "It smells like chocolate." I yelled, "MY BUNNY!" I ran down stairs to the basement, opened up the furnace door and watched my bunny melting in the hot furnace.

My foster mom hoped I had learned that sharing my bunny with the other children would have prevented this disaster. Basically, I learned never to hide things in the furnace!

Bob, biological, adoptive, and foster parent and former foster child.

Out of the Mouths of Babes

30 April

"The essence of our effort to see that every child has a chance must be to assure each an equal opportunity, not to become equal, but to become different—to realize whatever unique potential of body, mind and spirit s/he possesses."

John Fischer

My kids have come to understand that families come in all different shapes, sizes, colors, and combinations. My girls are very open and don't make the assumptions that most of us make about families. So, when they meet a white mom, a white dad, and a white child, they are still curious about the other children. They are eager to find out if the kids are "brown" or "peach," what color hair they have, what they like to play with, and whether they have any "problems with their bodies" (which comes from being exposed to persons with different abilities or medical problems).

It pleases me that my girls are so open. I do have to laugh when they get curious about our pregnant friends. They both understand the difference between a birth, foster, and adoptive mother. I have explained to them many times that generally when a white birth mom and dad have a baby, the baby will be white. I have also explained that when a black birth dad and mom have a baby, it will generally be black. But being children who delight in diversity, they still cannot wait to see what color baby the parents end up having!

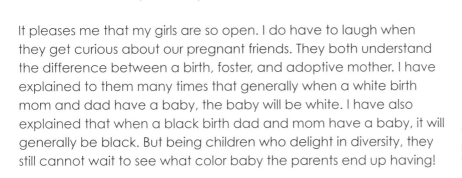

Valerie, adoptive parent and foster parent for medically fragile children for 10 years.

May 1 Quarantine

*"God is our refuge and our strength,
an ever-present help in distress."*
                                Psalms 46:1

There was a period of time when my little two-year-old, shaken baby vomited every day for several months. We never knew when or where it would happen. It was difficult to go anywhere with him. I finally got to the point where I took him, yucky clothes and all, to the doctor's office and told them I wasn't leaving until the doctor did **something** to help us.

He told me to go home, pack a bag, and meet him at the hospital. They tested and tested, called in specialists, and kept us in quarantine for about five days. They thought he had whooping cough. They called in the Health Department and began dispensing medication to all his classmates at preschool – "just to be safe." After a nose culture and a few days to complete the test, whooping cough was ruled out.

Eventually, the vomiting stopped as mysteriously as it had begun. The neurologist said it was possibly due to his brain growing and developing.

My faith in God is all that kept me going through that ordeal. Looking back, I realize it helped me take doctors down off the pedestal and realize we are all just human. They were as frustrated as I was, with no answers, only questions. Even now, it is a mystery and, thank God, a memory.

Dargie, mother and grandmother of many step, birth, foster, and adopted children.

Families Like Ours

2 May

"Yesterday is history, tomorrow is mystery, today is a gift."
Eleanor Roosevelt

On a recent drive home from the store, my six-year-old birth daughter and her four and a half-year-old foster brother were bickering in the back seat. He said he was never going to marry a girl, only himself, but he was going to have kids. She told him he can't ever be a dad because when she grows up she is going to have ALL the kids.

Thinking I might need to become involved in this conversation, I asked the typical "do you know where babies come from" question. Without hesitation she replied, "Of course I do, Mom. You just call the case worker!"

Only in families like ours.

Teresa, birth, adoptive, and foster mom specializing in fostering mentally ill children.

May 3 — Advice to Myself

"You can never take for granted what you have always known."
Angie Walker

It would be wonderful to be able to take children into your home and treat them like your own. I have the greatest admiration in the world for adults who have that temperament. But not all of us are born with that strength of heart or selflessness or whatever label you might care to assign.

In my extended family, there are children who live in foster care. The two girls live with foster parents less than an hour away. Often I ask myself rather guiltily what I assume others would also ask of me: Why can't I just have them live with us? The answer is always complicated, but usually winds up with something like: It's all I can do to handle my own life, let alone interject more lives into the equation. I do what I can—sharing holidays, small trips, band instruments and gentle ribbings about our tastes in music. It's not a lot. But it's something. And we all get something positive from it.

Awkward? Selfish? Unforgivable? Maybe all true on some level. But then I think about how well they are doing. They are living in a stable home with people who thrive amidst the busy little population. The girls never lacked for love, but they needed structure and predictability, which they now enjoy.

The truth is, it's worked out far better for me to be an uncle than a father. Better for them, because this is what I can give freely and lovingly. And better for me, because I've accepted my own limitations. We all can live with that.

Steve, birth parent, uncle to 2 nieces in foster care.

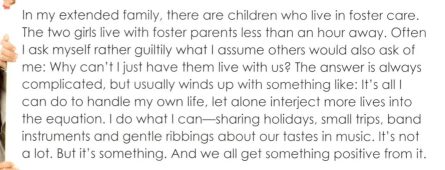

Baby Holders

4 May

"My mother had a great deal of trouble with me, but I think she enjoyed it."

Mark Twain

Several years ago we took a four day trip to visit family in North Carolina. It was the first time in nine years that I had traveled with an infant. It was my first time ever traveling with a hyperactive infant.

My brother and sister-in-law were there when I loaded the car. We took the play pen for inside/outside play and sleep, the walker for meals and such, the stroller for walks, and the car seat for travel. They laughed as we packed and joked about us taking the kitchen sink.

I was kind of embarrassed and considered removing something. On second thought however, I decided I knew my child and I knew that I needed everything I had packed.

On the way home, I was so thankful that I had stuck to my original plan. The trip was very enjoyable, mainly due to the "baby holders" where my child was safe when he wasn't in my arms.

Dargie, mother and grandmother of many step, birth, foster, and adopted children.

May 5 — The Observation Room

"God chooses to become present to and through us. It is up to us to rescue one another."

Nancy Mairs

The caseworker and therapist explained TPR (termination of parental rights) to the four sisters as we watched through an observation window. The girls ranged in age from preschool through early adolescence and their level of understanding varied.

I tried to imagine being a child who is learning that you are going to become an orphan. I tried to put myself in their place and see if I could even come close to understanding how it would feel. Of course, it was useless.

The oldest child cried silently signaling her understanding of the process. The second oldest girl scowled and made a few angry comments. The next sister demanded the judge listen to her and let her go home to her mom.

In the observation room we hardly breathed and all our hearts broke as the youngest child spoke. "You know," she said in her little girl voice, "some parents who love their children just aren't able to take care of them."

As she spoke, her foster mom started crying and said, "Oh, my, she really has been listening to me all along." I placed my arm around her shoulder, allowing her to release some of her pain. You know, she was right, they all do really hear what we say whether they let us know or not.

Susan, foster and adoptive parent, grandparent, and former foster family recruiter and trainer.

Material Possessions

*"What the heart gives away is never gone…
it is kept in the heart of others."*

Robin St. John

When I first began doing foster care I thought that I would never give my children thrift store clothes or anything less than what I would give my own children. I wanted to provide them with exciting toys and things they would not have access to in their birth homes. Later, I learned how much of a disservice this can be to a child.

I made things easier, newer, crisper, and cleaner than they had ever experienced before. The message I unintentionally sent them was that there was something wrong with their birth family's level of income. Eventually, I learned to encourage them to save, purchase items on clearance, and even accept donations. I kept presents and holidays to a reasonable level and helped them enjoy the non-expensive, noncommercial parts of the holidays and celebrations. I realized they could still be proud and accept their level of income as well as learn ways to increase it if they chose to do so.

I could buy them brand new this or that, but when it came right down to it, I couldn't give them brand new circumstances. If I spoiled them with material things they wouldn't have when they returned home, it only made the transition more difficult for them. I certainly did not want to do that.

Robin, foster mom to 30 children over 5 years.

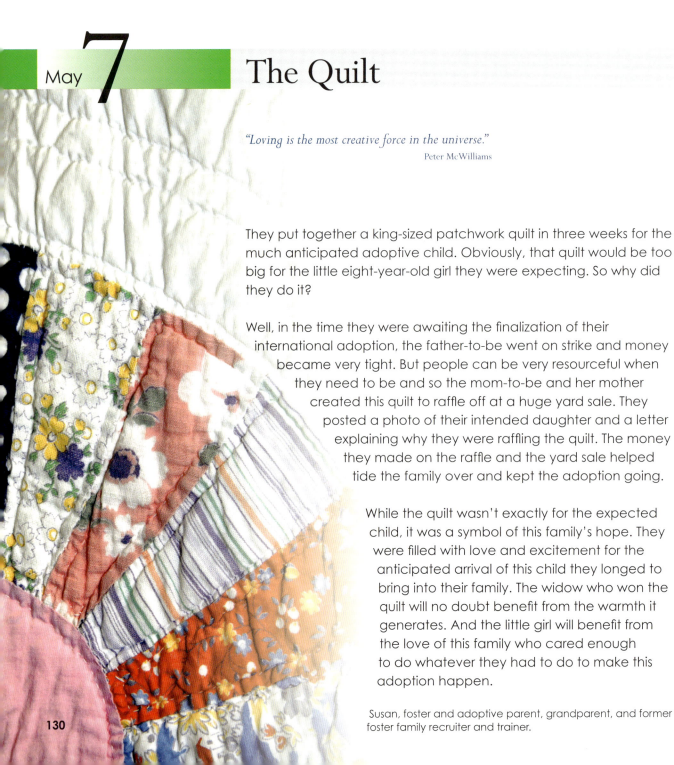

May 7 — The Quilt

"Loving is the most creative force in the universe."
Peter McWilliams

They put together a king-sized patchwork quilt in three weeks for the much anticipated adoptive child. Obviously, that quilt would be too big for the little eight-year-old girl they were expecting. So why did they do it?

Well, in the time they were awaiting the finalization of their international adoption, the father-to-be went on strike and money became very tight. But people can be very resourceful when they need to be and so the mom-to-be and her mother created this quilt to raffle off at a huge yard sale. They posted a photo of their intended daughter and a letter explaining why they were raffling the quilt. The money they made on the raffle and the yard sale helped tide the family over and kept the adoption going.

While the quilt wasn't exactly for the expected child, it was a symbol of this family's hope. They were filled with love and excitement for the anticipated arrival of this child they longed to bring into their family. The widow who won the quilt will no doubt benefit from the warmth it generates. And the little girl will benefit from the love of this family who cared enough to do whatever they had to do to make this adoption happen.

Susan, foster and adoptive parent, grandparent, and former foster family recruiter and trainer.

Weed Eater

"It's always something."
Gilda Radner

A while back we moved into a great house with a wonderful yard that has something in bloom from the first hint of spring until way into summer. Our first spring here, I was amazed and quite pleased.

We trimmed the branches that scratched the van as we drove down the driveway and mowed what we knew was grass. That is until my fifteen-year-old foster son got hold of the weed eater. There had been beautiful flower beds and vines surrounding several trees in the yard. One in particular flowed down the hill to the right of the driveway. The vines and little purple flowers had cascaded down the hill hiding rough chunks of cement.

I went to check the mail one day and there with the beautiful green and purple blanket was chopped away to reveal the cement pieces. My foster son had seen something growing on cement and trimmed it back. It took an entire year, until the following spring, for the vines to grow back. I have to admit I don't trust him with the weed eater any more. Perhaps he saw beauty in the cement or maybe he was a fifteen-year-old with a tool that could alter nature, maybe it was a power thing. However, in this case my power overrides and he is now banned from using the weed eater and in charge of mowing!

Dargie, mother and grandmother of many step, birth, foster, and adopted children.

May 9

Simplify

"The greatest gift we give each other is the quality of our attention."
Richard Moss

As parents, we have become increasingly aware of the pitfalls of over-programing our children. It begins innocuously enough; scheduling our child for one enriching activity, then another, and another… Until we begin to realize that our child is on sensory overload and that "quality time" with our child has been reduced to rushed, disjointed chats in the car on the way to endless indistinguishable destinations.

At times like these, it may help to reflect upon the words of Ralph Waldo Emerson, "Life is frittered away in detail: Simplify, simplify!" We would all be wise to heed his words. A backyard camp out, complete with flashlights, campfire and s'mores is many times more meaningful to a child, and certainly less stressful to parents, than an arduously planned and intricately scheduled, costly vacation.

Many times the endless, mundane tasks we feel obliged to perform, upon reflection, prove to be exactly as they seem - unnecessary and borne completely of habit and misplaced obligation!

Judy

Is It Worth It?

"My heart... reflecting back... each child adds a piece to my heart and then takes a piece away, making for an unending supply."

Dargie Arwood

The knowledge that you can give a child a home and love, even if for a little while, is the thing that keeps us fostering over and over. Sometimes it is terrifying to send that same child back to the people who hurt him to begin with, sometimes there isn't a choice. At least for the time they are in my home, whether it be for a day or a couple of years, they are loved and cared for and safe.

The joy we have received in doing this has by far outweighed the pain. We have literally saved children's lives. We have contact with many of them and with their adoptive or birth families. Our home has been filled with children, many of them delightful, some of them so hurt our hearts break over them. We love them as our own while they are here, and they take a part of us with them when they leave.

Marjie, adoptive parent, foster parent for 26 years to over 200 children.

May 11 — Mommy, I Love You

"It is astounding in this world how things don't turn out at all the way you expect them to."

Agatha Christie

"There are so many things I missed out on before I started the process of adopting my daughter—coloring Easter eggs, carving pumpkins, trick-or-treating, reading stories together, brushing hair, and of course, going to see Santa. But nothing is more rewarding than when, at the end of a tough day, your daughter says, 'Mommy, I love you' and hugs you so tight. God, how I yearned for someone to call me mommy and to feel that selfless love of a child. She is the best thing that has ever happened to me. I believe that there is a reason for everything that happens in life, things may not have worked out the way I thought they should, but they worked out better than I could have imagined."

Pat, foster parent for over 2 years, currently in the process of adopting.

A Rainbow of Children

12 May

"In praising or loving a child, we love and praise not that which is, but that which we hope for."

Johann Wolfgang von Goethe

I have fostered since 1993; I have also worked for the social services as a social worker for nearly ten years. I have done most of this work on my own as a single parent. I usually have five boys at any given time, so my life can get a little crazy trying to keep up with it all.

I have raised a lot of other people's children—all ages, sizes, colors, and cultures. I've had a rainbow of children at any given time. I have laughed, cried, danced… and a few times let out a good yell at them. I have a million memories and a zillion thoughts in regard to my children.

I have taken in children with Attention Deficit Disorder, children who are Obsessive/Compulsive, kids who have problems with drugs and/or alcohol, kids with sexually transmitted disease, and kids who have been unruly, and on probation or house arrest.

Sometimes it sounds impossible, but it isn't. I have done it and others will do it after me. We can't give up on our kids. We are their hope for tomorrow and, in many ways, they are our hope also. In their effort to live better lives we glimpse what is possible.

Carolyn, social worker and foster parent to teen boys.

May 13 — Mother's Day

"It isn't the great big pleasures that count the most; it's making a great deal out of the little ones."
— Jean Webster

On Mother's Day it is really nice. You would think the kids would want to give the things they make to their real mom, but I get a lot of gifts and cards from my foster kids and natural kids. They make me breakfast and watch the babies if we have any, clean house and try to make supper. It feels wonderful because their actions show that they do love and appreciate me.

Patty, foster parent to approximately 70 children in the last 11 years, biological parent of 2, step parent of 2, and grandmother to 6.

Mother by Choice

14 May

"This song of mine will wind its music around you, my child, like the fond arms of love."
— Rabindranath Tagore

One day we came home and our adopted daughter was not there, and she did not come home for the next two years. During that time, I had many opportunities to reflect on what made me her mother.

It certainly was not genetic makeup or the fact that she grew inside my body. It wasn't that she called me "Mom," because she had always called me by my first name. It was not the papers we had laying in a box someplace that said she was legally our daughter. So, what was it?

Near Mother's Day of the second year she was gone, I finally decided that no matter what she thought of me, no matter how distant our relationship had become, no matter if I ever saw her again or not, I would always be her mother. I was her mother because I had decided to be her mother. I had decided to think of her as my daughter, love her even when I did not like her behavior, and worry over her life as most mothers do.

When she returned home, she brought with her a nearly one-year-old son. I am his grandmother because I choose to be. When she brought him to meet us for the first time she told me she wanted him to know what a real family was like, and the mother in me smiled broadly and welcomed them both with open arms.

Susan, foster and adoptive parent, grandparent, and former foster family recruiter and trainer.

May 15 — The Towel

"Always be a little kinder than necessary."
James M. Barrie

It was a sunny day in May, and I was nervous as we turned into the drive of the simple block house to visit my fifteen-year-old daughter's half-sister. I had never met any of my daughter's birth family and she had not seen her sister, Dorothy, in the two years she had lived with me. Dorothy, a very active older woman, functioned as the hub for her extensive family.

She was warm and friendly as she ushered us into her clean but cramped home. She took great joy in telling us about each of my daughter's nine siblings, including their current whereabouts and how they were getting along. Kindly, she also shared with my daughter how her birth mother was doing. Their father, the parent they had in common, had died several years before.

When the visit was over and we got up to leave, Dorothy went into the next room and returned with a brightly wrapped package. I was astonished when she handed the package to me. Then she looked me straight in the eye and said, "Happy Mother's Day," and she thanked me for taking care of her sister.

As an infertile woman who adopted a very challenging teenager, I constantly wondered if I was doing things correctly. Dorothy's acknowledgment of my role as a mother touched me deeply. I have never dried a dish with the kitchen towel that was in that box because it is much too precious to me. It has come to symbolize the day I became a mother.

Susan, foster and adoptive parent, grandparent, and former foster family recruiter and trainer.

Making a Difference

16 May

*"So I began to stop and think when somebody entered the room:
If I loved this person, how would I behave toward him or her?"*
                                                    Bernie Siegel

A foster family who had not planned to take any teenagers because they had small children in the house was approached about taking in a parenting teenage girl. This was to be temporary since she was going on to another placement to learn parenting skills, so they said yes.

Despite her history of lying and stealing, the teen mom was always nice and polite and tried to follow the rules, but that got more difficult as time went by. When she finally left, the foster mother felt it was really time for her to go. She was sure this was one placement where she hadn't made one bit of difference. However, on Mother's Day that year she was deeply touched when her former foster daughter called her.

The girl had told her foster mom she would never finish school because of the baby. Two school years later however, the foster daughter called to invite this foster mom to her graduation, stating that the encouragement she got from this woman helped her finish.

We never really know the effect we may have on these children who enter our lives for a brief but powerful moment.

Susan, foster and adoptive parent, grandparent, and former foster family recruiter and trainer.

May 17 — Purple

> "You are your most valuable asset. Don't forget that. You are the best thing you have."
>
> Gary Paulsen, Hatchet

In first grade, Mr. Lohr said my purple teepee wasn't realistic enough, that purple was no color for a tent, that purple was a color for people who died, that my drawing wasn't good enough to hang with the others. I walked back to my seat counting the swish, swish, swishes of my baggy corduroy trousers.

With a black crayon, nightfall came to my purple tent in the middle of an afternoon.

In second grade, Mr. Barta said, "Draw anything." He didn't care what. I left my paper blank and when he came around to my desk, my heart beat like a tom-tom while he touched my head with his big hand and in a soft voice said, "The snowfall. How clean and white and beautiful."

Anon

Birth Parents

"In all endeavors strive to celebrate the spirit of the warrior…
Calm, Centered, Certain… whether tending to the flower garden
or searching for the heart of the divine."

Jo-Anne Rowley

I know you sometimes worry that, as a foster parent, I might try to take your child or turn him against you, but that's not what I want. I desire with all my heart that you would see how precious a gift you have been given. I wish that you could see the strength in your child, learn from it and, no matter what the reason, make the necessary changes for his sake. I wish that you could feel the joy and passion, privilege and honor of loving, comforting, holding, and raising this gift from God. I wish that you would look into the eyes of your gift and say, "I'm sorry," and mean it.

But, until you are ready to do that, I will do it for you. I will be grateful for your child and try to show him his goodness. I will continue to hope you will come home to him someday soon, healthy and willing to work hard to keep him. When that time comes, I will hand him over to you with sadness because I have loved him and with joy because he will be back where he belongs.

Joanne, foster parent.

May 19 — One Hour Speed Clean

"Snowflakes are one of natures most fragile things; yet look what they can do when they stick together."
Vesta M. Kelly

Get the kids involved. Put jobs (or rooms) out on slips of paper on the kitchen table. The first one to get to the kitchen gets to pick first and so on. Even the little ones can help.

Sometimes we have to clean up in a hurry (for company or whatever), and sometimes I get the kids to help first thing in the morning so we can spend the rest of the day doing fun things. This is their reward. Besides, there is something about all of us doing it together that makes it more fun.

This technique teaches them teamwork and housekeeping skills. I am always willing to do my part to help the kids learn.

Dargie, mother and grandmother of many step, birth, foster, and adopted children.

Group Homes

"I wanted the perfect ending. Now I've learned the hard way that some poems don't rhyme and some stories don't have a clear beginning, middle and end. Life is about not knowing, having to change, taking the moment and making the best of it, without knowing what is going to happen next. Delicious ambiguity."
Gilda Radner

I have been newly educated on the fact that there are some children that do not have the ability to thrive in a family setting. There are some children that, for a variety of reasons, simply need the total structure and predictability of a group home setting.

Families often make unscheduled changes; spur of the moment things like leaving the laundry for another day so that they can do a fun activity. This is too much inconsistency for some kids. The emotional drain of the closeness with a family, or even the perceived requirement for closeness, is too much for some.

It was difficult, but I have had to acknowledge that my home isn't the right setting for all kids. It hurts, but in retrospect I feel better about acknowledging it and allowing those children to leave for a placement that is more right for them

Wendy, biological and foster parent.

May 21 — It's a Scream

"Laughter is the key to survival during the special stresses of child-rearing. If you can see the delightful side of your assignment, you can also deal with the difficult."

James Dobson

The kids and I sometimes need to "vent." So when we're out on the open road (never in town) we say, "One, two, three, scream!"

We don't do it often, but sometimes you just need to scream. On days that have been particularly stressful for them, the kids will even ask, "Can we scream?" It can be very therapeutic.

Some people may think we are crazy, but it does relieve stress. And most of the time we end up laughing. Try it sometime. If everyone does it, it doesn't hurt your ears. (We don't do it with small children in the car.)

Dargie, mother and grandmother of many step, birth, foster, and adopted children.

Hellos & Good-byes

22 May

"...fear points the way for the opportunity to grow."
Edmond E. Frank

If you know nothing else about life know that it is a series of hellos and good-byes in some degree or another. There is no need to fear the good-byes if you address them head on and are truthful about your feelings.

There is no need to avoid hellos simply because you know there will be a good-bye someday. Embrace every opportunity to say hello and create the best relationship you can for whatever time you have. It will be your learning ground for the next relationship and the one after that. And finally, know that any unresolved pain you may carry from a previous incomplete good-bye can be further released when the next good-bye comes along. Such is the miracle of the cycles of life.

Susan, foster and adoptive parent, grandparent, and former foster family recruiter and trainer.

Fear always comes on the winds of change.
For mankind always fears what he does not know.
Yet fear points the way for the opportunity to grow.
Only those who fly on the wings of courage...
Those willing to use the winds... the currents of change...
Will soar with the joy of knowing themselves.
For they have come to know that awesome wonder,
By being an eagle in the skies of life.
Edmond E. Frank

May 23 — Believe in Yourself

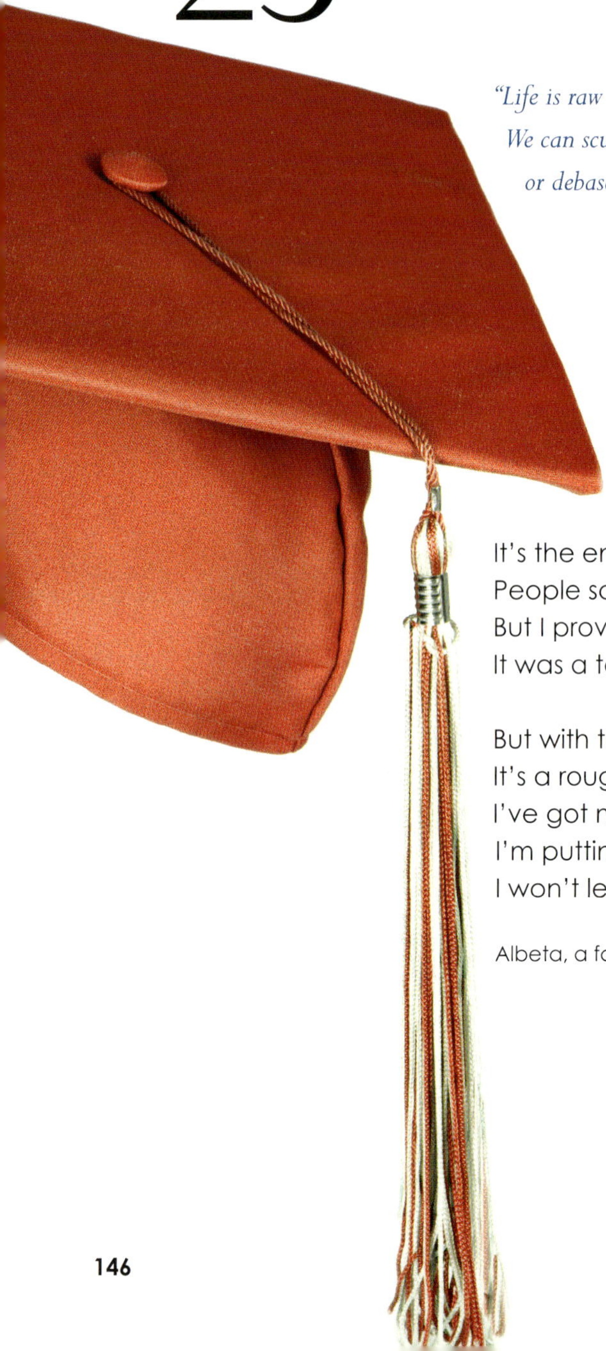

*"Life is raw material. We are artisans.
We can sculpt our existence into something beautiful,
or debase it into ugliness. It's in our hands."*

Cathy Better

It's the end of my high school year.
People said I wasn't going to make it.
But I proved them wrong 'cause I'm graduating.
It was a tough battle, I can't lie,

But with the help of my counselor and true friends I made it by.
It's a rough road ahead of me, but there's no stopping me now,
I've got my head up high and my feet planted on the ground.
I'm putting my best foot forward, I'm striving to succeed,
I won't let anyone knock me down because in me I believe.

Albeta, a foster youth

Love with a Pure Heart

24 May

"The difference between commitment and involvement is like ham and eggs. The chicken is involved and the pig is committed."
Rita Mae Brown

Relationships are challenging even under the best conditions. There are so many feelings, and they often come in floods. Everyone is in a different place, feeling different things. Everyone has their own agenda. Sometimes we say things we shouldn't, or we don't say things we should. It makes me wonder how relationships survive.

Maybe the chance of survival would increase by doing things like waiting to talk until you're calm; and making it a point to share feelings, hopes, dreams, and fears. It's important to be there when there are no words, only tears. Keep in touch with reality by dealing directly with the unfairness life sometimes brings. Try to be on the same page, look for that place of common ground.

I have learned that some things get easier with age and that it is important to love with a pure heart. I believe it is important to pray for each other when you are apart. The most important thing is to BE THERE, and never let each other go.

Dargie, mother and grandmother of many step, birth, foster and adopted children.

May 25 — Our Kids

"Praise is like sunlight to the warm human spirit; we cannot flower and grow without it. And yet, while most of us are only too ready to apply to others the cold wind of criticism, we are somehow reluctant to give our fellow man the warm sunshine of praise."

Jess Lair

We feel that God put us on earth to help children who desperately need it. When our kids come to us, they are usually so beaten down that constant reassurance is the most important thing they need.

They need to know that no matter how angry we get with them, and it does happen, we would NEVER hit them. How sad it must be to grow up in a family that is constantly fighting. It hurts your heart to see them flinch when you accidentally approach them too quickly.

A lot of our kids have been homeless and they are thrilled with the smallest things, from a hug to a computer. With many of these kids, food is a major issue. They mostly want to gorge and we let them for awhile, until we are sure they have finally eaten enough, which can sometimes be a couple of months. Then we tell them they do not need to eat so much because we will always have food for them. A sad moment for me was when my twelve-year-old adopted son told his caseworker, "They cook three meals a day, and we can have all we want! We can even have snacks!"

Praise is also important to our kids. They need large daily doses of it. Praise is what keeps them going in a world that has been so cruel. Praise is the one thing that all the medication in the world cannot replace.

Shirley & Tom, adoptive parents, foster parents to 19 kids (mostly teens) in the last 6 years.

What Makes a Family?

26 May

"The ache for home lives in all of us, the safe place where we can go as we are and not be questioned."
Maya Angelou

I was raised in a family with one mom, one dad, one sister, one brother, four grandparents, with an assortment of cousins, aunts, and uncles thrown in. So, in my mind that is the first thing I see when I think of "family."

Life though, has taught me that the broader definition of family is probably a more realistic one. I have seen families of people who had no blood relation at all but just came together through some series of happenings. These people love and care for each other when it is convenient and when it is not.

I have seen single parents with children who work together to make life have a sort of tender-sweet meaning, even though the environment they live in may be harsh. I have seen gay and lesbian couples raise happy and healthy children with very traditional values in the midst of a society often unaccepting of their choices.

I have seen aunts who become mothers and uncles who become dads, and cousins who took on children they hardly knew to give them a good home. Also, I have seen strangers reach out to children they do not know and offer them a home where they will be safe. One of the greatest rewards of fostering and adoption is developing the ability to understand, through experience, that "family" is not created with blood—it grows with loving commitment.

Susan, foster and adoptive parent, grandparent, and former foster family recruiter and trainer.

May 27 — Never Too Old

*Happiness is like a kiss—
in order to get any good out of it
you have to give it to somebody else.*
— Unknown

We got a call this week from our adoption worker saying the FBI had finally cleared my fingerprints. We have been waiting so long to finalize the adoption of our son and we were all thrilled!

He is only a few months away from turning 18 and some people may wonder why it is so important since he will soon be of age and out of the system anyway. It is important to all of us though, we are his forever family, and now it is almost official.

We called a family meeting and discussed everything from possible name changes to party plans. Everyone was excited—expectant even. After two and a half years of getting to know us, he still wants us to be his family. His wish is about to come true. He will finally be out of the system and an official member of our family.

He may shout louder now for his turn at the computer. He may demand his turn in the front seat of the car. He may feel differently when he calls us Mom and Dad. I may feel free to hug him more and longer. Changes may come, but we are in it forever now.

Dargie, mother and grandmother of many step, birth, foster, and adopted children.

Summer Job

28 May

*"Learn from the mistakes of others,
you can't live long enough to make them all yourself."*
Eleanor Roosevelt

I was speaking to my fourteen-year-old foster daughter about getting a summer job with the local youth summer employment program. She asked hesitantly what type of work she would be doing. She didn't seem excited or interested so I dropped it until I brought the application home which she signed compliantly.

My husband and I had just bought a house and one evening we were discussing how tight our budget would be when I noticed my foster daughter looking at me. She approached us and said, "I really don't mind working, you know. I know things are expensive and we need the money."

Suddenly, I realized what she had been thinking all this time. I put my arm around her and smoothed the hair hanging in her face. I explained that our budget was for the adults to worry about and that we would be okay. I told her that her summer job would be for her and that she would be earning money to spend on herself and save for her future. Then I saw the relief of a child who had, for too long had carried adult burdens, as she smiled and hugged me tightly.

Robin, foster parent to over 30 children in the last 5 years.

May 29 — Advice About Advice Giving

*"Advice-giving should avoid criticism, yet provide feedback;
avoid pontification, yet offer alternative opinions;
avoid dictating, yet provide encouraging suggestions;
advice-giving should not settle for the quick solution
at the expense of talking things out."*

Richard J. Delaney

Adoptive and foster parents have questions, especially during crisis times, about whether they are doing what is right for their child(ren).

It reminds me of the story of the man who was learning to parachute. On his first jump, he counted to three and pulled the rip cord. Nothing happened. He calmed himself and pulled the cord for the backup chute. Nothing again. Just then, a man streaked by him going straight up. As they shot by each other, the parachutist yelled out, "Do you know anything about parachutes?" "No," the skyward man screamed back. "Do you know anything about propane?"

When a family is in free fall or when there is an explosive situation, it's nice to have someone to turn to with questions. How and when to give advice to others is more art than science. Offering advice, should not replace or overshadow the task of compassionate listening. WE are not the problem solvers. Though we want to impart wisdom when needed and requested, we must respect the decisions of the family in need. In some cases advice giving should be avoided all together and replaced with encouragement and support.

Rick, clinical psychologist, trainer, and consultant who has worked with foster and adoptive children and their parents over the past 20 years.

How Many Kids Do I Have?

30 May

"Life is playing a violin solo in public and learning the instrument as one goes on."
Samuel Butler

Recently, I was lining up a baby-sitter. She asked how many kids she would be watching. I said, "Just a second I need to count them." She replied, "Don't you know how many kids you have?" So, I told her this story:

I came home a few months ago to find several children, including mine, playing in the yard. I told the kids that I didn't recognize that it was time for them to go home. As I was sending them out of the yard my wife called out, "They just got here, they are our new foster children."

A few days later my wife was leaving as I came home. She said dinner was on the table. There was a new kid, Kim, sitting at the table. After dinner, I asked Kim if she had pajamas. When she said that she didn't, I asked Rachel, who was about the same size, to get her some. Rachel said, "But Dad, she doesn't need pajamas." I told her that we all shared whatever we had here. Later, while the kids were watching TV, Rachel took me aside to thank me. I told her that's what a family is all about—helping kids in need. Then she told me that Kim was a friend from school and she was thanking me because we never allowed friends to stay over on a school night. So, when people ask me how many kids I have, I tell them I can't be sure because it changes from day to day.

Bob, adoptive parent of 6 children, biological parent to 6 more and foster parent to over 125 children in the past 22 years.

May 31 — Child's Play

"You can learn more about a person in a hour of play than in a lifetime of conversation."

Plato

There is a famous study about children using play to process trauma. The children played with their food, broccoli to be exact, to recreate a hurricane they had survived. They blew the broccoli around their plates and made it fallover and they held it in place with their utensils. It seems they were able to process the emotions related to the trauma with this sort of play.

When you watch foster and adoptive children at play they tend to include things other children would not. One child takes on the role of a "birth mom," a term most children have never heard. Another child may take the part of a caseworker or a police officer, while yet another may assume the role of a therapist. Some children even replay their traumas, mistreating dolls and calling Child Protective Services or rushing the "baby" to the hospital. They move their barn yard animals and their stuffed dinosaurs through the intricate web of social services they have experienced.

While it is sad that these kids have gone through these experiences, it is good that they can create positive outcomes in play. In many cases, the story is over when the plastic frog goes to live in his "forever home" with a sock monkey and the mistreated doll is placed in a foster home where she is safe. Thank goodness the children know enough to create the happy ending.

Susan, foster and adoptive parent, grandparent, and former foster family recruiter and trainer.

Typical Siblings

1 June

"Our greatest power is the power to change the way we see."
Stephen Covey

I have two seven-year-old adopted daughters, one is white and the other black. They have been together for about six years and they are what I call "typical siblings" the best of friends, and the worst of enemies.

One Sunday we were visiting a new church and running late as usual! I dropped the girls off at the door to their classroom and headed to the nursery with the baby, so I didn't really make introductions. I was not worried because the girls were old enough to pass along any necessary information.

The teacher got their first names and, since the girls arrived together and obviously knew one another, she asked them if they were friends. They said, "No." She asked them if they knew each other, and they replied, "Yes." Being somewhat puzzled, she took the question back up again later. The older of the two girls was frustrated at the repeated questions and finally blurted out, "No, we are not friends, we are SISTERS!" Apparently, that possibility had never occurred to the teacher.

My daughters are frequently mystified when people don't know automatically they are sisters. They know they have different skin colors, they know that they have different birth parents, but they are SISTERS and they think everyone should see that fact.

Valerie, adoptive parent and foster parent for medically fragile children for 10 years.

June 2 — When the Student Is Ready

*"Wake up with a smile and go after life…
Live it, enjoy it, taste it, smell it, feel it."*
— Joe Knapp

Many years ago, during a time of extreme stress in our family, we saw a family therapist. One of our therapeutic tasks was for my teenage adopted daughter to teach me to ride a ten speed bike. We never accomplished that task, but I was reminded of it recently by another situation.

My daughter's son is now teaching me to roller blade. He is a patient teacher and I am a willing student. He says things like, "You are doing great!" and I feel so encouraged. He shows me how to move my feet and he will not allow me out of the house without my protective gear. He offers to let me lean on him as I learn. He steadies me and gives me faith that I can do it.

My heart bursts with joy and pride as the observer in me watches the two of us accomplish a task his mother and I could not do all those years ago. I've grown up some since then, let go of my need to always be the teacher. He is doing a wonderful job and I know it is because his mother and I eventually worked through most of our differences and came to a place of genuine love and respect for one another. We have been able to pass that on to him and he is able to be both a teacher and a student as we continue to learn about life from each other every day.

Susan, foster and adoptive parent, grandparent, and former foster family recruiter and trainer.

Laundry

3 June

"For peace of mind, resign as general manager of the universe."
       Larry Eisenberg

We all have it—sheets, towels, pants, shirts, dresses, socks—laundry. Some have more than others, but we all have to find a way to deal with it. I do it every day and still it is never "finished" for more than a few hours.

I have come to the conclusion that as long as everyone has something to wear that's clean, I've done my job—at least for that day.

Dargie, mother and grandmother of many step, birth, foster, and adopted children.

June 4

Positive Addiction

*"Sometimes it is necessary to reteach a thing its loveliness...
until it flowers again from within."*

Galway Kinnell

I have been fostering for twenty-six years, and I love it. Yes, we have had some children that were hard and caused some damage to our home, colored on walls, spread feces; most of the horror stories. However, I will say that the majority of our foster children have been a joy, and we have loved doing it.

Once in a while a child comes into our home that doesn't fit here for one reason or another. It happens; and, hopefully we realize it, and they move to a more appropriate placement.

We love being foster parents, and we will only stop doing it when we are too old and decrepit to manage any more. I can't possibly describe our feelings when we took in a little child in a body cast, with blankness in his eyes, and then experienced the joy of seeing that child become a happy, healthy, bright-eyed child. Yes, it breaks your heart, over and over again, but it is something you get addicted to.

Marjie, adoptive parent and foster parent for 26 years to over 200 children.

From Russia with Love

5 June

"Faith isn't so much to believe that God is as to believe that God is for you."
                                                Richard Rohr

After many years of friendship, I finally married the love of my life in 1998. We felt that God had put us together and that we were definitely right for one another. We were both in our mid thirties and desperately wanted to start a family but found we were infertile. We considered adoption, but the long wait and chances of a parent coming back and taking the child made domestic adoption less preferable.

We started looking at international adoptions on the internet and decided on an agency that specialized in Russian adoptions. After many months of jumping through hoops and lots and lots of paperwork, we received a call from the adoption coordinator that a baby girl with blond hair and brown eyes was available. We waited with anticipation for the video and, after viewing it, told the coordinator we definitely wanted her. After more paperwork and a maze of legal requirements we left for Russia.

When we saw and held her for the first time she was sick and had a bad rash, but she seemed glad to see us. We knew we had made the right decision because she needed us as much as we needed her.

Our daughter now has a large family that loves her. It is hard to imagine she came from an orphanage thousands of miles away. But once again, God put us all together and we are definitely all absolutely right for each other!

Troy, adoptive father.

June 6 — I'm Not the Enemy

"To handle yourself, use your head; to handle others, use your heart."
— Eleanor Roosevelt

I pray that the memories of the time a child spends in my home will be fond ones. Often times the more comfortable children become in the home of a foster parent the more guilt they feel about "betraying" their own family. There is no age limit on these feelings.

So the kids can relax, I make sure all of my foster children know I do not want to replace their parents. I hope that coming to understand that I am not the enemy will help them enjoy their time with me without feeling they are betraying their folks.

Dargie, mother and grandmother of many step, birth, foster, and adopted children.

Fighting the Good Fight

7 June

"Forgiveness is the ability to give love away in the most difficult of circumstances."
Wayne W. Dyer

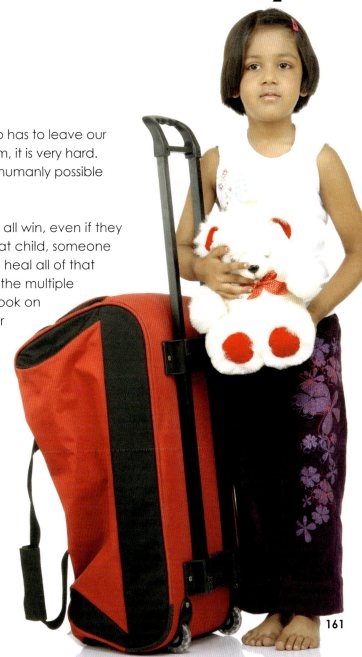

When a child we have loved and tried to help has to leave our home because it is not the best place for them, it is very hard. Even when we know we've done everything humanly possible to help, it still hurts.

I think it is in "fighting the good fight" that we all win, even if they have to move on. For during our time with that child, someone really loved them, really went all out trying to heal all of that accumulated pain from the abuse, neglect, the multiple losses, the grief beyond measure. We really took on the world on their behalf and kept trying over and over again even when the child was fighting against our trying to help because she couldn't accept our love. We grieve deeply, but our scars show how much we tried, how much we love, and by some miracle we are left able to love again.

Nancy, social worker and foster parent.

June 8 — The Day We All Got Married

"Love is the only thing that can be divided endlessly and still not diminish."
　　　Joanne, foster parent for reactive attachment disorder children

On our twentieth wedding anniversary, my husband and I renewed our wedding vows along with two other couples. It was a wonderful celebration of family. One couple exchanged vows they had written, another wife sang a beautiful song to her husband.

We chose to involve our entire family in our special part of the ceremony. My husband and I lit a unity candle. We then invited each of our children (foster, adopted, natural, etc.) to come and light a candle of their own from the flame of our unity candle. There was an awesome glow on our side of the church.

Hugs and kisses were exchanged as we publicly renewed our commitment as a family with the music of Celine Dion's *Because You Loved Me* playing in the background. I was told by many who attended that this was the most moving part of the ceremony for them.

It meant more to our entire family than our guests will ever know. No signing of adoption papers in judges' chambers will ever compare to the day that we all got married.

　　　Dargie, mother and grandmother of many step, birth, foster, and adopted children.

Persistence

"Example is not the main thing in influencing others, it is the only thing."

Albert Schweitzer

Some days when I am being smug and pompous, I think I have more to offer my grandson than his mother does. Of course, on the days when I am sane I know this is not true. And when I spend an extended period of time with him I see her positive influence in him everywhere.

This is most remarkable, because she was in foster care for eight years before she came to live with me. Her life was torn apart more than once, and she suffered greatly at the hands of relatives and even some of the foster families with whom she stayed. Her birth family was not able to care for her adequately, but I watched her take cooking classes and child care classes so that she could do a better job.

Once, after she became an adult she told me she would have a nice house someday. She has worked hard to break the cycle of poverty and dysfunction and she is winning.

On my last visit with my grandson he found a golf ball stuck in between the metal pieces of a grate across the drive. He was determined to get it out. I kept saying, "It is useless, it is hopeless, it isn't worth the effort." But, he persisted, he found something he wanted and was determined to do whatever it took to get it. He got that trait from his mother; we are both lucky to know her.

Susan, foster and adoptive parent, grandparent, and former foster family recruiter and trainer.

June 10 — Trust

"The most important thing that parents can teach their children is how to get along without them."

Frank A. Clark

I recently put together an independent living program for my two girls. One of them is moving into the final stages of her program where she is having weekends alone with her two sons while I go away. The purpose of this is to ready her to go out on her own with the boys in an apartment with no help or supervision. I had to prepare her for what it would be like to be alone and all that she needed to do while I was not available to assist her. When it came time to have her first weekend I had written out a list of what she needed to do, but I still found it extremely difficult to leave her and trust her to take care of the boys and the house.

Considering everything, she did a fairly good job. Each weekend that I have to leave I have to trust her to do what needs to be done and to follow through on her plans. It is always difficult, but I have found that if I pray about my worries it is easier to trust her. Thus we both have been less stressful about the situation.

I have come to trust her and to trust God to take care of what I cannot.

Tonya, foster parent for more than 120 children over 20 years.

Empty Nest?

11 June

"Love is a fruit in season at all times, and within reach of every hand. Anyone may gather it and no limit is set."
Mother Teresa

No matter how many kids remain, when children leave my home it's a sad occasion for me. It doesn't matter if they are with us for a weekend or a year, I grieve when they leave.

It is amazing how many individual rooms are available in a human heart. Each child that comes along occupies a place no one else can fill. My friend teases me by saying that I am the only person she knows who suffers from Empty Nest Syndrome with four kids still in the house.

Dargie, mother and grandmother of many step, birth, foster, and adopted children.

June 12 — The Long Road

*"Heroes come in every shape and size.
Making special sacrifices for others in their lives.
No one gives them medals, the world don't know their names.
But in someone's eyes they're heroes just the same."*

Paul Overstreet

When I get discouraged because results seem so small, I remember my first foster care experience. The two sisters, nine and eleven, had major deficits in their social skills. Their history included sexual abuse and severe neglect. They were behind in school, emotionally and developmentally delayed, and suffered from nightmares. What hope, I wondered, did these two have of growing up to become healthy adults?

A year passed as I struggled to teach the girls appropriate behaviors and new skills. Parental rights were terminated, and adoptive families were sought. Progress had been made, but was it enough to help an adoptive family want each of the girls? Would they be successful? To avoid disrupting the girls lives again before they moved in with their adoptive families, I delayed taking a new job in a different city.

Finally, the transition was completed, and continued contact was encouraged. I received a few letters, phone calls and visits over the next seven years and learned of successes and trials along the way. Then came the invitation to the older one's high school graduation! Both girls were delighted to see me. They had successfully adjusted to their families and social life, and they wanted to thank me for my role in their lives. The seeds of love and patience sown seven years earlier were coming into full bloom.

Lesa, therapeutic foster parent and foster parent trainer.

Wrapped in Safe Arms

13 June

*"Things are not untrue
just because they never happened."*
Dennis Hamley in Hare's Choice

"About eighteen months ago we were putting our home on the market to sell. Our most recent placement had lived with us about a year and had been in multiple homes prior to that. One day when I was washing dishes he asked me, 'When you move, will I be going with you?'

"I just about dropped face first into the sink. My heart just sank thinking of his true concern and fear of being left behind AGAIN."

Darlene, birth parent, adoptive parent, and foster parent to 35 children over the last 10 years.

We often take for granted the sense of security that comes from growing up in a stable family. Children who have been abandoned or shuffled from one home to another cannot emotionally afford the luxury of relaxing into the belief that they have a safe place to stay. One of our main goals with foster and adoptive children is to wrap them in the secure arms of safety and help them come to believe the world can be a good place for them.

Susan, foster and adoptive parent, grandparent, and former foster family recruiter and trainer.

June 14 — Because You Loved Me

"You must carry the chaos within you in order to give birth to the dancing star."
— Nietzsche

You don't know me, I'm just a face in a sea of nothing, a never ending race

Violence, abuse, drugs, destruction, ignorance, malice — alone in my room remembering all these elements of my world.

You don't know me, I can't describe the dreams I dream, the things I think, the tears I hide.

My past, my circumstances, my world is not my excuse! Faith in myself and Supernatural Love are the tools I'll use.

Those who hurt me I will thank, for they have taught me to be cautious with my heart. The things I cannot help I will forgive because now I have a new start.

If the world could only understand the abundance of hopes and dreams they hold in their hands. The past is gone and the future lies ahead, but the lives of others do not pass without their stories unsaid.

The person I'll be, the things I'll do, are because of the people in my life like you. You didn't know me, just the same the world will be a better place just because you loved me.

Stephanie, a foster youth.

Birdseed Blunder

15 June

"You're only human, you're supposed to make mistakes."
Billy Joel

My niece got married last week. My entire family was involved in the preparation. Monday we stuffed netting with birdseed and tied them with ribbon. Tuesday, mints. Thursday we decorated the church and baked the cake. Friday we decorated the cake. Friday afternoon—the big event, ushering, serving, and so on. I say we all helped, because when Mom has something special to do all the others take up the slack. We're a family, we work together.

Throughout the week, my fifteen-year-old foster son kept telling me that he had never been to a wedding. I explained about many of the traditions and told him to just have fun. As the bride and groom went outside, the photographer positioned them to throw the bouquet and garter. When the groom started to throw the garter, my fifteen-year-old pelted him with unopened bundles of birdseed. I was unaware until I heard the groom take him aside and instruct, "Buddy, they usually untie these and throw just the birdseed, otherwise it hurts."

We must never take anything for granted with these kids. Often they aren't aware they are missing some crucial piece of information, and this can leave them vulnerable to social errors. Luckily, in this case, a gentle and understanding groom eased the embarrassment of the faux pas and taught my foster son one more lesson in social interaction.

Dargie, mother and grandmother of many step, birth, foster, and adopted children.

June 16 — Feed My Lambs

"If you're going to care about the fall of the sparrow you can't pick and choose who's going to be the sparrow. It's everybody."

Madeleine L'Engle

As a child, I participated in my family's summer ritual of visiting relatives. The children in our family would take turns visiting each of our aunts and uncles and grandparents for a week at a time. Aunt Addie and Uncle Otis raised sheep. One of my favorite activities was feeding the baby lambs who had either lost or been rejected by their mother. I recall hanging tightly onto that giant baby bottle so the lamb I was feeding would not pull it from my hands. It would make me so sad when a tiny lamb would refuse to take the nourishment I placed before it.

I remember Uncle Otis continually reminding me to lock the gate to the barnyard so his lambs could not escape the safety of the fenced lot. He knew how vulnerable they were to the dangers of the outside world.

Looking back, I realize my favorite activities haven't changed all that much. Except the lambs I am feeding and watching over these days are my foster children.

Lesa, therapeutic foster parent and foster parent trainer.

Daddy's Home!

*"To laugh often and much;
to win the respect of intelligent people and the affection of children;
to earn the appreciation of honest critics and endure the betrayal
of false friends; to appreciate beauty; to find the best in others;
to leave the world a bit better, whether by a healthy child, a garden patch,
or a redeemed social condition; to know even one life has breathed easier
because you lived; this is to have succeeded."*

Ralph Waldo Emerson

My husband is a truck driver, so he is gone more than he is home. My five-year-old adopted son thinks his dad is the greatest, and the look of love on my son's face when he sees his daddy is something to behold.

As a matter of fact, last week my husband came home and seemed really disappointed. When I asked him what was wrong he explained, "I was hoping to get here before bedtime. Seeing the look on his face when I walk in makes my day."

However, his disappointment was premature. It wasn't long before my son was in bed with us, touching his daddy's face and smothering him with kisses. "Is that you, Daddy? I love you, Daddy. I missed you!"

Together again, safe in Daddy's arms, they went back to sleep. On the days when we feel sorry that we can't do it all, we can feel satisfied that we have indeed done something wonderful for this child...and he has done the same for us.

Dargie, mother and grandmother of many step, birth, foster, and adopted children.

June 18 — His, Mine & Theirs

*"Give what you have.
To someone it may be better than you dare think."*
Henry Wadsworth Longfellow

When my husband and I married eleven years ago we decided not to do a "yours, mine and ours" family by bringing more children into the world since our children were already teenagers. We chose instead to do a "his, mine and theirs" family by becoming foster parents. We have had over fifty high risk teenage boys in nine years.

It has been the most challenging full time career I have ever had; we averaged five to six kids at all times. We both feel every young man in our home has been placed here by Divine purpose. Our commitment to each child was to provide a functional family experience. And we have accomplished that goal.

Two years ago we decided to stop fostering as the boys we had grew up, moved out on their own or were placed with biological families. We may not have a house full of kids living with us but they are now coming back with their newborn babies and introducing us as their "grandparents."

Cathy, foster parent to teen boys for 9 years.

The Treasure Chest

19 June

"Success consists of a series of little daily victories."
Laddie F. Hutar

It must be difficult to have a body that says you are nearly grown when on the inside you crave the simple joys of childhood. When we love children with troubled pasts, we come to learn to look beyond their physical beings and into the needs of their hearts.

"Our two fifteen-year-old foster sons were at a point where they needed encouragement and nurturing more than ever. So, I got an old box at a junk store, pasted macaroni on it and sprayed it with gold paint to create a treasure chest. Then I filled it with inexpensive treasures including things like a half hour of reading alone with the child and sharing a favorite television program. Each day the boys get to celebrate a success from their day by drawing from the treasures. It is so heartwarming to see a 260 pound fifteen-year-old who has spent time in jail get so excited about such little things. My goal is to help create the 'magic' of childhood in their lives—lives that have been so devoid of such magic. Even on the worst of days, we can find a success to celebrate." "C" does correctional therapeutic foster care for her state youth center. She and her husband have cared for 11 teenagers in the 6 years they have been doing foster care.

Susan, foster and adoptive parent, grandparent, and former foster family recruiter and trainer.

June 20 — Satisfying the Hunger

"No longer forward nor behind
I look in hope or fear;
But, grateful, take the good I find,
The best of now and here"
  John Greenleaf Whittier

All children come into foster care hungry, although they may not always be hungry for food. However, no matter what sort of hunger they really have, it often presents itself as some kind of "food problem."

My children have stolen food, picked through dumpsters for food, and stashed food under their beds. I have had children eat until I thought they would burst at the seams. I had a child once who circled his plate with one arm, put his head down and shoveled in food as if the fork was an earth-moving machine. And yet these same kids will go without lunch at school rather than admit they are in foster care and do not have to pay for their meal. I try to make sure there is plenty of food available and plenty of leftovers.

I suggest new foster parents check out the movie *Heidi*. There is a scene in the movie where her clothes closet is opened and a dozen little hard biscuits come tumbling out. Why did Heidi hoard food? She had lost the most precious of all things, her home in the Alps with her beloved grandfather.

And then there is the fact that dealing with all this has caused me to resort to some pretty odd behavior myself. I may be the only woman in town to take a pan of Rice Krispie® treats to the bedroom at night! If I don't they will mysteriously disappear—and no one will know how that could have happened!

Carolyn, social worker and foster parent to teen boys.

Summer

Oh, I do think it's the pleasantest thing
Ever a child can do!

June 21 — What It Takes

*"As the old man walked the beach at dawn,
he noticed a young man ahead of him
picking up starfish and flinging them into the sea.
Finally catching up with the youth, he asked him why
he was doing this. The answer was that the stranded starfish
would die if left until the morning sun.
'But the beach goes on for miles and there are millions of starfish,'
countered the other. 'How can your effort make any difference?'
The young man looked at the starfish in his hand
and then threw it to safety in the waves.
'It makes a difference to this one,' he said."*

                          Minnesota Literacy Council

The statement of the year
is to truly be sincere
and to accomplish the goals that you make.
When that's all done,
you'll become number one,
because you've shown that you've got what it takes.

Matthew, a foster youth.

What's It Really Like?

22 June

"To succeed all you need to give is all you have."
Unknown

When people ask me about fostering I am very honest. I tell them what it is really about. I say that you need to look at fostering as the greatest challenge you will ever undertake and know it will mean getting in touch with every feeling you can imagine having.

I tell them it takes understanding and considerable coping skills to foster. The ability to walk away from a situation long enough to gain control over your feelings is a powerful learning experience for most foster children and you will likely get a chance to demonstrate this more than once a day.

If people come to me thinking they can save the world through fostering, I tell them they need to reconsider. What I have learned is that we are lucky to save a tiny piece of each child we contact; but, that tiny piece brings that child closer to becoming a whole person.

I tell them that it will sometimes hurt more than death and that it can also bring happiness and joy far greater than anything they have ever experienced. They must simply be willing to give love unconditionally, never expecting anything in return for the love and hope they are willing to give. Eventually, we all learn that the reward is in the giving.

Tonya, former foster parent for over 120 children in the last 20 years.

June 23 — Respite

"We should consider every day lost on which we do not dance at least once."
Nitzsche

Foster and adoptive parents are generally very caring people. They care for the children they love with the utmost devotion. However, it is sometimes difficult for them to care for themselves in meaningful ways. One way parents care for themselves is to take occasional breaks from parenting. Going away for a weekend, or out for an evening, or simply trying to get time alone at home to take a bubble bath can be a challenge for any parent. However, it is necessary to model self-care if we want the children to learn how to care for themselves someday.

"Although we found the children had difficulty at the very beginning with going to respite, after awhile it became a very nice break for everyone. It was kind of like going to stay at an auntie or grandma's house since we were able to choose who we wanted to do respite and they agreed to follow our schedule. These kids can be both emotionally and physically exhausting and we do have to think of ourselves. If we are overworked all of the time we are no good to the kids either."

Deena, mom to a great bunch of kids (ages 21, 19, 17, 15, 8, 7, 6, 5, 5, 3)

Susan, foster and adoptive parent, grandparent, and former foster family recruiter and trainer.

Patience

"It's the action, not the fruit of the action, that's important. You have to do the right thing. It may not be in your power, may not be in your time, that there will be any fruit. But that doesn't mean you stop doing the right thing. You may never know what results come from your action. But if you do nothing, there will be no results."

Gandhi

"Foster care is commitment, caring, loving, holding on, accepting, teaching, praying, coping, being patient, repeating as often as necessary, realizing limitations, and giving totally of oneself. Maybe you might hear a thank you or see changes, but you have to be patient. It won't happen over night and it may not come at all until they are out of your home, an adult, with their own life."

Trish, birth parent to 3 children, foster parent to nearly 600 children in the last 20 years, and grandparent to biological and foster grandchildren.

June 25

Mommy, Don't Leave Us!

"Those who bring sunshine to the lives of others cannot keep it from themselves."
Sir James Matthew Barrie

Two brothers came to me for emergency care. They were enrolled in a preschool not far from my home and were to stay in that program in order to help keep some consistency in their lives.

About fourteen hours after their arrival, I dropped them off at the preschool. As I started to leave, they clung to my legs and cried, "Mommy, don't leave us."

I didn't know what to say or do. It was like playing a part in someone else's dream. I stood there for a moment trying to get hold of myself and make a plan. I decided to be "Mommy" and just say what my own kids would need to hear in this situation.

"Boys, I will be back by 3:30," I promised. "You go ahead and have lots of fun and make something for me today; I'll take you to the park and spend some special time with you this afternoon." With that, I hugged and kissed them and they went to start their day.

I went to my van and cried, but not for long. Pulling myself together, I created a plan to keep these little guys busy and start a routine that would prevent a scene like that from happening again. Then I took a minute to thank God for the chance to be their "Mommy," even for a short time.

Dargie, mother and grandmother of many step, birth, foster, and adopted children.

My Dream for the Children

26 June

"Whatever you do, put romance and enthusiasm into the lives of our children."
Margaret Ramsey McDonald

There are over a half-a-million children in out-of-home placements and only a small percentage of those are available for adoption. Lots of these kids were traumatized by parents or by moving around so much in foster care. Trusting adults is not something they do easily.

The dream I have for the kids who come into my home is for them to reach for their goals in every way they can. I plan to help them and let them know they can become anything they want to if they work very hard. When I think of this it makes me work harder to help them. It also makes me think more about adopting kids that do not have a family of their own to do this for them.

Sharon, foster mom for 2 years.

June 27 — All They Need Is Love?

"Fatherhood is the single most creative, complicated, fulfilling, frustrating, engrossing, enriching, depleting endeavor of a man's adult life."

Kyle D. Pruett

A foster family I trained came into the office to talk to me about how things were going with their latest placement. It was their third placement in the 18 months they had been foster parents. Prior to taking on this task they had cared for the children of friends and neighbors, but never had any children of their own.

In the beginning the staff had wondered if they were going to be able to be realistic enough about what they would have to do as foster parents. They were so inexperienced, but they had a very positive attitude and a sense of humor that just made you want to cheer them on.

While they sat in the office, the foster father described how they were setting up behavioral plans and using consequences and reinforcers to help their foster daughter change her behavior. She had only had a short "honeymoon" period and was in full swing testing limits and pushing boundaries. From everything they described, they were doing a wonderful job and I told them so.

Then the foster dad looked at me and with a chuckle, he said, "Remember in the classes when I kept saying all these kids needed was a little love? Well, I was wrong, they need a lot more than that." We laughed together and then I told him that maybe love wasn't all the kids needed, but it was a darn good place to start.

Susan, foster and adoptive parent, grandparent, and former foster family recruiter and trainer.

To Adopt or Not to Adopt

"We're all in this together… alone."
Lily Tomlin

He was fifteen. Before we met, we talked on the phone. I brought up the subject of adoption. "Someday," I said, "if you want us to adopt you…"

"No, I would never want that!"

A year or so passed, he was family, and he brought up the subject again. "I want to be adopted, my mom and dad (deceased) would want me to go on and have parents."

We started processing—months went by—final meetings, "I don't want to be adopted. I feel I'm turning my back on my parents."

Pros—out of the "system," officially family, new parents can sign for drivers' licence…

Cons—leave "real" family behind, biological parents removed from birth certificate…

His seventeenth birthday is five months away. Time is so short. The years fly by. Time drags. He wants to drive. We go in circles. It's his life, his decision, his heartache. It isn't as big a decision as marriage, but then again, it's bigger. We seek advice, ask questions, get answers.

Bottom line: He loves us and we love him, but it's hard. Does anyone really know how hard? He does.

Dargie, mother and grandmother of many step, birth, foster, and adopted children.

June 29 — A Time & a Season

"Don't bother to give God instructions, just report for duty."
Unknown

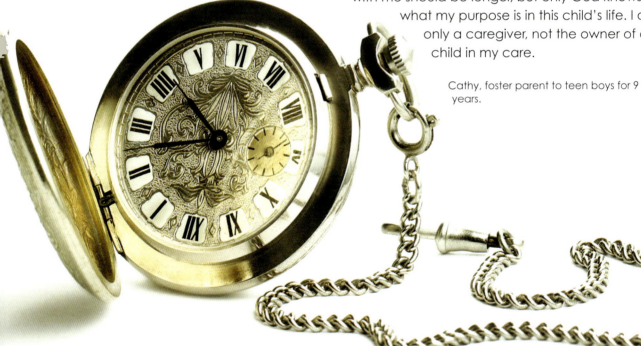

I try to never forget that when I am called to be a foster parent it is only a gift from God for a time and a season. The children placed in my care are guests, like my own children, until they are old enough to be on their own or ready to move on. I may believe their stay with me should be longer, but only God knows what my purpose is in this child's life. I am only a caregiver, not the owner of any child in my care.

Cathy, foster parent to teen boys for 9 years.

To Go Up in a Swing

30 June

"Only as high as I can stretch, may I grow;
only as far as I can seek, may I go;
only as deep as I can look, may I see;
only as much as I dare to dream, I can be."

Sipri Cuthbert

How do you like to go up in a swing,
Up in the air so blue?
Oh, I do think it's the pleasantest thing
Ever a child can do!

Up in the air and over the wall
Till I can see so wide,
Rivers and trees and cattle and all
Over the countryside—

Till I look down on the garden green,
Down on the roof so brown—
Up in the air I go flying again,
Up in the air and down!

Robert Louis Stevenson

In some ways I believe that is exactly what foster parents do for children. They help them go up in a swing and see over the wall to the possibilities that lie on the other side.

Susan, foster and adoptive parent, grandparent, and former foster family recruiter and trainer.

July 1

Life Book

"Success is a journey not a destination."
Unknown

"My wish for each foster child is that they would have a beautiful 'life book' filled with photos, poems, handprints, awards, drawings and art projects. They need something to document their childhood, something beautiful." Jean, birth, foster, and adoptive mom

When my daughter came to me at the age of fifteen, she could not distinguish her biological family from her many foster and adoptive families of the previous eight years. She would tell a story from her past and not know her relationship to the people involved. This phenomenon may seem strange to the general public, but it is all too common with children who have been "in the system" for a long time.

When you have lived in several homes and have foster siblings, natural siblings, extended family members, and in some cases family members from a disrupted adoption, how do you remember who is who? One remedy to the confusion is to help children create something concrete they can use to keep track of the process of their lives.

This might be done through journaling or with a scrap book filled with mementos of significant events. There are commercially prepared books which help foster children record memories and families as well as feelings related to being in care. Whatever format is chosen, it can be an invaluable tool to help the child keep an otherwise fragmented life tied together.

Susan, foster and adoptive parent, grandparent, and former foster family recruiter and trainer.

Insta-Party

2 July

"Bringing up a family should be an adventure, not an anxious discipline in which everybody is constantly graded for performance."

Milton R. Sapirstein

Birthdays are special at our house. We might even roll someone out of bed to open their gifts - just to make sure they are surprised.

We have such a large family that we call ourselves an insta-party. Usually we have a family thing (favorite restaurant or favorite meal at home, etc.), and then something with friends like skating or bowling. The youth group at our church also has a celebration for our teens when they have a birthday.

Some may think the kids are spoiled, but I just want them to know they are loved—by family, friends, and church family.

Dargie, mother and grandmother of many step, birth, foster, and adopted children.

July 3 — Macaroni & Cheese

"Success is failure turned inside out."
Unknown

Our eight-year-old foster daughter had been with us about three days. We were on our way to the grocery store and she asked me if I knew how to cook macaroni and cheese.

I said, "Sure, why do you want to know?" She said, "I was once so hungry, I put the macaroni and cheese into the water but it never got soft so I ate some of it anyway."

That evening as I cooked supper, I called her into the kitchen and, together, we made macaroni and cheese. She said it was the best she had ever eaten. So when she sees that yellow and blue box, I hope it reminds her of the fun time we had on the day she learned to cook macaroni and cheese. Also, I hope the time spent teaching her this simple skill helps her feel confident that she won't ever have to be that hungry again.

Nancy, a foster parent for special needs children.

Missingmomitis

"Never let your head hang down.
Never give up and sit and grieve. Find another way.
And don't pray when it rains if you don't pray when the sun shines."
                                    Leroy "Satchel" Paige

Late in the day on the Fourth of July the boy staying with me began to whine about feeling bad. After getting more information I determined something else was going on that he could not verbalize.

To be safe, I put him to bed and sat with him rubbing a cool cloth on his forehead. He cried as he lay there and I could see his pain was genuine, but I was puzzled as to the source. Then he began asking me questions about how I celebrate Independence Day. I quickly discovered he had a very strong family connection to the holiday. So, I placed a call to his mother and told her I thought he was suffering from a little "missingmomitis."

She talked to him and explained that she had some sparklers and things for him that she would save until their visit on the weekend, and they would have their own Fourth of July celebration together. They talked briefly about other things and within ten minutes he was sleeping soundly.

I often forget that the feelings, needs and connections of the children in my care are not the same as my own. I realized in that moment that we never completely know the joys these children experienced in their birth family even when we are aware of much of the tragedy.

Susan, foster and adoptive parent, grandparent, and former foster family recruiter and trainer.

July 5 — Just for Today

"Do not be anxious for tomorrow, for tomorrow will look after itself."
Matthew 6:34

Some things seem bigger than all of us. I personally wish there was no abortion, that dads could force moms to deliver if they wanted to be responsible for their child, that everyone had to take parenting classes to be a parent, that if you abused your children they were taken away with no second chances, that there were no guns, wars or illness.

But, for today, I will foster children, love them, hug them, let them feel safe, help the parents learn to do better in any way I can, and let the rest of the world worry about the BIG stuff I have no control over.

Cheryl, mother of 3, home daycare provider, new foster mom.

A Simple Blessing

6 July

"All happenings, great and small, are parables where by God speaks, the art of life is to get the message."
                                              Malcolm Muggeridge

Last summer we went to see my newborn niece at the hospital. As we wound our way through the hospital corridors bearing gifts, we passed a room with two blue ribbons representing twin boys. As we passed, I felt impressed to touch the door and offer a simple blessing.

Later, while we were enjoying holding and photographing the new baby, I got a phone call to pick up two little brothers. After the call, my daughter had one request. "Mom," she said, "don't touch any more doors on the way out."

Dargie, mother and grandmother of many step, birth, foster, and adopted children.

Fresh Perspective

"The person with dreams is more powerful than the one with all the facts."

Unknown

A child can always help you see things from a fresh perspective, and they can freshen up your sense of humor in the process. A couple of examples follow:

"I wanted to be a supportive foster mother and give my preschool-age foster children something special about themselves to always remember. I wanted to instill self-confidence and hope. So, if they said they wanted to be an astronaut, or they wanted to learn how to tie their shoes, I would encourage them by saying, 'You can do anything you really want to do.'

"When one of my foster children was adopted by his grandmother, I received a call from her. She asked if I could talk with him. Apparently, anytime she tried to discipline him, he would respond, 'Cindy said I can do anything I want to.'

"And then there was the time when my husband and I were foster parents to preschool-age children. We exclaimed to our foster son, 'You're a smarty pants!' To which his younger sister replied, 'Me a smarty dress!'"

Cynthia

Instant Know-How

8 July

"Prayer is the place where burdens change shoulders."
Unknown

"I wish I knew then what I know now." How many times have I thought that in working with children? How many times have I wished parenting had come with some can of instant "know-how" for difficult situations. However, it doesn't and we just learn as we go.

But even today, as long as I have worked with children, when I come across some new program or a great resource, I find myself wishing I had been able to access it for some child I worked with years ago.

They never leave me; the lessons I learned in their presence are burned into my heart. I pray daily that I will do the best I can with the children in my care at this moment, and I continue to pray for those who have moved on. It is my way of letting go and still acknowledging the eternal connection I have to all the children I have had the honor to serve.

Susan, foster and adoptive parent, grandparent, and former foster family recruiter and trainer.

July 9

False Allegations

"He drew a circle that shut me out—heretic, rebel, a thing to flout.
But love and I had the wit to win: We drew a circle and took him in."

Edward Markham

Allegations of abuse happen to just about every foster parent at some time. Most foster children believe nothing good will ever happen to them and they do not deserve to be loved. So, if you love them, there must be something wrong with you. It is often uncomfortable for them to be loved, they are more used to being abused or neglected. Children who feel this way will try to push you away, to show you how "unlovable" they are. Making an allegation is one way to do this.

The best thing you can do when you have an allegation is to cooperate with the investigation. It will be uncomfortable and people will ask you all sorts of questions when the answers seem obvious to you. The process is different in each state, but the need to be patient and cooperate honestly is the same everywhere. Understand that you need to let your caseworker know what is going on, but you probably need to look for your day to day support from other foster parents.

There are many channels an allegation must move through and it goes much slower than it should. It takes a lot of courage and love to be a foster parent and not everyone has what it takes. An allegation of abuse can be frightening, but you can survive it and in turn you may be able to support one of your fellow foster parents through it too.

Liza, foster mom.

Reality Check

10 July

*"The door of success is marked 'push' and 'pull.'
Achieving success is knowing when to do what."*
— Yiddish Folk Saying

I had a call last night from a kid I "kicked out" of here over four years ago. I hadn't spoken to him since then, and he called me to say thanks.

We talked for three hours, and he will stop by today because he wants my opinion on some of the things he is doing. He still calls me "Dad," even though he has one (he doesn't see his birth parents much).

This young man lived with us from age twelve to almost eighteen, and it really hurt when I had to ask him to leave our house. However, at the time I believed it was the reality check he needed to turn his life around. Last night's conversation confirmed I was right.

Allen, corrections-based foster father for older teen boys for over 30 years.

July 11 Laughter

"If the only prayer you say in your entire life is "Thank You," that would suffice."

Meister Eckhart

Our (now adopted) shaken baby is developmentally delayed. The first few months we had him, he showed no emotion except to cry.

On Labor Day weekend, we had gone to the home of my nephew and had a great meal and visited. Everyone officially welcomed our new baby into the family. On the way home, we decided to rent a movie. My husband and the older kids went into the store while I waited in the car with the baby.

I began to play with him, singing his name. Even though doctors had told us he couldn't see, I hoped that he could at least hear me. He did! As I sang his name over and over, he started laughing. I kept singing and he kept laughing. Even when the family returned, we just sat there making him laugh. The car was filled with laughter, his and ours, and our hearts filled with hope for his future.

Dargie, mother and grandmother of many step, birth, foster, and adopted children.

Angels & Witches

12 July

*"You take something out of your mind,
garnished in kindness out of your heart
and put it into the other fellow's mind and heart."*

Charles H. Burr

My six-year-old foster daughter was in her bed, sitting up, her eyes red with tears. She said, "The witches are going to get me!" She had just awakened from a nightmare, and she was still crying when I came into the room. I held her on my lap and she sniffled and sobbed until she finally began to rest and became quiet in my arms.

I asked her what had caused such a dream and she said, "I never got to say good-bye to my Mommy. I couldn't talk to her because she was breathing funny when I walked into the room." Her mother had died with AIDS and she had basically drowned from her lungs filling up with fluid.

I rocked her and said that mommies know when their babies are there, even if they don't hear them. I told her that her mommy was an angel now and could watch over her and keep the witches and all the bad things away. She looked at me and smiled. "Do you really think she is an angel?" I told her I was sure of it because she was so special that any mommy would want to be her angel.

She climbed back into the covers and went to sleep. Later, I found a song by Alabama with the line "there are angels among us" and she loved to listen to it at bedtime. Pretty soon the witches were all gone, and she was able to sleep through the night. I'm sure her guardian angel was watching over her and smiling.

Robin, foster mom to 30 children over 5 years.

July 13 — In the Greenhouse

"Our days are a kaleidoscope. Every instant a change takes place…
New harmonies, contrasts, combinations of every sort…
The most familiar people stand each moment in some new relation
to each other, to their work, to surrounding objects."

Henry Ward Beecher

Recently I started a part-time job at a greenhouse. It is labor intensive work but very satisfying. Working with the earth and tending to the plants seems to stimulate the more creative side of my thinking.

The tomato plants we grow from seed remind me of the many children I have cared for. We plant these children in our home, we tend, fertilize and help them along in every way we can think of. Yet, they all grow differently; some taller, some shorter. Some are sensitive to light or fertilizer, while others grow anywhere with very little attention. Some grow better alone, while others do best in groups. There are so many variables.

Being a parent of any kind—foster, adoptive, birth, step, or just a nurturing adult in a child's life—requires providing individual attention. We have to be consistently aware of how each child responds to the environment we provide. We have to watch how they acclimate as they grow and adjust to their changes by making adjustments in our nurturing.

In the end, the goal is the same as gardening. We gardeners want our plants to grow, blossom, and bare the most delightful fruit. When it comes to our children, this fruit is a good life, healthy relationships, and ultimately the ability to be a good nurturing adult.

Susan, foster and adoptive parent, grandparent, and former foster family recruiter and trainer.

What Mountains?

14 July

"I have always loved to go new places in the world outside, because somehow it helped me to go to new places inside myself where I hadn't been before."

Laures Van der Post

I once fostered a young brother and sister for a few months. As a treat, we decided to take them for a short camping trip to the Smoky Mountains. They were very impressed with the tourist towns of Pigeon Forge and Gatlinburg.

As we drove further up into the Smokies I asked, "So, what do you think of the mountains?" The boy replied, "I can't see any mountains, all I see is a bunch of trees!" At first I laughed, and then I thought how many times I'd heard the saying, "He can't see the forest (or in this case, the mountains) for the trees."

It made me think of how it can be like that for foster parents. Sometimes we get so caught up in looking at the child, we don't consider the larger family. We must be sure not to miss seeing the family because we are so focused on the child.

Dargie, mother and grandmother of many step, birth, foster, and adopted children.

July 15 — Surprising Therapeutic Moments

"When you build bridges you can keep crossing them."
Rick Pitino

My eleven-year-old foster son displayed strong symptoms of Reactive Attachment Disorder. As a very young child, he had been severely neglected, and now he was very anxious and fearful. He refused hugs or took them very stiffly. He constantly lied and manipulated family and school situations so he felt in control.

One day, my husband, Jeff, and I took him and his two younger brothers on a hike. The trail followed a creek, crossing it several times on the way to a waterfall. The first creek crossing was small enough for the two younger boys to jump over. The eleven-year-old frantically searched for a way to cross. His brother ended up showing him where to cross the creek. The next crossing was wider and the eleven-year-old refused to cross. He was afraid he would fall, hit his head and die. Once again, only his younger brother was able to convince him to cross with his assistance.

At the third crossing, the eleven-year-old sat down on the bank and sobbed. He was petrified. Finally the two younger boys convinced their brother to walk across holding hands with Jeff and me. This was tough for a child who believed that when adults are in control, bad things happen.

At the fourth crossing, this child actually let Jeff carry him across the creek piggyback style. And, at the next crossing he walked across by himself with the adults and brothers close by. By the end of the day, he was wading in the creek, laughing, and enjoying the water. He even asked if we could hike this trail again. Who says therapy only happens in an office? Real life is full of the most wonderful therapeutic experiences ever.

Lesa, therapeutic foster parent and foster parent trainer.

Finding the Inner Child

16 July

"Anyone can help a child become an adult. It takes a special person to be one who can help a broken child grow into a whole adult."

Keven Harrington

There is talk in the media these days about connecting to one's "inner child." For most people that means remembering the part of us that still feels the emotions we felt as a child, remembering the good times, the fun, and the freedom of innocence. It may also mean allowing the inner child of our past to grieve losses and experience long-hidden pain.

Some very young foster and adoptive children come to us already very old because they have buried that innocent child so deeply. This is done for survival so that the tough exterior will protect the vulnerable child inside. And it works extremely well. Even though it works and we understand why they do it, we still find it difficult to watch a child struggle with being a child in a world that is sometimes unsafe for children.

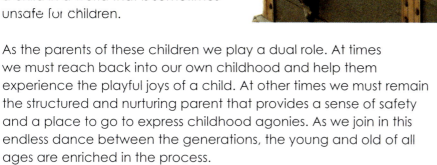

As the parents of these children we play a dual role. At times we must reach back into our own childhood and help them experience the playful joys of a child. At other times we must remain the structured and nurturing parent that provides a sense of safety and a place to go to express childhood agonies. As we join in this endless dance between the generations, the young and old of all ages are enriched in the process.

Susan, foster and adoptive parent, grandparent, and former foster family recruiter and trainer.

July 17 — A True Miracle

"When God is going to do something wonderful, He begins with a difficulty. If He is going to do something very wonderful, He begins with an impossibility."

Dewey Cass

When we saw our Russian-born son we were told we didn't have to take him. At twelve months he weighed only twelve pounds. He was unable to sit up or even bear any weight at all on his legs. We did not know if he would survive the trip home, but we knew he was our son.

He made it home and even our doctor was at a loss for words. We didn't know what problems he would have but we knew that God would equip us to handle them. We knew he had moderate hearing loss so we signed to him from the very first moment we met him. We already had one hearing daughter and one deaf son and daughter.

Of course, we signed "mommy" and "daddy" and "I love you" to him right away and I continued to sign "mommy" practically all day every day! When he finally signed "mommy" we were all ecstatic. And later, on my birthday, he signed it all day and I know he knew what he was saying.

Since then he has learned to walk, run, stand on one foot and play basketball. He even says, "sink it!" He is two-years-old now and he is signing and even speaking in broken sentences and our entire family treats him just like he has always been here. What a blessing this child has been to our family, a true miracle.

Jennifer, biological, adoptive, and foster mom.

Watch What You Say

18 July

"What after all is a halo?
It's only one more thing to keep clean."
Christopher Fry

I had a five-year-old that was quite a character. He had an amazing understanding of adult conversation and a very mature sense of humor. At that time in my life, when I was exasperated with the kids, I would jokingly say, "What do I have to do, write you a letter?"

One day he was sent home with a note from the teacher. He had gotten in trouble for saying that to her. I felt so bad and embarrassed as I called to talk to her about the situation. She laughed and actually thought it was cute, but she couldn't tell him that.

I disciplined myself with his help, and told him how sorry I was that my inappropriate behavior had caused a problem. He was forgiving, and we agreed that neither of us would use that phrase anymore. From then on I was careful about what I said.

Dargie, mother and grandmother of many step, birth, foster, and adopted children.

July 19 — After They Leave

"God does not comfort us to make us comfortable, but to make us comforters."
— Jowett

When a foster child leaves my home, I am not the only one who feels the loss. My children and grandchildren bond to these temporary family members also.

I used to ask my children when they were grieving, "Would you rather you had never known them?" I encourage them to think of the joy we all received from taking care of these beautiful children. I tell them I know they hurt now and remind them that these children will always be in our hearts.

My six-year-old grandson missed one little foster baby so badly because she was very special to him. After she had gone he said, "But, Grandma, she will always be in my heart won't she?" It was so cute and also very sad.

He understands that these children need us, and he knows it hurts when they leave. None of my children or grandchildren has ever been willing to say they wish they had never known them.

Marjie, adoptive parent and foster parent for 27 years to over 200 children.

My Angel

"The great use of life is to spend it for something that outlasts it."
William James

When Sissy came to me she was a pretty little seven-week-old, very small, weighing in at six pounds. It was the dead of winter and she was wrapped in a urine soaked blanket and wearing only a little dirty diaper. She was hungry and crying and had sores all over her body from a skin infection. She also had numerous cigarette burns and smelled terrible.

Several days went by before a hearing took place, but the court decided that Sissy and her siblings would come home with us. At the time we had two beautiful children ages eight and four. When I told my wonderful, little four-year-old daughter she said, "Mommy you got a baby, which is what you wanted. Bubby got a brother, and Daddy got a new son. I will have two new sisters. You know Mommy, we have all kinds of love to share so I think it is okay."

Later, we adopted those three beautiful children. Oh yes, we have had our trials and tribulations, but they have added joy and love to our family that I didn't think could exist. Several years later my beautiful little four-year-old who would be twenty-four now, passed into the hands of God. Not a day goes by that I don't think about her and the year we added these three children to our family.

Willie, biological and adoptive parent, foster parent for 7 years.

July 21 — Unnecessary Moves

"Courage… is when you know you're licked before you begin but you begin anyway and you see it through no matter what."
— Harper Lee

Susan, foster and adoptive parent, grandparent, and former foster family recruiter and trainer.

"Our eighteen-month-old foster daughter came to us when she was twenty-eight days old. She had a sister, but they had never been placed together and it appeared that the girls would never know each other. Then we found out the worker was planning to move both girls from the homes they were currently in and place them in a home together while they awaited adoption. Now, I didn't get into foster care to adopt every child that came through my door, but I could not imagine giving up this beautiful light in my life to another foster home. To an adoptive home, yes, but not to another foster home only to be moved again when they found an adoptive home. Finally, after much arguing with the caseworker and her supervisor, I convinced them to place both girls in my home."

Wendy, birth mom of 3 children, adoptive mom to 1 child, and foster mom to 11 children over the last 5 years.

Foster children are often moved without the input of the foster family in which they are currently residing and we hope there are good reasons for the moves to take place. Sometimes we KNOW the move is not the best choice and almost every foster parent who does this for any length of time will have a case where they are in a struggle with a caseworker to try and prevent an unnecessary move. I heard once that there is nothing more fierce than a mother bear protecting her cubs, but I might vote for a foster mother who knows injustice when she sees it.

Shooting Bullets

"Before speaking, ask whether it is true, necessary, or kind."
Unknown

With the disruptive bad habits and/or inappropriate roles foster children may have acquired, their arrival in the foster or adoptive home can produce a great deal of turmoil. As a result, the parenting family can become discouraged and sink under the weight of the child's negative influence on them.

Which reminds me of a story. A mother found her three-year-old boy playing with a box of bullets. She was shocked to find that he had swallowed a couple. Panic stricken, she sped him to the local hospital. The emergency room doctor examined the boy thoroughly, fed him a heavy duty laxative, and released him to his mother with these instructions. "Take him home and keep him quiet. And whatever you do, don't point him at anybody for the next few hours!" As with this little boy, many of our foster and adopted children have swallowed a lot of things they shouldn't have. And, when it comes out, these kids are often pointed directly at the adoptive family.

The overall hope is that these families will look to more experienced foster and adoptive families for a better understanding of their situation. It is imperative that a supportive group of family and friends is established to help you see how the child's past has impacted him and will impact everybody around him; to try to inject more enjoyment and pleasure into the sometimes laborious task of parenting troubled kids; and to offer a vision of a brighter future for the family and child.

Rick, clinical psychologist, trainer and consultant who has worked with foster and adoptive children and their parents over the past 20 years.

July 23

Perfect

"It is only those who are willing to endure the pain of the struggle that will ultimately enjoy the rewards of success."

Unknown

I just went through my most difficult challenge as a foster parent. It took more than six weeks for me to get through it, and I am still not free to discuss details, but I do want to share my healing process.

1. I talked to my husband, we prayed.
2. I talked to my pastor's wife, we prayed.
3. I cried to my favorite niece, we prayed.
4. I cried to my best friend, we prayed.

I asked them all to hold me accountable to do what I said I would do.

Keeping things to myself and beating myself up did **not** help anyone. Sharing my feelings, fears and tears helped tremendously.

I found out that nobody is perfect, and nobody expects me to be perfect—even when they joke that I am Supermom. Many people care about me and my family! I can ask for help and they will help me. It's okay to ask for help.

I cannot control the children in my home. I can love them, pray for and guide them, but they make the choices. I can and do, however, control my reactions to those choices. Even if the choices are hurtful to me, I have learned we can work through it and still be family.

Dargie, mother and grandmother of many step, birth, foster, and adopted children.

Focus on the Positive

"If our children deserve a thousand chances, and then one more, lets give ourselves a thousand chances—and then two more."
Adele Faber & Elaine Mazlish

Working with children who are emotionally unstable, as are most children coming into care at this time, is a very difficult job. Each of these children desperately want and need to have someone who will hold on and support them no matter what; but they are very afraid that you will quit, that you will abandon them too.

No matter how well equipped you are to parent, there are always other avenues to explore when working with these special children. The mental, physical and emotional damage takes time to mend. You need to ask for help. Don't quit at the first sign of adversity. Accept where the child is, and go from there. Unrealistic expectations can only lead to frustration on both your part and that of the child. You've got to focus on the positive.

Trish, birth parent to 3 children, foster parent to nearly 600 children in the last 20 years, and grandparent to biological and foster grandchildren.

July 25 — Group Outing

"When kids are acting their worst, that's when they need you the most."
Richard J. Delaney

The young boy had worked hard on his behavior plan because he was really motivated by the reward of taking his friends to do something special. Then over spring break, when he had earned enough points, we planned an outing with him and three of his friends. All week he kept asking how many days until it was time to pick them up. He reminded me to call their parents the night before so they would be ready on time. He was really excited about the whole thing.

After I had all the kids in the car the fighting started. First it was arguing, then it was calling names, then it turned into punching and crying. We had all been together less than thirty minutes. The mood would calm and then wind up again and near explosion until I broke the group up. The young boy who had looked so forward to this event was sabotaging it before my very eyes. I couldn't figure out why he was being so aggressive with these kids.

The day ended with the friends going home early and the young boy angry and pouting. We had a long talk after it was over. He said, "I really tried to control myself, but I just couldn't." I grieved with him over the loss of the planned fun, and I assured him there would be another chance to try again, and again, until we figured out together how we could make this work.

Susan, foster and adoptive parent, grandparent, and former foster family recruiter and trainer.

Creativity Abounds

"Seeds of discouragement will not grow in the thankful heart."
Unknown

It is no secret to most foster care providers that our children are very creative. When the result of their creativity is a piece of art, it is a wonderful thing! I have had many boys who lived with me who were artists. As I glance at the top of my computer I see a terra-cotta sculpture one of my boys made and proudly brought home to me.

At one time I had four boys who were very good artists. What a thrill it was for me to see them share and learn from each other. I encouraged them at every opportunity. I bought paper, pens, pencils, and watercolors. There was a great sense of camaraderie as they created their masterpieces. The older boys taught the younger ones, and while there were certainly some times of loud discussions, they all had fun.

I was the grateful recipient of their labors. How I love those treasures! I have a paper tower holder, a pair of lizard earrings, pencil holders, drawings, and on and on. Wherever my life leads, these are the things which will always travel with me. These are the things that bring a smile to my face and tears to my eyes.

Carolyn, social worker and foster parent to teen boys.

July 27 — Passing Time

"Blessed be childhood, which brings down something of heaven into the midst of our rough earthliness."

Henri Frederic Amiel

One summer my sister and I packed up the kids and headed for a Florida beach. It was about a twelve-hour drive so we stopped quite a few times to let the kids run and play. They didn't mind too much being in the van because they were excited to be going to the beach for the first time ever.

I had purchased some art supplies, several games, toys, and books to help pass the time. The trip was enjoyable and the kids were putting great effort into behaving themselves.

About three-fourths of the way there, I looked into my rear view mirror and saw four sets of toes resting on the back of the third seat in my fifteen-passenger van. They had decorated each other's toes with markers and there were forty little faces staring at me. They were putting on a puppet show… singing and dancing. That moment of fun and laughter became one of my fondest memories of traveling with the kids.

Dargie, mother and grandmother of many step, birth, foster, and adopted children.

A Mouse in the House

"Look out for mercies.
The more we look for them, the more of them we will see."
Maltbie D. Babcock

Recently I've had a mouse in my house. I put out poison, and I felt terribly guilty about trying to kill the little thing. I did not want it in my house though.

I would lie in the bed at night and hear it, gnawing or running across the carpet. I would wake in the morning and find evidence that it had been in my living room or my office. A few times I actually saw it running across my floor. I was afraid it would get into my bed at night or run across my foot when I was sitting at my desk. I jumped at every sound I heard and I was hyper-vigilant, taking notice of every tiny movement I saw. Getting up in the dark to go to the bathroom became a thing of the past!

One of the things that came from this experience was the realization that there are so many families in the world who live in conditions much worse than my home. The kids we work with may have lived with rats and roaches and who knows what else. They often learn to be unaffected by their environment as a matter of sanity. I suppose if you are dealing with things crawling around in the house, you may wonder why it is important to put your dirty socks in the hamper. I suppose even a mouse can teach us something.

Susan, foster and adoptive parent, grandparent, and former foster family recruiter and trainer.

July 29 — Chosen

"You cannot touch love…
but you can feel the sweetness that it pours into everything."
Anne Sullivan, found in *The Story of My Live* by Helen Keller

After the birth of our first child, we were told I couldn't have any more children, so my husband and I decided to adopt. Our doctor informed us that he knew of a child that was about to be born and was going to be available to adopt. He was ten days old when he came to live with us.

Since he had been without constant attention for so many days, I worried about him being unattached to us as his parents. From day one he had already started sucking his thumb and did so for a long time. But from the first moment that we held him we knew he was ours and that he belonged to our family.

We would often forget that he was adopted and wanted to make sure he never felt that he wasn't ours. It has been thirty years since we adopted our son, in that time there were challenges with successes and failures, as with all children. Our lives have been blessed and enriched by the extra love we have given and received from him. I have never regretted adopting this child that was chosen to be ours.

Margaret, birth and adoptive parent, parent of special-needs child, and grandparent.

Love Only Multiplies

"The best way to know God is to love many things."
Vincent Van Gogh

I had been concerned that my biological grandchildren would somehow seem different and closer to me than the adopted ones. As I sat holding my adopted granddaughter, stroking her hair as she drifted off to sleep my concerns lessened.

I remember with a rush of emotions the first time I held her in my arms. Her mother was getting dressed to take her to the hospital because she was having trouble breathing during the night. Both the young mom and her child were new in our home, and they were facing many changes; but first we had to get through a hospital visit. After hours of tests and paperwork they admitted her. She spent the entire night in an oxygen tent clinging to her mommy. After their hospital stay I think they were both very glad to come "home."

The baby always liked and went freely to my husband. Their relationship quickly blossomed into a loving one, and now she calls him Papa in a way that makes his chest swell with pride. I have a new name too, Neena, and I love it. My concerns have vanished now. I do not think my love can do anything but multiply to include all the children yet to come, no matter how they come into our family. Each child is unique and very special, just like each child who has passed through our home. What I have discovered is that it doesn't matter how they became a part of my life, for me, it would be much harder to try not to love them.

Dargie, mother and grandmother of many step, birth, foster, and adopted children.

July 31 — Grace

"It is in the shelter of each other that the people live."
Irish Proverb

We grew very discouraged when one young man living in our home refused everything we offered. This fifteen-year-old preferred to sneak downstairs after we had gone to bed and raid the refrigerator rather than share in family meals. He preferred hanging out in his room to joining in on a game or family activity. He preferred sleeping to going out with friends or watching television. We tried to give him space, but never gave up trying to engage him in relationship.

One evening we took in a five-year-old on an emergency basis. I had him bathe and began the bedtime routine. I read a story, and he cried big tears. I rubbed his back, and he said he missed his mama. I sang a lullaby, and he said he was afraid. And so it went, until I began to worry that I would run out of ideas. Then I looked up and there in the doorway stood our fifteen-year-old recluse with the football we had given him for his birthday.

"Want to play catch?" He asked the five-year-old.

I watched in amazement as this wounded teenager played with this hurting child and then tucked him in bed. Where my husband and I could not reach, these two had been able to connect. I had been given the privilege of witnessing grace in action.

Lesa, therapeutic foster parent and foster parent trainer.

A Special Family

1 August

"The doors we open and close each day decide the lives we live."
Flora Whittemore

Every child that has passed through my home has taught my family something and blessed us in some way. The good, in my opinion, has far outweighed the bad. It takes a special family to do foster care. I have been blessed by **the most special family**.

Choosing to become a foster family was something we decided together. When a call comes asking us to take in a child without a home, we discuss it as a family. The response is usually, "When do we pick them up?" My family has learned to share their rooms, food, clothes, love, and each other with those that are sent our way.

Learning to make good choices is an essential life skill. Living those choices is sometimes difficult, but it is one of the best legacies we can leave our children.

Duryle, mother and grandmother of many step, birth, foster, and adopted children.

August 2 — Stability

"I don't think of all the misery, but of all the beauty that still remains."
Anne Frank

"I was in the system on and off until I was eighteen. I was in nineteen foster homes, two group homes, and two psychiatric hospitals while in care. The longest I was in one home was thirteen months. In a way this was a bad thing for me because now I am always on the move. Today, I don't think that I would really change anything about growing up in the system except the fact that I did not have any stability."

Stacey, former foster child who was in care for 14 years.

One of the biggest problems with the system of caring for children who cannot live with their birth families has been the lack of stability. Children have been removed from their homes and then shuffled around to overcrowded or unprepared foster homes and then removed again when "things didn't work out." We must do a better job of serving these children. In order for them to blossom we must give them time to put down roots.

Susan, foster and adoptive parent, grandparent, and former foster family recruiter and trainer.

The Rewards of Fostering

3 August

"'Hope' is that thing with feathers that perches in the soul…"
Emily Dickinson

I foster because I find it so rewarding. There are the adult foster children who come back to say, "Thanks for saving my life." The first steps of a child that everyone thought would never walk. The first words from a kid who refused to talk to anyone, but decides to talk to you. Then there is the teen that says, "It was really neat how you fought for me that way, no one has ever done that before. There are the thankful parents, the great people you meet who foster, and the possibility that you will foster a child who will stay forever.

Dianne, biological and foster parent for 21 years, and adoptive parents of 6 special-needs children. Have reunited over 90 children with their birth parents.

August 4 — Hurt Feelings

"Remember, when they have a tantrum, don't have one of your own."
Judith Kuriansky

I have often been hurt by an adult "adopted child." It seems to hurt more and be harder to forget with this child. There is a wall I can't get past, issues never completely laid to rest, baggage always packed and ready to run with if she is held accountable.

Lord, help me get past my pain and understand hers.
Help me love her no matter what and keep my heart from hardening.
Help me to move on and not dwell on these hurts.
Give me the peace that passes understanding that I sang about as a child.
Lord, teach me to love unconditionally.

This is by far one of the hardest things I have ever done. And, when I am able to see things clearly, I know that choosing to be in an ongoing relationship with all its challenges is even harder for her.

Dargie, mother and grandmother of many step, birth, foster, and adopted children.

Right Time, Right Placement

5 August

*"There are only two ways to approach life—
as a victim or as a gallant fighter—and you must decide
if you want to act or react... a lot of people forget that."*
— Merle Shain

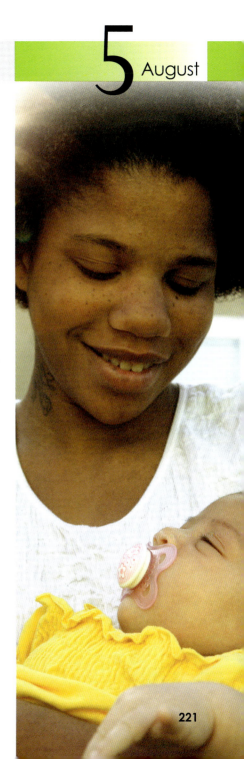

Last night we picked up our first emergency placement in over two years. We had stopped taking emergency babies when our fourteen-year-old foster (now sixteen-year-old guardianship) daughter decided to find an adoptive home for the baby she was carrying. We didn't feel it was fair to her to have babies around while she was dealing with all of the emotions associated with her decision and the hormonal changes from the birth of the baby. About eighteen months later however, she wanted us to start again.

When the placement worker called with an eighteen-month-old girl and her six-year-old brother, our foster daughter was in the room saying, "Yes, yes, yes." So we said, "Yes." She went with me to pick them up and talked about how this little girl was the same age as her birth daughter. She was a big help with both children as we drove home. She even helped comb the lice nits from their hair, putting to use "tricks" she had learned growing up.

It felt so good to see the joy on her face as she "mothered" this little one, content in the knowledge that her birth child has a wonderful home with a sister, mother, and father that she selected. The frequent e mails, pictures, and even a trip to their home in another state to visit them for "their" baby's first birthday reconfirm the rightness of her decision.

Bobbi, birth, foster and guardianship mom.

August 6 — A Special School

"Excellence can be attained as you: care more than others think is wise; risk more than others think is safe; dream more than others think is practical; and expect more than others think is possible."

Unknown

Today I have hope. Today I went to a school and entered a classroom where the teacher was teaching in a way my child could learn. I could see it, I could feel the energy of learning taking place. I also saw that the children in this classroom had great difficulty sitting in their seats and were struggling with concepts. They were not struggling with the structure of the school though. It was a special school, where over two hundred children who learn differently come together to be taught in ways that work for them.

I was impressed. I was also a little sad for all those children who grow up thinking they are defective because they do not fit into the cookie cutter approach often used in public school settings.

Today though, I will celebrate. I will celebrate the smiles I saw on those children's faces as they participated in a learning process that helped them feel successful. I will celebrate the teachers who are willing to go that extra mile and create that special activity for the one child who needs it. And, I will celebrate the joy I felt at finding a place where they do not look at my child with dread, but embrace him and all his hidden talents.

Susan, foster and adoptive parent, grandparent, and former foster family recruiter and trainer.

Little Skater

7 August

"Those who do not know how to weep with their whole heart don't know how to laugh either."

Golda Meir

One day I sat gazing out my kitchen window. I noticed that my little five-year-old was skateboarding down the drive way. He was going at a snail's pace… but he was actually riding it! This child that didn't walk until he was two, has limited vision and permanent brain damage was learning, jumping, and balancing!

At first I sat in amazement, alternating between laughter and tears. I called the other kids in to witness this wonderful event. They, too, were surprised and delighted as they watched him.

Looking back, I don't think I have ever been so proud of one of my children. He has had so much to overcome. He is an inspiration to us all.

Dargie, mother and grandmother of many step, birth, foster, and adopted children.

August 8 — Roles

"Parenting... goes both ways. We have a lot to impart to children... about teaching them the ways of the world. And they also have things to tell us, things that we may have forgotten, or we get so busy... that we forget to focus on the things that truly matter. And children can teach us too."

Judy Ford

What makes a mother or a father? We are often taught roles like MOMS do the bandages and cooking while DADS do the fishing and fixing. But in our case we both do it all. Sometimes he gives the hugs and I do the discipline and then it changes.

When we create these rigid "roles" we make people less flexible and less resilient. If we can teach that people work together in a family and that everyone gets chores done together we have taught the meaning of team work.

Roles are for Hollywood; in a family we need to work together.

Jim, foster parent to teen boys.

Family of Choice

9 August

*"I wonder why it is that we are not all kinder to each other...
How much the world needs it! How easily it is done!"*

Henry Drummond

My siblings and I first went into foster care when I was seven. We only stayed for about six months, and then we went home. Two years later, however, we were placed again. I was told we would only be there for another six months which made sense to me since that is the way it worked the first time.

Years later we were still in the foster home. During that time we came to believe we were going to stay in that foster home forever, and we started calling the foster parents "Mom" and "Dad." The children were referred to as our brothers and sisters; we were part of their family. Eventually, one of my brothers did go back home, but the rest of us did not. My parents refused to allow me to be adopted by my foster parents.

The people I call my "family" are the people who took me when I was nine years old. All together there are nine of us kids, seven biological, and two not. I don't really know how to refer to them because they are not my adoptive family and they are no longer my foster parents because I'm too old. I guess they are simply my family of choice, we all chose one another.

Sharon, former foster child.

August 10 Sisters

"The questions is, 'If we as a human community want children, how does the total society propose to provide for them?'"

Jean Baker Miller

They are sisters, born to recovering alcoholics and mentally ill parents of different ethnic backgrounds. Their mother struggled as a single parent, unable to keep her own life together, much less provide the kind of consistent, healthy care needed for the two girls. What chance did they have?

The younger one called me "the grandpa who brought candy." The older one would call to inquire when her Christmas check was coming. I am the birth grandfather of these girls who have been in foster care for two years now.

It was a painful, soul-searching time when the extended family realized the girls were being removed from their mother's care and placed in foster care. I realized that due to my age, stamina, and current life situation it would be unfair to all involved for me to try to take on the responsibility of their daily care. It's been my personal choice not to interfere and pull the girls in yet another direction.

Having seen recent photographs, it's clear the girl's foster parents are doing a fine job. The girls are thriving on the love and consistent care they are receiving. I would like to express my admiration and thankfulness for foster families who give of themselves to this kind of parenthood. In particular, I send my deepest appreciation to that Kansas, foster family that is making the time and sacrifices needed to provide a home for two sisters.

PaPa Duane, birth grandparent.

Foster Parent Pledge

11 August

"I believe God is in me as the sun is in the color and fragrance of a flower—the Light in my darkness, the Voice in my silence."
— Hellen Keller

F   is for a Future without fear
O   is for a way Out when times get rough
S   is for a Safe place to stay
T   is for Trying to help them understand
E   is for trusting Everyone involved
R   is for a Rest from harm

P   is for a Person who cares
A   is for only an Arms distance away
R   is for Reassurance in their lives
E   is for Everything they do good or bad
N   is for Nurturing them with our hearts
T   is for all the Tender Loving Care

pledge by Karen

Foster parents are a remarkably diverse group. They are rich, poor, tall, short, college graduates, and high school dropouts. One thing they have in common is their focus on the children. This focus causes them to draw on whatever experience they have to provide whatever the child needs.

Susan, foster and adoptive parent, grandparent, and former foster family recruiter and trainer.

August 12 — The Need to Nurture

"We never get to the bottom of ourselves on our own. We discover who we are face to face and side by side with others in work, love, and learning."

— Robert Bellah

Several years ago I took my foster children to an empty playground for the afternoon. They were having a wonderful time and two of the girls even persuaded me to play with them on the seesaw.

On one trip up into the air they bumped the ground and I fell, hitting the ground hard between my shoulder blades. The children circled around me, helped me to the van, and I drove to the nearby home of a friend.

As I was recovering from that fall, the children became concerned. They were afraid they were in trouble, afraid they had hurt me badly, afraid I was angry with them and would send them away. The girls who had been on the seesaw with me were particularly worried so I let them take care of me. It was not easy to find things for them to do; but, they brought me lunch, changed the channels on the television, and other minor things that helped them feel as if they were being useful.

That incident reminds me that, even though our children need to be nurtured, they also need a chance to nurture. When they feel they have done something hurtful, we can sometimes help by creating a structure for them to make amends in healthy ways. We must not forget that being able to feel legitimate compassion for another human being is a high level achievement.

Susan, foster and adoptive parent, grandparent, and former foster family recruiter and trainer.

Jamie

13 August

"This is the beginning of a new day. You have been given this day to use as you will. Tomorrow, this day will be gone forever; in its place you will have left something behind... let it be something good."

Unknown

My son, Jamie, came to me as a foster child over twenty-eight years ago. He was ten weeks old, the baby of five siblings, and he had been neglected due to a very ill mother. In our family he was the youngest of three boys (my sons were nine and five at that time). We loved him immediately, and he thrived with us. We put his seat in the center of the dining room table where he would be stimulated constantly as the family and many visitors surrounded him with conversation and activities. He was the center of our world.

He was seven before we were able to adopt him; a wonderful day in all our lives. Jamie had developed into a beautiful, friendly and self-confident child with a smile for everyone. He loved playing sports and was the mascot of his older brothers' football and baseball teams.

As with any child, all has not been easy. Jamie was diagnosed with a brain disorder and was extremely hyperactive. He had many operations and allergy treatments, but he continued to be happy and outgoing. He experienced the usual difficulties during his teen years, but eventually found his way.

Jamie has grown to be a loving and thoughtful son and a terrific father. He could not be more my son if he was born of my womb. I will always be grateful that he came into our lives.

Judy, adoptive mother, former foster mother, grandmother of 6.

August 14 — I Just Like Surprises

*"For a happy life, three things are necessary:
Something to hope for.
Something to do.
Something to love."*

William Barclay

I have noticed that the larger my house is, the more places I have to put things "up." For instance, there is a high cabinet or shelf in almost every room where we have "put up" balls, plastic bats and toys that might be used as a weapon. You can also find those toys that make loud or irritating noises up there.

I don't get rid of them. I just take them down when I find them and allow the children another chance (they think it's Christmas). Eventually though, one of us tall people usually puts them up again.

I also put up important papers and tapes. You know those things where you think, "This is the only copy we have and we need to guard it with our lives." It's not lost, I just have it "put up" in a very safe place. I know the kids can't find it because I can't. I put up gifts that I buy before holidays and can't find them until after the event.

It's not that I'm disorganized, I just like surprises. And besides, I've never lost anything really important... like a kid.

Dargie, mother and grandmother of many step, birth, foster, and adopted children.

Alphabet Soup

15 August

*"God has not called me to be successful;
He has called me to be faithful."*
— Mother Teresa

An IEP, which is written by the ARC and based on the child's PLOP, will include the SDI and related services necessary to provide a FAPE for the child in the LRE available.

Advocating for the educational rights of a special needs child can be a challenging and often frustrating task. It is like learning a new language in order to play the game well. It can be quite intimidating.

Yet foster and adoptive parents who walk into the middle of a child's life jump in and take on this task every day. In some ways it is akin to the struggles their kids have in the classroom. Rules don't make sense and logic doesn't apply. Frustration abounds as parents wait for the next meeting or person before a task can be completed. Sometimes the child moves on to another placement before the educational evaluation is even complete.

So why bother? Why struggle with the school when the child may not cooperate at all with the plan? Why insist on their right to a Free and Appropriate Public Education in their Least Restrictive Environment? Why attend a meeting of the Admissions and Release Committee to write an Individual Education Program and create Specially Designed Instruction considering their Present Level of Performance?

Well, because it is the soul work of foster and adoptive parents to shine the light of worthiness on each and every child. When we treat them as worthy, some of them even come to believe it themselves, and that is the point.

Susan, foster and adoptive parent, grandparent, and former foster family recruiter and trainer.

August 16 — Raising Boys

"It (motherhood) is the biggest on-the-job training program in existence today."

Erma Bombeck, *Motherhood, the Second Oldest Profession*

I have fostered boys since 1993, and I have learned volumes about the male species! I have found out they have various plateaus of growth, and for some reason they seldom change from one generation to the next.

The ages I find especially challenging are the twelve to fourteen year olds. This is the scruffiest age group I have ever encountered. Hygiene is NOT one of their concerns. I remember one time I asked a twelve-year-old boy if he had brushed his teeth, and he looked at me in a perplexed fashion. Then he put his finger on his cheek, rolled his eyes toward heaven and stated, "let me think." He answered my question without even answering it.

They will wear the same underwear and socks for days, and doing their laundry can be quite a chore! I can remember boys going into the shower room and coming out without one drop of water touching their hide. Once I asked a counselor, "What do I do with these boys who don't want to take a shower?" He answered me with the wisdom of experience by saying, "wait until they discover girls."

Actually, I've come to understand the truth of his words over the years, but I still find this age group very challenging!

Carolyn, social worker and foster parent to teen boys.

Does It Ever Get Easier?

17 August

"It is gratefulness which makes the soul great."
Abraham Joshua Heschel

When we entered the world of foster care we were filled with the thoughts of happy beginnings. We did not yet know the feelings that come when a child leaves. Does the leaving ever get easier?

My first instinct is to say no; but, in a way, I think it does. We learn more about how to heal and move on each time we feel the loss of another child.

I still grieve over the first child I lost. I dearly loved her, and I still wonder how her life on a reservation has been. And then there was the boy who came to us when he was two days old. We planned to adopt him, but the worker didn't like the idea of him being adopted by a family of a different culture. He left when he was five-months-old and my heart still hurts for him even though I know he is in a great adoptive home.

I have learned so much with each child I have lost. As much as it hurts, I wouldn't give any less than I did with the first child because I know I'll always reap the fruits of my labor. Sometimes it comes right away in the form of another child we have the privilege of adopting. Other times we wait and hear years later that what we did made a difference. I am grateful for the pain as well as the joy because it is through the pain that we grow.

Kathy

August 18 — The Highchair

"He loves each of us, as if there were only one of us."
St. Augustine

My youngest biological son was nine, so it had been quite a while since my house was filled with baby furniture. When we got our first foster child my parents traveled six-hundred-fifty miles to bring him a highchair. He wasn't even able to sit up at the time, but we all knew the time would come when he would need it.

I had no idea we would be blessed with more babies when I disposed of the furniture, but through the years we have had more babies sit in that chair than I can even count. We have since adopted that first child who sat there and he has loved each baby who came after, just as we have loved him. We only hope these children have been blessed by their time with us. We know we have been blessed by each of them.

Dargie, mother and grandmother of many step, birth, foster, and adopted children.

Taking Time

19 August

"There is something infinitely healing in the repeated refrains of nature—the assurance that dawn comes after night, and spring after the winter."

Rachel Carson

One of the moms I know says she wishes children didn't have to mold into time frames set by adults. I know what she means when I watch her six-year-old color. He bends intently over a dinosaur he has stenciled onto blank paper and sticks his tongue out as he moves the marker across the page.

Too often we are forced to interrupt an exploration or a curiosity so that children can catch the bus or get to soccer practice. I often wonder if they would get to the same place eventually if we just let them explore the world naturally.

I know that we must be careful and that predictability and structure often give a sense of security like nothing else, but have we overdone it? I suppose we put spelling and science and math in their separate spaces because it is too difficult to take thirty first graders outside and teach them to spell water by letting them use a brush and bucket of water to paint the word "water" on the sidewalk and then watch it evaporate.

When we work with children who have been forced to lose their innocence, we can do them a great service by helping them rekindle their sense of awe. The world we live in is a wonder and by reconnecting them to that they begin to sense the wonder in themselves. So, go out with your child someday soon and pick a flower or skip a rock and revel in the magic the world offers.

Susan, foster and adoptive parent, grandparent, and former foster family recruiter and trainer.

August 20 — The Perfect Match

"I don't remember how I spent my time before loving this child. We thank God for him everyday."

Dargie Arwood (on the one year anniversary with her foster child).

I had a foster child who came to me at age three, weighing only fourteen pounds. I did physical therapy with her, played with her, talked to her and told her how much I loved her. After the first month, the doctor didn't recognize her when she went back for a checkup. That goes to show you that these little ones have great potential. It is our job to help them reach it. It may take extra time and care, but it is worth it.

This child came to me at a time when I was going through a personal crisis, and I needed her as much as she needed me. God knew who we were and what we needed, and He placed us together for a reason.

Eight months later this child died, and I wondered why I was not able to keep her. However, in my heart, I know that now she is running and playing without a wheelchair or feeding tubes and that she has no worries. We just do the best we can with these children in the time we have.

People ask me, "How can you care for someone else's child like that?" The answer is simple. When I get foster children, I take them as my own. I don't have to, I want to.

Marie, adoptive parent and foster parent for over 20 years caring for more than 50 children, many of whom were handicapped.

Comparisons

21 August

"We destroy the love of learning in children, which is so strong when they are small, by encouraging them to work for petty and contemptible rewards (gold stars, or papers marked with 100 and tacked to the wall, or A's on report cards, or honor rolls, or Dean's lists) in short, for the ignoble satisfaction of feeling that they are (somehow) better than someone else."

John Holt

Many of the children we work with are delayed in their development. It may feel quite natural to make statements like, "My child doesn't read as well as the other first graders." On the surface these comments seem harmless, indeed they are a way of helping others understand quickly something significant about the child in question.

In my family, as in most families, this sort of thing goes on all the time. My father, however, is appalled when one child is in anyway compared to another. When I adopted my daughter, she did many things I associated with a much younger child. I would say things like, "It seems to me she should be able to tell time." My father would then respond with something like, "What is she doing today that she couldn't do yesterday?" I figured he was just missing the point. I was partly right, one of us was missing the point.

I have come to understand that each child grows and learns in an individual way depending on his life experiences, his talents, his challenges, and his support systems. And, as the wise man in my family puts it, "The only fair comparison for a child is to compare him to the child he has been in the past... and even then you must be careful."

Susan, foster and adoptive parent, grandparent, and former foster family recruiter and trainer.

August 22 — Up in the Air

*"Happiness comes of the capacity to feel deeply,
to enjoy simply, to think freely, to risk life, to be needed."*
Storm Jameson

What I try to think about when things get up in the air: This child is safe now, and I'm blessed to be able to help and care for him or her.

I can always go to my prayer closet–that helps a lot when I'm in need and others are in need. I also think back to my childhood and how I wasn't wanted. Even though those memories hurt, it reminds me that children need to know that we need them.

I have this posted in my kitchen:

and another one:

Good Morning, this is God, I will be handling all of your problems today. I will not need your help. So, relax and have a great day!

I can do all things through Him who strengthens me.

Philippians 4:13

Tish, foster parent to approximately 25 children in the past 3 years, biological parent, adoptive parent, and grandmother of 5.

Keeping Promises

23 August

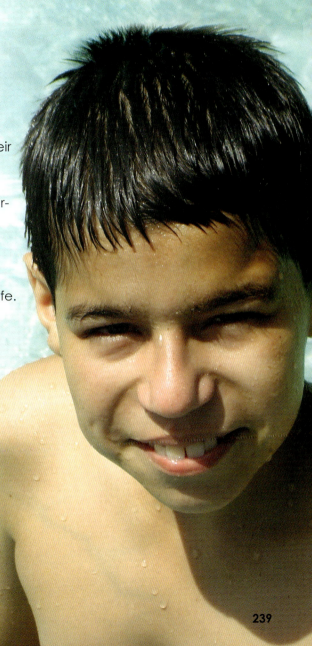

"The truth is that life is delicious, horrible, charming, sweet, bitter and that is everything."

Anatole France

One summer, I got two young brothers for a short respite. My other children and I were packing for a trip during their stay, and it was a busy time.

We had a lot of trouble with the behavior of the four-year-old, so I promised that if he wouldn't run away, I would take him for a swim. His behavior improved immediately, he had something special to look forward to. He had never been to a pool before, and I assumed from the reports I heard that he had little to look forward to in his life.

While little brother napped and the older kids packed, I took him to the pool. He jumped and kicked, splashed, and rolled. I watched him, not sure if it was sweat or tears rolling down my cheeks.

When it came time to go, he didn't once ask to stay longer or complain that it was brief; he thanked me for taking him. He had been rewarded for good behavior, and now he behaved even better. It is so important to keep the promises we make to these children. What was a twenty minute hold up for me was a dream-come-true for this boy… and I was blessed to have been part of it.

Dargie, mother and grandmother of many step, birth, foster, and adopted children.

August 24 — Sea Monkeys

"Everything we fix for our kids, our kids will be unable to fix for themselves. If there's more than a ten percent chance that our child might be able to work it out, we should keep clear of the problem."

Foster Cline & Jim Fay

My sixteen-year-old daughter had been living with me for one year when she mail-ordered a package of sea monkeys and promptly tried to bring them to life. Although it was difficult for her, she read aloud, "Put two cups of boiling water into a clean clear container such as a goldfish bowl." Then she measured two cups of cold water into a saucepan and put it on the stove.

"What's the deal here? I put two cups of water in that pan," she mumbled as she measured after boiling it for several minutes. She repeated this process at least six times before finally running into the living room saying, "I think some of the water is getting out of the pan in the steam."

We briefly discussed the process of evaporation and then she returned to the kitchen saying that she knew what to do now. She then measured exactly two cups of water, boiled it, poured out exactly one cup of boiling water, threw away the rest and repeated the process to get the second cup of boiling water.

It wasn't the way I would have done it, but it worked. We live in a world that puts us all in boxes and asks us to walk in straight lines; but, some of us have been fortunate enough to share life with children who have survived by living outside the box and seeing labyrinths where others just see a line.

Susan, foster and adoptive parent, grandparent, and former foster family recruiter and trainer.

Christmas in August

25 August

*"Remember to listen to the flowers…
to taste the rainbows…
to embrace the song that makes you uniquely you."*

Thomas P. O'Hay

One night I awoke to the smell of bacon frying. It was late and I thought I might be dreaming, especially when I realized there was Christmas music playing and it was summertime. Then my somewhat troubled teen foster daughter began waking the family up for her surprise.

She had been up making muffins, scrambled eggs and lots of other breakfast foods. She had set the table with the best china, put up Christmas decorations, and even had place cards for each family member present. She escorted us proudly into the dining room for the feast.

It was 3:00 am in the middle of August. We were touched but puzzled. We wanted to laugh but we controlled it and simply enjoyed the meal.

The gifts our foster children bring us are often unusual and unexpected, but they are gifts none the less. Each day I try to accept those gifts for what they are… the heartfelt offering of someone reaching out and trying to connect. Sometimes we get a macaroni necklace and sometimes a marvelous Christmas breakfast in the middle of a hot summer night.

Caroline, as told to Dargie, mother and grandmother of many step, birth, foster, and adopted children.

August 26 — Borrowed Child

"God is in the details."
Ludwig Mies vander Rohe

I went to a training session last night for new foster parents. A case manager, a therapist, another seasoned foster parent, and I participated in a panel discussion for the new recruits. The other foster parent (on the topic of how our biological children react to the foster children) shared that one of her youngsters asked, "Mom, how long are we gonna borrow this kid?"

Since I think of the word "borrow" as referring to taking something I need (with permission) for a period of time, the child's choice of words seemed funny. At first I laughed, but then I thought about the hidden wisdom in that choice. After all, the fostering of children is supposed to be temporary. Sometimes it is hard to remember that concept when you begin to love a child. Children, once loved, are not easily returned. If we kept the children until we were ready to return them, the foster care system would look very different!

It is one of our greatest challenges… letting a child go. By the way, after over three years, that family is still "borrowing" that particular child.

Dargie, mother and grandmother of many step, birth, foster, and adopted children.

Powerful Words

"Between stimulus and response, there is a space. In that space lies our freedom and power to choose our response. In our response lies our growth and happiness."

Unknown

It was not my proudest moment. After a long, harrowing day filled with rebellion and obstinate frivolity aimed at getting out of doing anything I asked, I had finally agreed to a trip to the park.

The next thing I found infuriating was a lie that was so obviously a lie I couldn't imagine it even being told. At that point I lost my mature, foster parent thinking. My master's degree in social work might as well have been shredded. I could hardly believe my own ears when I said, "Well I had hoped you would be different. Your mother is a liar, and I suppose you are choosing to be one too."

The moment those words came out of my mouth I regretted them. I know they were a result of personal stress, taking on more than I could handle, and holding on to lots of unexpressed anger—but none of that mattered.

The child did not seem to be effected, but who knows what long-term scar my pronouncement will leave. If I could take it back I would. If I could explain it to him I would. If I could rewind time I most certainly would.

I cannot do these things though, so I will remember this anguish the next time I'm feeling stress. I will work at making amends to this child in a real way that matters. And, I will pray that I will never, never make an error like that again.

Susan, foster and adoptive parent, grandparent, and former foster family recruiter and trainer.

August 28 — From the Heart of Kids

"Children have never been very good at listening to their elders, but they have never failed to imitate them."
— James Baldwin

In my years of working with kids, the most valuable tool I have implemented is to actively listen when they speak. Most kids are more than willing to share what they believe they need from their caregivers. This can include ice cream for breakfast as well as unconditional love. Being a good, discerning listener is one of the most valued parenting skills. In addition our kids need from us a sense of direction, consistency and leadership.

The following brief list is gleaned from some suggestions shared by those youngsters. These ideas come from the heart of kids, prompting us as caregivers to keep in mind what is important to them, and of what is truly important in life.

- Remember that you are a role model.
- Show me what it means to have a true friend.
- Remember, I am watching everything you say and do.
- Be creative in your thinking, so that I can too.
- Show me how to forgive.
- Feel good about yourself, so that I might feel good about myself.
- Demonstrate honesty.
- Teach me the value of boundaries.
- Demonstrate empathy by showing others that you care.

Gina, counselor, mentor, mother, and author of "For the Kids."

Family Tree

29 August

"So one thing I want to say about life is don't be scared and don't hang back, and most of all, don't waste it."
Joan W. Blos

As we were riding into town my grandson asked me, "Who is my momma's daddy?" We adopted his mother when she was fifteen and he knows that, so I knew he wanted to know who her birth father was.

I was so glad I knew the information! I gave him his grandfather's name and told him about what kind of work he did. I told him how old his grandfather was when his mother was born, and we figured up how old he would be now if he were still alive.

Every time we were interrupted by some traffic situation he would direct the conversation back to his family tree. We talked for almost a solid hour about people he did not know and probably would never see. It was so important to him to hear this information, so important for him to have something to connect with in all of it.

He asked me if he would be adopted some day and I assured him that most likely that wouldn't happen because his mother was able to take care of him. And then he got to the real question. "If I did need to be adopted one day, would you sign the papers?" My eyes filled with tears and my heart swelled in my chest and I said, "Of course I would." I wish the answers to all his life questions would come that easily.

Susan, foster and adoptive parent, grandparent, and former foster family recruiter and trainer.

August 30 — May You Have

"We are pilgrims in a strange land, but God has placed remembrances of heaven along our way."
— Don Hudson

Enough happiness
    To keep you sweet,

Enough trials
    To keep you strong,

Enough sorrow
    To keep you human,

Enough love
    To keep you joyful,

Enough hope
    To keep you happy,

Enough failure
    To keep you humble,

Enough success
    To keep you eager,

Enough friends
    To give you comfort,

Enough enthusiasm
    To look forward,

Enough faith
    To ease your fears,

    Enough determination
        To make each day better than yesterday.

Stephen

My Butterfly

31 August

"A child is a butterfly in the wind:
Some can fly higher than others,
But each one flies… the best that it can.
Why compare one against the other?
Each one is different, each one is special,
Each one is beautiful!"

Unknown

After being told that I couldn't have any more children and adopting one child, I was anxiously awaiting the birth of my third child. When he was born we learned that he had Down Syndrome. Although I felt blessed to have given birth for a second time, I was disappointed at first, especially with doctors telling me that there was no hope for this baby.

I struggled with depression for a long time. I kept asking myself why this happened to me and what had I done to deserve this? Then I realized that God only gave these types of children to special people, and it didn't matter if he wasn't going to be like other children, he was still a miracle and he was my child. It was my job to prove the critics wrong.

At that time, I decided I would do everything I could to help this child reach his human potential. Kyle is now twenty-six years old. He loves music, movies, and food. He has starred in many local high school plays. Just because someone says you can't do it, doesn't mean it can't be done.

Margaret, birth parent, adoptive parent, parent of a special-needs child, and grandparent.

September 1 — Tea Party

"The strength of my children is what sustains me, they are the true heroes."

Patti, foster parent for medically fragile infants

"After nearly two years of being separated from their fourth sibling, the foster children in our home were looking forward to being reunited with their sister. We were working diligently to make it happen although we hadn't said anything to the children. Of course we were foolish to think they wouldn't suspect the plan. I watched them during visits, and it was pure joy to see them fill up and become whole people again when she was there, especially the seven-year-old who seemed to be the most connected with his separated sibling.

"It had been several weeks since her last visit when the seven-year-old found out another one had been cancelled. I overheard him talking to himself about the quickest ways to die. The depth of feeling and anguish these kids can suffer is astounding. Later, I stood outside the bedroom door and eavesdropped as he had an imaginary tea party with his missing sister. He told her how much he missed her and what they would do when he saw her again and then he seemed very comforted. How did he know to do that?" Deena, mom to a bunch of great kids (ages 21,19, 17, 15, 8, 7, 6, 5, 5, 3).

As foster or adoptive families we learn from these survivors and honor them when we work to help the system that cares for them become more accountable for meeting their real needs, like the one that would cause a seven-year-old to consider dying.

Susan, foster and adoptive parent, grandparent, and former foster family recruiter and trainer.

Family Meetings

"Listening is a form of accepting."
Stella Terrill Mann

A family meeting is one way to work together as a team. In our house it doesn't matter if kids have been with us two days or two years, they are all welcome to attend and be heard at our family meetings.

We have family meetings about everything. We might discuss what movie to see, where to go for a vacation, a phone bill, or something as serious as a move. The kids don't have the final say, but they are welcome to state opinions and concerns. They often have interesting and worthwhile things to add, and this is an invaluable tool.

In family meetings we are modeling decision making, planning, and negotiating compromise. Most importantly though, it makes them feel like they are a part of the family, and that is the best benefit of all.

Dargie, mother and grandmother of many step, birth, foster, and adopted children.

September 3 — The Phone Call

"If we could sell our experiences for what they cost us we'd be millionaires."

Abigail Van Buren

When you reunite a child with biological family it can be so bittersweet. You prepare them and help them adjust. You go through the behaviors after each visit. You answer the myriad of questions from both the child and birth family. Sometimes you are treated with respect and other times you are not.

On that last day you drive away after unloading the boxes and in their excitement you may or may not get a "thank you" or a hug. It depends on the situation. They are just glad to be together, excitedly unpacking and you leave feeling almost embarrassed at their happiness. It feels so empty, like you want an ending, the credits to roll down the screen, theme music or something.

You drive home, put the keys on the counter, walk into your house and begin again. You think of the child often and wish they would call. Some do and some don't and most youngsters aren't great at letter writing.

Then it happens… that unexpected phone call. You listen to an excited and happy child tell you the latest news and ask carefully about your "new kids." You laugh and chat for awhile and afterward you know you did the right thing. You were part of a new beginning. It can boost your day, your week, your month! It is part of the experience of being a foster parent.

Robin, foster parent for 30 children over the last 5 years.

Saving Grace

4 September

"God speaks to those who take time to listen."
Unknown

While at the computer one evening, I heard soft giggles fill the air and assumed the girls had awakened and were playing. Then something about the gentle breeze and the tender voices I heard drew me toward the sounds.

As I walked into the living room, Grace was sitting there with a sparkle in her eyes and a big smile on her face. I asked, "Who are you talking to sweetie?" I felt a chill run over me as she said, "My angel."

The next morning she told me her angel's name was Sally. Grace said, "She has brown hair and was dressed in white, and she comforts me and plays with me when I am lonely. She knows when I am bad and she wants me to be happy." I was shocked because I didn't think she would remember what had happened the night before.

I saw definite changes in Grace after she found Sally. She was able to give hugs and she showed love for others she had not been capable of showing before. I had heard that little children can communicate with and see angels, but I wasn't a believer until then.

Today Grace's angel lives here with us and protects her. My life has changed too. I needed a boost from a higher power and I found it through my "Saving Grace."

Donna, foster mom.

September 5   For the Money?

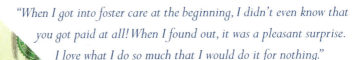

"When I got into foster care at the beginning, I didn't even know that you got paid at all! When I found out, it was a pleasant surprise. I love what I do so much that I would do it for nothing."

— Anonymous Foster Parent

What foster parent has not heard the "foster parents just do it for the money" comment? It is enough to make even the most mild mannered caregiver fume with rage. Foster parents do receive a check for their willingness to care for children who cannot live with their birth families, but this check is a reimbursement. The IRS doesn't even consider it income; that should be proof positive that people aren't getting rich off the system in this way.

Yes, there are some foster parents out there who take in lots of children and use the money they receive to meet their own needs, not those of the children. There is corruption in most every institution. However, it is more common to find foster parents who spend their own money so their foster children have a nice Christmas or a stylish pair of shoes or a fun vacation.

Becoming a foster parent is something people may investigate as a way of making money, and it is sometimes even promoted in those terms by recruiting agencies. However, the rewards of fostering tend to be found in other places, not in the measly amount of money one receives to meet the needs of a child.

Susan, foster and adoptive parent, grandparent, and former foster family recruiter and trainer.

Serving Up Spaghetti

"…I finally figured out the only reason to be alive is to enjoy it."
Rita Mae Brown

One night we were serving spaghetti, buffet style. I was filling plates and handing them to the kids as others poured milk, served salad and gathered utensils. My sixteen-year-old foster son was standing in front of the silverware drawer getting a fork when his spaghetti slid off his plate and into the drawer.

He didn't know what to say or do. As the rest of us became aware of what had happened, we began to laugh. My other son admitted that he almost did the same thing. We helped him clean it up and went on with our dinner.

Life is way too short to make a big deal of a little tomato sauce and a few noodles. By choosing laughter over anger when we can, we'll have more energy to deal with the really hard things when they do come along. Besides, now we have another funny, family story to share.

Dargie, mother and grandmother of many step, birth, foster, and adopted children.

September 7 — No Fame, Fortune, Glamour

"We can do no great things—only small things with great love."
Mother Teresa

It seems to me that the only people who understand why someone wants to foster are the people who are already doing it. There is no fame, no fortune, no glamour. It is harder than anything you have ever done before. You will spend more energy and effort on attempting to do something that ought to be simple because several people are involved and it becomes more cumbersome.

And after all of that, it will also bring the greatest joy, especially when you see the little changes occur. They will only be small things but you will have the joy of knowing that you helped someone. It will change your outlook on life.

Sandi, foster mom for one year.

Opening Every Door

8 September

*"Don't try to make pigs sing.
It's a waste of time, and it annoys the pigs."*
                                        Mark Twain

I came home one afternoon to find my front and back doors open, the stove burner lit and on high, every cabinet door and drawer open, and the refrigerator ajar. My first thought was the Second Coming, but when I saw my cat looking at me expectantly I knew that wasn't it.

I scratched my head and reached for the phone. My sixteen-year-old foster daughter was at the youth center a block away and "had wanted to cook something" but changed her mind. It was just another day of caring for this creative child.

She could quote Shakespeare, write like Isak Dineson, and she had a better knowledge of the English language than I did on my best day. She also left all the drawers open, papers turned up, magazines open, shoes in the hallway, the bed unmade, and she wore more food than she ate.

She taught me so much about the gifts that God bestows on us. She had her own priorities and daily maintenance was not one of them. However, friendships were high on her list. She sought knowledge from people she admired, she was always the teacher's pet and learned more from what she wrote than anything she ever read. It was disconcerting, like being in the presence of an alien at times. I would be so frustrated about some minor chore not done, and she would be trying to figure out her place in the universe. In other words, she was a typical teenager doing her job opening every door just to see what was inside.

Robin, foster parent for 30 children in the last 5 years.

September 9 — To Medicate or Not to Medicate

"Do what you can, with what you have, where you are."
Theodore Roosevelt

During my eight year career of working in Day Care/Preschool, I dealt with many kids diagnosed as Attention Deficit Hyperactivity Disorder (ADHD). It wasn't until I had one of my own that I was faced with the decision of whether or not to medicate.

It was one of the hardest decisions I've ever had to make. The more "capable" my little shaken baby became, the more dangerous his impulsivity became. The slightest noise would wake him up at night, and I had to apply dead bolt locks to my outside doors so he wouldn't go outside. He knew no protective fear.

Many people encouraged me to try medication even though I was unsure. We chose to try the medication and, as a result, the quality of his life and the peace I feel as a mother are wonderful. The medication literally enables him to learn and follow directions. He now actually has a healthy sense of fear to help keep him safe. We can both rest easier now.

Not all families will choose medication, and each parent of an ADHD child must make that decision. One thing I know is that I am grateful that the medication is available so we at least have a choice.

Dargie, mother and grandmother of many step, birth, foster, and adopted children.

Moving In

14 September

"Whenever I go on a trip, I think about all the homes I've had and I remember how little has changed about what comforts me."
— Brian Andreas

It is easy for well-meaning caregivers to sometimes forget how it feels to a child to come into a foster home. And, in reality, we may understand intellectually what it is like to be unable to live with our birth parent, but unless we have actually lived that experience we cannot truly know the perspective of the child.

"The hardest part about being in foster care is you don't feel as though you are part of a family. Sometimes foster parents and staff members need to understand this. Yes, you may be living in their house, but being a foster kid you never forget that it is not your house, you are just sleeping in a bed."

Stacey, former foster child who was in care for 14 years.

One of the first, and most difficult, tasks of any foster family is to help the foster child feel as "at home" as possible given the circumstances. We can never assume they will feel like family just because we hope they will. We have to reach out to them and teach them it is emotionally safe to move in with us. We ask them to risk their hearts and in doing so, we also risk our own.

Susan, foster and adoptive parent, grandparent, and former foster family recruiter and trainer.

September 15 — Guilt

"One of the secrets to a long and fruitful life is to forgive everybody (including yourself) everything right before you go to bed."
— Unknown

A comedian once said that guilt is the gift that keeps on giving. As we all know, good parents can usually find things to feel guilty about. Where did we go wrong? Was it that time we accidentally dropped Johnny on his head?

One of the most predictable areas of guilt concerns the lack of feeling love for a child. Why don't I love this unfortunate child? What kind of parent does not love a child? There is also the guilt parents feel about their anger toward a child. What kind of parent can be angry at a child who has already been the focus of so much rage and abuse in his past?

It is important to connect with other foster or adoptive parents to reduce the pressures that guilt produces. Being able to frankly communicate about the soul-searching that parents engage in at these times with someone who has experienced similar feelings can free you to look at the situation with a whole new perspective. Knowing that others have faced these same feelings can help eliminate the discouragement and isolation that guilt produces.

Rick, clinical psychologist, trainer, and consultant who has worked with foster and adoptive children and their parents over the past 20 years.

Rare Moments

16 September

"At fifteen life had taught me undeniably that surrender, in its place, was as honorable as resistance, especially if one had no choice."

Maya Angelou

She ran away. After the police reports and hours of worry, it was painful news for us to hear that she was refusing to live with us any longer. It's hard to not take the rejection by foster children personally. We soothed our wounds.

And then came the call. "Mom, I need help." After several months at a residential facility, she was on the run again. Running away seemed to be her favorite coping skill. The details regarding how she managed to travel hundreds of miles, crossing state lines were not important. She knew she had broken the rules, she wanted to return to the facility, and she was looking for an advocate. She called me, she shared her story, she acknowledged she needed me.

As I made the necessary phone calls, I reminded myself that some children have been too badly wounded in the intimate relationships of family to feel comfortable getting too close to anyone. I would not reject her. I would find grace and contentment in those rare moments when she reached out.

Unknown

September 17 — The Unpacked Ornament

"Nothing is impossible to a willing heart."
John Heywood

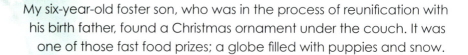

My six-year-old foster son, who was in the process of reunification with his birth father, found a Christmas ornament under the couch. It was one of those fast food prizes; a globe filled with puppies and snow.

One night in May my son watched me carefully as we sang songs before bedtime and then he sat up, his palms holding his head. "Mom, will you come like Santa Claus did in that movie whenever I shake the globe?" He had watched a movie that told of a father who became Santa and would return to his son at any time he shook a Christmas globe.

I sat motionless and stared at him in the darkened room with the hallway light shining on his face. What should I say? How could I possibly explain that his father would most likely never let him contact me again?

I smiled and said gently, "No, I won't be able to, Honey, because, unlike Santa, I have to take care of children instead of toys and I can't disappear and leave them all alone. But whenever you shake the globe I'll be thinking of you and be giving you a big hug and kiss in my mind." He grinned and lay back down on the pillow with the globe in his hands.

Sometimes I think of him and close my eyes sending him my hugs and kisses, remembering that innocent face and the blessing of magical thinking.

Robin, foster mom to 30 children over the last 5 years.

Adjusting the Focus

*"He told me that once he forgot himself,
and his heart opened up like a door with a loose latch
and everything fell out,
and he tried for days to put it all back in the proper place,
but finally he gave up and left it there in a pile
and loved everything equally."*

Brian Andreas

When it seems like things are not working, it is possible that you are expecting too much, too soon. Focus on the positive.

Ask others that you trust to be objective and tell you what they see. Perhaps you are being too hard on yourself or on the kids. Focus on the truth.

Take a deep breath—go away for a little while and get a new perspective. Keep a clear focus.

Remember, it takes someone special to do what you do.

Dargie, mother and grandmother of many step, birth, foster, and adopted children.

September 19

Seeing Below the Surface

"I've learned that under everyone's hard shell is someone who wants to be appreciated and loved."
Andy Rooney

In South America there is a tiny fish that has eyes which are adapted to see both above the water and below the surface. I think this would be a wonderful adaptation for foster parents; indeed, I believe some foster parents actually develop this trait over time.

It is one thing to look at a child's behavior on the surface, but that is only part of the picture. We may see tantrums, lying, stealing, and sexual inappropriateness; or, we may see clinging, indiscriminate affection, over-pleasing, and attempts at perfection.

All these behaviors are rooted in some set of experiences we were not able to witness. So, as parents to our children we must function on two separate but related levels. We address the inappropriate behaviors, attempting to motivate the child toward more acceptable choices and at the same time we use our inner eyes to look for the possible root cause of the behavior.

The ability to look behind the behavior for the need that is being expressed is the mark of a sensitive parent. The goal is to reach the point where we can consistently respond to inappropriate behavior and, at the same time, identify and find healthy ways to meet the needs being expressed. Until we develop that dual purpose eyesight though, we can reach this process through experience and trial and error. Every child who passes through our lives becomes our teacher as we learn more and more about how children express needs.

Susan, foster and adoptive parent, grandparent, and former foster family recruiter and trainer.

Did Anyone Ever Tell You…?

*"A life of value is not a series of great things well done;
it is a series of small things consciously done."*

Joan Chittister

20 September

My husband, Jeff, worked at developing positive rituals with our foster boys, brothers, ages nine and eleven. He "counted their ribs" and played "horsey." He worked on their self-esteem. He would say, "Hey, you've been at school all day - around teachers, students, and cafeteria workers. Did any of them tell you today what a neat boy you are?" Or he would say, "Wow, you've been busy today. You've ridden your bike and played with your friends. I just have one question for you. Has anyone told you today that you are one neat boy?"

After ten stressful months of working with the severe emotional and behavioral problems of the brothers, the treatment team decided that one of the boys needed to be moved. The time came for us to tell the child about the new placement. We told him he could still come to visit and call any time he wanted. He took the news pretty well and when we were ready to go, he hugged his foster dad and said, "Hey, has anybody ever told you what a neat dad you are?"

Tears welled up in our eyes when we recognized that somehow, amid all the struggles, the message of affirmation had broken through, and now our foster son was able to pass it on. That is the power in family rituals, a means of connection for a lifetime.

Lesa, therapeutic foster parent and foster parent trainer.

September 21 — Children Learn What They Live

"It has been wisely said that we cannot really love anybody at whom we never laugh."

Agnes Repplier

One evening we were sitting around talking after dinner when I saw a tiny black streak head under the stove. I was horrified and jumped onto my chair after seeing the mouse. Everyone laughed at first to see me screaming from my perch, baby close to my chest. And then the little critter got brave and ran back out across the kitchen floor.

My daughter, son, and granddaughter then joined me on the table while my older sons and daughter-in-law chased the mouse around the house with a broom and a bowl. I'm not sure what they would have done if they had captured it with a bowl. They did try, but it took a trap to get rid of the mouse once and for all.

Later, my daughter told me that the two-year-old was standing on a chair with her doll clutched tightly to her chest screaming, "Oh my God! Oh my God!" At first I was embarrassed about how ridiculous I must have looked to all my children. Children learn how to react to the things that happen in life by watching how we react. What an awesome responsibility, even in what seems like the most insignificant moments.

Dargie, mother and grandmother of many step, birth, foster, and adopted children.

Fall

Up in the air and over the wall,
till I can see so wide

September 22 — Losing Mother

"Mothers have as powerful an influence over the welfare of future generations as all other causes combined."
— John Abbott

There are many words for "mother." Mother is the nurturing caregiver who is the center of a home, the provider of all basic needs. Mom is the one who takes care of us when we are sick, picks us up from school, and chaperones our dances. Ma is the one we tease, nag, and cajole when we want our way.

It is Mama we seek out when we are feeling small, she is the one we go to when our best friend finds a new best friend. Mommy is the one that takes us to school on our first day, puts up with the stray puppy, and delights in the bundles of wild flowers we bring her.

What loss could be worse than that of a mother? That is just what has happened to our children in foster care. I have taken in boys that lost their Mothers to drugs, alcohol, AIDS, and some who just don't know where they went.

I could never keep track of all the fights I have broken up when the "yo mama" talk brought everyone to their feet, fists swinging. These boys hold their mothers on a pedestal. The worst of the worst was still the best to them. This is a hard concept for people to understand. Mother's Day and birthdays are very difficult when you are dreaming of the mother you lost, thinking of the pain you feel, and sometimes blaming the system for taking you away from your mother.

Carolyn, social worker and foster parent to teen boys.

Peer Pressure

23 September

"Keep strong if possible; in any case keep cool."
Sir Basil Liddell Hart

As I walked through one of those huge super stores, I could hear a child screaming and crying. This is certainly not unusual, we have all had kids get upset in the store. The little girl, who was about four-years-old, was screaming, "Go back, Mommy. I want it."

Her mother continued to shop as she patiently and lovingly explained to the girl that she could not have the desired item. This mother did not appear disturbed at all. I was in awe!

The cashier in my lane said, "Geezz, you'd think that lady would just give the kid a cookie or something." That comment and the stares of others in the store made me powerfully aware of how society often pressures us to reward negative behavior. I admired that mother because there are times when I might have marched right back there and bought that item just so I could finish my shopping without so many people in the store looking at me.

Foster and adoptive parents often face this sort of task as they attempt to provide consistent, firm, and loving limits in the midst of an often out-of-proportion rage. Providing guidance within the context of unconditional love is a challenge, but it yields great rewards - maybe it was the mother who deserved a cookie!

Susan, foster and adoptive parent, grandparent, and former foster family recruiter and trainer.

September 24 — The Right Reason

*"It takes the eye of faith
to see the beautiful butterfly in the caterpillar."*
Chinese Proverb

I've often asked myself "What is the 'right' reason for someone to adopt a child?" I have taught several classes for people who want to adopt over the years and I have noticed that many people adopt for their own issues, not because of a child's loss in life.

Sometimes these well-meaning people want to adopt because of a loss of fertility, or the loss of a child in their own family. Sometimes they are looking for a child to love them or searching for a way to keep a dead marriage alive.

It is important for adoptive parents to face the fact that the majority of the children who are available for adoption have many problems. They lose the most significant relationship in their lives when their connection to their birth parents is severed. It is very difficult for them to be loving when they have lost everything they came into this life with. It is important for adopting parents to remember that having two or more families to adjust to in the early years of life is a lot to cope with for a child.

Adoptions can be successful, wonderful experiences, but parents must go into the adoption for the right reasons. And it is important for them to have lots of patience and realistic expectations for the challenges ahead.

Carolyn, social worker and foster parent to teen boys.

Like Everyone Else's Kids

*"The tree on the mountain takes whatever the weather brings.
If it has any choice at all,
it is in putting down roots as deeply as possible."*

— Corrie Ten Boom

I find my life as a foster parent full of questions these days. Do the kids who have been taken from me know how much I loved them? Do those children remember me? Do they cry for me as I cry for them? Are they loved as I loved them?

My goal in life has always been to make the children in my care feel like they are the most important people in the world. I believe there is no other like them and people would be honored to know them. I always felt confident in my own self-esteem—until I started fostering.

I live in a fish bowl where my every move is up for criticism. Unfortunately, none of us are perfect. We are human beings with love in our hearts for children and we have opened up our homes to children who need us. We make mistakes just like everyone else. Our kids sometimes have dirty faces just like everyone else's kids. Our kids sometimes eat their lunch on the bus and make things up that aren't true, just like everyone else's kids.

And because I choose to foster, total strangers have lots of control over my family's life and happiness. Their decisions surround me daily. Many times I end the day with the question, "Why am I doing this?" Each time I see one of my beautiful children, I remember why.

Deena, foster, birth, and adoptive mom to a great bunch of kids.

September 26 — My Child Would Never Do That

"O God, Creator of Light: At the rising of your sun this morning, let the greatest of all light, your love, rise like the sun within our hearts. Amen"

Armenian Apostolic Church

Foster, biological and adoptive parents have all gotten alarming phone calls concerning their children. I learned very early in parenthood NEVER to say, "But my child would never do that, he knows better."

My child certainly does know better, but that doesn't mean he or she will make the right decision, especially when peers are watching. I have been called into schools, police stations, and other parents' homes to hear news that made me want to crawl under a table.

In these situations, we must take a deep breath, don't blame anyone (it won't help), and think of the fact that how you handle this situation will greatly affect this child's life. Keep in mind that you can deal with this, the sun will come up again tomorrow and life will go on.

We are not alone. Get help for you and the child. Someday—and I know, because it has happened to me more than once—most of the kids will thank you. I try to look at the positive side. Thank God that they got caught and not hurt or killed. It gives everyone a second chance.

Dargie, mother and grandmother of many step, birth, foster, and adopted children.

What Every Kid Needs

"I believe that we will not merely endure; we will prevail... because we have souls, spirits capable of compassion and sacrifice and endurance."

William Faulkner

We had just started as foster parents and our first child was a nine-year-old boy. On his first evening with us, over a "Welcome!" dinner of pizza with extra cheese, we were discussing his stay with us. We asked him what he wanted to call us, explaining we would be fine with either "Mom and Dad" or "Linda and Steve." His answer and the intent look in his blue eyes are forever burned into my heart.

"Well," he said, "if it's really okay with you, then I'd rather call you 'Mom and Dad.' Every kid needs a mom and dad, you see." Those words, and the depth of his need and his awareness of it, grabbed my heart in a way that has never let go.

Those words sustained me in the midst of many frustrating times ahead, and gave me the courage to let him go back to his birth mom when it was time to do so. But they did something else to, something that occasionally still causes me intense pain. They made me his MOM, and letting him go still hurts.

Linda, birth mom, adoptive, and former foster mom.

September 28 — We Care

"One's life has value so long as one attributes value to the lives of others, by means of love, friendship, indignation and compassion."

— Simone De Beauvoir

One of the great frustrations of foster parents is the low level of respect they sometimes receive from the system within which they work. Often caseworkers seem to disappear due to an overwhelming caseload. Financial reimbursements for meeting all the needs of the child, twenty-four hours a day, seven days a week, are less than one would receive for babysitting a few hours. Here is one foster parent's idea of a way to change all that.

"I wish each and every elected official would be required to follow the case of just one child from pickup to leaving the system. I wish they had to go into foster homes, emergency homes, shelters, meetings with the caseworkers, and biological families. I wish they had to walk babies withdrawing from drugs during the night, restrain teens out of control, provide all those kids' needs, and feel all the emotions that go along with that. And I wish they had to do all this with the little money the system provides. I know they will not do that but maybe just the idea will make them realize we are not a bunch of emotionless people doing a low class job. We care!"

Kathy, foster parent.

Susan, foster and adoptive parent, grandparent, and former foster family recruiter and trainer.

Egg Drop

29 September

"Empowerment (to enhance another's power) happens as others come to see themselves as competent, as not missing anything essential, as already intact. Bringing people to this view is possible only as we see them that way. Empowerment begins and ends with seeing others as already able and whole."

Arthur Edendorf

When one of my foster teens was in seventh grade, they had a contest in Science class. They were to make something that would keep an egg from cracking when it was dropped from the eighth floor of the bank building. He had to fill a six inch cube with something that would pad the egg. We all put our heads together and came up with an idea. He used two pieces of foam rubber with a spot hollowed out in the center for the egg. He taped it together with duct tape.

I met him the morning of the competition, camera in hand. They dropped hundreds of eggs from the bleachers, the top of the ladder of a fire truck, and then from the top of the bank building. His egg was one of seven that survived. He won a trophy with his name engraved on it. He asked his teacher if all our names could be engraved on it. He wanted us to be recognized for our part. We just wanted him to succeed and be a winner.

It was probably one of the best times in his young life. We keep the foam cube on a special shelf and when people wonder what it is (and they do), we relive the victory.

Dargie, mother and grandmother of many step, birth, foster, and adopted children.

September 30 — Great Expectations

*"A pint can't hold a quart—
if it holds a pint it is doing all that can be expected of it."*
— Margaretta W. Deland

One of the largest barriers to healthy relationships that I have found is the unspoken and often unrealistic expectations we have as parents. Foster and adoptive children are often experts at sucking all the fun out of families. They remain unsatisfied even when their new parents and caretakers give and give and give, expecting the child to be grateful.

An example I often use in training is that when a new baby comes home from the hospital we don't require the baby to earn a diaper change or a bottle. The parent gives the baby what s/he needs simply because the baby is in need. They don't expect the baby to say thank you. When bringing a child or teen into a new home, it is most beneficial to the relationships to use that same logic. Parents need to unconditionally provide food, shelter, and FUN without making the child earn it or be grateful.

Sally, foster care professional.

Roller Coaster

1 October

"Whatever did not fit in with my plan did lie within the plan of God. ***I have an ever deeper and firmer belief that nothing is merely an accident*** *when seen in the light of God, that my whole life down to the smallest details has been marked out for me in the plan of Divine Providence and has a completely coherent meaning in God's all-seeing eyes. And so I am beginning to rejoice in the light of glory wherein this meaning will be unveiled to me."*

St. Teresa Benedicta of the Cross

I keep this quote in my purse or somewhere on me at all times. It is a constant reminder that when life is pulling you by the seat of your pants you can sit back and enjoy the ride. Just remember that someone else is controlling the roller coaster, and He is not going to let you fall off.

So often it is a struggle to see the big picture when you are in the midst of chaos and the bumpy road of life. It's like when you are on an airplane and you have the window seat. You can see miniature houses that look like a toyland and lakes the size of water droplets. You stop and think about how amazing it is to see the world from this point and you somehow feel at peace. You know that no matter what struggles lie ahead when you reach the ground again, you will recall your vision from the clouds and see a glimpse of the bigger picture. The road that lies ahead of you opens up and doesn't seem as bumpy as it used to.

Canela, sibling of an adopted and special needs child.

October 2

Leaves

"Strong people are made by opposition like kites that go up against the wind."
Frank Harris

I once had a beautiful, little girl that should have been at school in second grade instead of home with me. She was in transition, coming from an abusive situation and waiting for a permanent foster home.

It was in the Fall of the year, and the leaves were changing color and falling, carpeting my front lawn. It was windy, and every time we would open our front door leaves would scurry into the entry way.

My little helper and I were cleaning up before the other kids came home from school. She offered to sweep the steps and entry way while I vacuumed. We were working away when I turned off the vacuum and heard her shouting, "I said, get out! I said get out of here and stay out!"

I ran to see why she was shouting and there she was, trying to sweep the leaves out the door. Every time she opened the door, more leaves would blow in. For awhile, I just watched her trying to outsmart those leaves. She wasn't frustrated, she was having great fun. When she finally tired, I helped her sweep up the last bunch into a dustpan and dispose of them.

I prayed that she would handle all that life would bring in such a positive, creative manner.

Dargie, mother and grandmother of many step, birth, foster, and adopted children.

I'm in the Way

3 October

"People will forget what you said,
People will forget what you did,
But people will never forget how you made them feel."
— Unknown

Sometimes I wonder how my foster children view their lives. They pick up some things so quickly and take them to heart. Many times the ideas they incorporate into their belief system become clear in unusual ways.

We were fostering a little girl one summer and she was attending Vacation Bible School. She had learned a song that went something like, "I am the Way, the Truth and the Life. No one comes to the Father, but through Me."

Later I heard her singing, "I'm in the way, the truth and my life." I don't really believe she knew what she was singing, but I wondered how true those words had been for her in her short three years. I certainly hoped whatever came before, that she no longer had that view of her importance and worth.

Fortunately, other adults saw her worth and she was adopted into a wonderful family where she now has a little brother and a mom and dad forever.

Jen, biological, adoptive, and foster parent.

October 4 — Fantasy Date

"You must look into people as well as at them."
Lord Chesterfield

One cool fall evening I sat on a front porch swing with a pregnant seventeen-year-old foster child. She told me about her life, the incest she suffered, and the years she spent working in the sex industry. This beautiful child-woman was no stranger to a wide variety of sexual acts, and she discussed them with a vacant stare. She also talked about the love she felt for her toddler who she voluntarily placed in foster care because she could not care for her.

When I asked if there was anything she wanted now that she had never experienced I was not sure what she might answer. She thought for awhile and a single tear trickled down her cheek as she told me about her fantasy date. "He would call me to make arrangements and then come pick me up in his car," she said. "And he would come in and meet my parents before we left to get a hamburger and go to a movie. And when he brought me home he would kiss me good night at the door."

She was seventeen years and eight months at the time of that conversation. Four months later she aged out of the system with a new baby and one in foster care, crossing that line between being a foster child and being the birth parent of a foster child. When I work with birth parents now I am reminded of her; and wonder what hills they've had to climb and what dreams they had that were never fulfilled.

Susan, foster and adoptive parent, grandparent, and former foster family recruiter and trainer.

Our First

"Love is a wonderful thing.
You never have to take it away from one person to give it to another.
There's always more than enough to go around."

Pamela J. deRoy

We had finished training, been given proof of everything needed, and were certified to be foster parents. They called and told us we could pick up a fourteen-year-old Hispanic boy at the shelter. We were excited; he was angry. We wanted to love him and take care of him; he didn't even want to know us. He had ideas of belonging to a gang and punishing someone or everyone for his circumstances. He was embarrassed to be seen with me because I was "white."

Six months later when he was allowed to return to his mother, he was very slow about wanting to go. He had come to admire our grandson who lived with us and looked to him as a mentor. As he prepared to leave, he walked around the house looking at all the pictures so he "would remember" them. He extended a pat to all the animals and was gone.

Last month, seven years after his departure, he came to visit. He was a tall, handsome young man who didn't smoke, drink, use drugs, or belong to a gang. He works hard to help support his mother and sisters. He was anxious to eat my biscuits and gravy and said he would be back. I'm thankful we have stayed in touch through the years. We love him and I believe he loves something about us and our home. We are proud of him.

J. C. & Neva, foster parents.

October 6 — Don't Come with Me to the Bus

"…self-hood begins with walking away, and love is proved in the letting go."
Cecil Day Lewis

When our five-year-old first came to us the doctors didn't give us much hope that he would see, or walk, or talk. Today he can do all of those things and so much more.

He is in a special education class at school where he is learning routines and rules. For months he worked on standing in a certain spot while waiting for the bus in the morning. Slowly, I started waiting farther and farther up the driveway after making sure he would stay on his "spot." After about three months, I started waiting in the carport because he was doing beautifully.

One day he stopped me at the door saying, "I am a big boy. Don't come with me to the bus." Hearing those words made me proud and very hopeful. I started to argue, but I realized he could do it so I agreed to wait by the window and watch to make sure he was safe. He has proven to follow all the rules while waiting for the bus. Most importantly though he has proven that doctors aren't always right!

Dargie, mother and grandmother of many step, birth, foster, and adopted children.

Concurrent Planning

7 October

*"There is always hope for tomorrow
if you believe in yourself today."*
Unknown

I think there are emotions that set pre-adoption homes apart from other foster families. For us, the wait is for a child that will stay forever. That brings with it a higher level of emotional turmoil. While we were completing our home study and classes I could think of nothing else. Every minute, every hour, it was all that was on my mind, even though I had four biological kids, four cats, one dog and an evil parakeet to fuss over. I worried about the right crib, the right room, and if we would get the right worker! I drove everyone nuts.

We are the willing victims of concurrent planning, setting our families up for possible loss, and feeling guilty if we pray for the babies to stay. It is a difficult life to live. I did not know how difficult until I became involved. Now I feel like the weight of my family's happiness rests on my shoulders because I am the chief negotiator dealing with DSS, a throng of therapists, and the birth family.

Many friends who foster told me that the home study and classes were only the beginning and there are some things you just have to experience for yourself. Since the babies have arrived, my husband says I really have something to worry about. I look longingly back to last summer when my biggest worry was if the house smelled good.

Deborah

October 8 — The Lifestyle

"One hundred years from now it will not matter what kind of car you drove, what kind of house you lived in, how much you had in your bank account, or what your clothes looked like. But the world may be a little better because you were important in the life of a child."

Margaret Fishback Powers

I have always been around children and worked with them, never even thinking about fostering or adopting until our sibling group of three showed up. I had heard about parents who abused their children but never knew many personally. After we took the kids in, I was like a magnet for others in the same situation. I remember telling a friend a few years ago that I knew twenty-four little kids who were not living with either parent. Now I know hundreds. It can be really heartbreaking.

Fostering is a life-style people don't understand unless they live it. I have truly been blessed by my second family. Some days it gets tough. I always thought that when I reached my forties I would be free to travel, pursue my hobby of genealogy, sleep late, spoil my grandchildren, and have a lot more money. Well, I still do my research, I just have three kids who go with me. I have not yet learned what sleeping late is. I have a beautiful granddaughter I spoil rotten, and hey, what is money good for anyway?

Linda, biological, foster, and adoptive parent.

Baggage

9 October

"Some people think there are angels whose sole purpose is to make people uncomfortable so that they do not fall asleep and miss their lives."

Anon folk artist

When we take in foster or adoptive children, we must realize most of them travel with a lot of baggage (though their possessions are few). When we look at where they've been and what they've seen, is it strange that these children have some behavior problems? Is it unreasonable that they take so long to change?

It takes a lot of patience, but if we can be strong and let them "unpack their bags" as they are able, it can make all the difference. In the end, we may find that it makes them, and us, better people.

Dargie, mother and grandmother of many step, birth, foster, and adopted children.

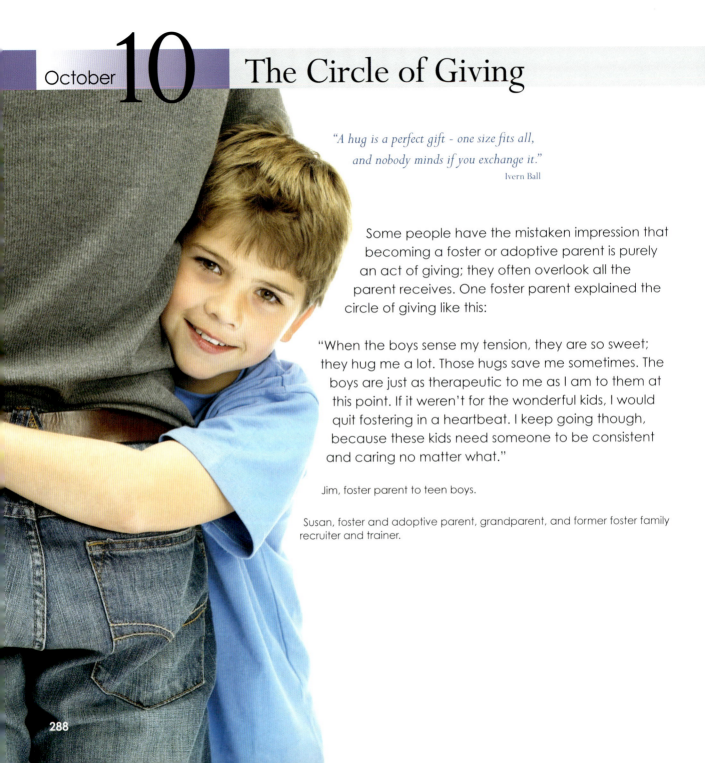

October 10 — The Circle of Giving

"A hug is a perfect gift - one size fits all, and nobody minds if you exchange it."
Ivern Ball

Some people have the mistaken impression that becoming a foster or adoptive parent is purely an act of giving; they often overlook all the parent receives. One foster parent explained the circle of giving like this:

"When the boys sense my tension, they are so sweet; they hug me a lot. Those hugs save me sometimes. The boys are just as therapeutic to me as I am to them at this point. If it weren't for the wonderful kids, I would quit fostering in a heartbeat. I keep going though, because these kids need someone to be consistent and caring no matter what."

Jim, foster parent to teen boys.

Susan, foster and adoptive parent, grandparent, and former foster family recruiter and trainer.

Investing in Humanity

11 October

"'Real isn't how you are made,' said the Skin Horse. 'It's a thing that happens to you. When a child loves you for a long, long time, not just to play with, but REALLY loves you, then you become Real.'"

Margery Williams, *The Velveteen Rabbit*

This has been the hardest job I've ever had, with the least financial reward and recognition and yet the most fulfilling. Talk about stretching and growing.... We foster parents get into foster care to rescue a child, but the truth is we rescue our own souls. We do this by investing in humanity. We think we're in this for the children's sake, but I have to confess, I'm not the same person I was before I started—and that's a good thing!

Cathy, foster parent for 8 years to teenage boys.

October 12 — Visual Identity

"The past is never completely lost, however extensive the devastation. Your sorrows are the bricks and mortar of a magnificent temple. What you are today and what you will be tomorrow are because of what you have been."

Gordon Wright

It can be hard to remember who you are if you have been in foster care for a while. Photos can be one of the most significant items in a child's life. They need photos of their families, photos of themselves as babies, photos of their parents. Children need to be able to remember who they are and where they come from. I have heard children say, "I am forgetting what my Mom and Dad look like." This can be a very frightening experience. As they become blurred and out of touch with their roots they lose part of their identity and that is not easily rebuilt.

Once I knew a boy who went on the run for a very long time. One of the few items he carried with him the whole time was his book of photos and the story of his life.

Take photos; make a lifebook for your children. Many of those children will keep them forever.

Carolyn, social worker and foster parent to teen boys.

Can Cows Jump Over the Moon?

13 October

"If a child is to keep alive his inborn sense of wonder, he needs the companionship of at least one adult who can share it, rediscovering with him the joy, excitement and mystery of the world we live in."

Rachel Carson

On our way home from church one night, my six-year-old pointed up and said, "Look at that!" We finally figured out that he was excited about the moon. Then he asked, "Can a cow jump over it?" I explained that cows don't really jump, especially over the moon. We talked about fairy tales, nursery rhymes, and pretending.

It amazes me when this child brings things to my attention that I take for granted. I love it that we can have wonderful conversations and he is asking the questions. We are thankful partly because we once thought this child would never talk, let alone ask these "why" questions.

It is important to remember not to cap the growth and development of our children. With lots of love, consistency, encouraging friends, and prayer, children can go a long way beyond what doctors might expect. Who knows, maybe one day I will learn that cows actually do jump over the moon!

Dargie, mother and grandmother of many step, birth, foster, and adopted children.

October 14

Until I Die

"The art of becoming wise is the art of knowing what to overlook."
William James

It was 9:30 pm, and I said no to fixing a baked potato for a boy that was in my care. He told me that was all right; he just wouldn't eat anything until he died. Inside I laughed, but outside I just said, "Okay, that's fine. Just let me know if you change your mind."

Now this incident came after several years of caring for children. Early on I would have been so worried, and I would have tried to cajole him into eating something more appropriate to the time of day. I started learning long ago there were some things not worth struggling over. There are plenty of areas to extend yourself and try working things out in a way that feels good, and we need not tackle each outlandish statement a child makes.

I knew this boy and I knew sooner or later he would want to eat something. I knew that he didn't have real suicidal tendencies, and that he often talked in extremes. I also knew if he didn't get the strange thing he wanted he would eventually let go of the idea and move on. In fact, later that night he decided he would have jelly toast and oatmeal for breakfast. It takes some maturity as a parent to be able to recognize the statements that require attention and the ones that require exactly the opposite.

Susan, foster and adoptive parent, grandparent, and former foster family recruiter and trainer.

Freedom Walk

15 October

"If you can't make it better, you can laugh at it."
Erma Bombeck

One year I had three foster children reunify with their birth families all at the same time. It was a triple heartbreak.

My husband and I knew what to expect having dealt with the loss and separation before. God always sees fit to have one of us strong when the other is weak so we have succeeded in not losing ourselves in our grief. We have no biological children so when the house is empty it's a shock and a relief at the same time. We can do what we want when we want, pretty much act like a young married couple again.

I am always unprepared for my husband's alarming habit when we are alone during these brief times. He will pull down all the blinds and walk into the living room completely naked. He does this little stroll to make me laugh. Gradually, as the years have gone by, this has become a tradition. I call it the freedom walk.

It makes me giggle to myself to think about that man strolling through our house at night, getting a glass of something to drink at the fridge, acting so nonchalant. It reminds me of why I married him: his good nature and his ability to make me see the lighter side of things even when life is really painful.

Robin, foster mom for 30 children over the last 5 years.

October 16 — Survivor

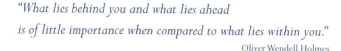

"What lies behind you and what lies ahead is of little importance when compared to what lies within you."
— Oliver Wendell Holmes

She was the only girl in a large family. From a very early age, she was the target of abuse and harassment from the "men" of the family. Her mother knew what was going on but refused to do anything about it.

She became increasingly self-destructive in her teen years. Her collection of behaviors ranged from eating-disorders to self-mutilation. Her foster family and friends worried for her safety and wondered whether she would physically survive, let alone emotionally.

After years of therapy, attending a support group, and the encouragement of friends and foster family members, she began to see herself as a survivor. She was able to put most of her past behind her and totally separated herself from her biological family. She learned to smile again. She learned to eat in front of other people.

She decided to make a family of her own. She married and is now committed to raising her children in a healthy, loving environment. She is not only alive, but able to enjoy life…and she gives much of the credit to her foster family and others who walked through the dark, scary times with her.

Lesa, therapeutic foster parent and foster parent trainer.

Adoption Announcements

17 October

"The hero of my tale, whom I love with all the power of my soul, whom I have tried to portray in all his beauty, who has been, is and will be beautiful, is Truth."

Leo Tolstoy

When we adopted our son we made copies of the picture of our family with the judge and filled out announcement cards that have lain in a drawer unmailed for five years. Growing up I had been sworn to secrecy about the adoption of my own sister. My family did not want her to know and we were never to tell. Years later, when my sister asked me directly, I eventually told her the secret. She has not talked to me since.

Now I find myself with all these conflicting feelings about adoption. If adoption hurts, why are we so happy? If adoption has to be kept a secret, why are we so proud? If adoption makes people feel unloved, why are we so in love with each other our hearts are bursting?

I think hiding the truth with lies is what hurts. I think it is the lies that make people feel unloved. Our adopted son looks more like my husband than any of our children, and we all delight in that twist of fate. Adoption is every bit as much a blessing as the births of my biological children. Actually, it took a little longer and was more painful at times.

Dargie, mother and grandmother of many step, birth, foster, and adopted children.

October 18 — Whatever Works

"Only those who attempt the absurd will achieve the impossible. I think it's in my basement. Let me go upstairs and check!"

— M.C. Escher

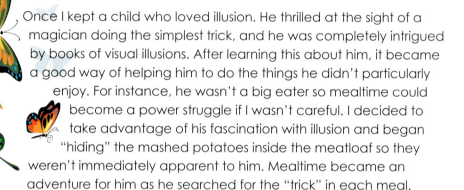

Once I kept a child who loved illusion. He thrilled at the sight of a magician doing the simplest trick, and he was completely intrigued by books of visual illusions. After learning this about him, it became a good way of helping him to do the things he didn't particularly enjoy. For instance, he wasn't a big eater so mealtime could become a power struggle if I wasn't careful. I decided to take advantage of his fascination with illusion and began "hiding" the mashed potatoes inside the meatloaf so they weren't immediately apparent to him. Mealtime became an adventure for him as he searched for the "trick" in each meal.

The best use of magic was for getting him up in the morning. If I waited until 7:30 it was always a struggle for him to eat and be ready in time to leave. So, I started getting him up at 6:00. He would eat, brush his teeth and get ready except for putting on his shoes, and then he'd go back to sleep until 7:45. Somehow this gave him the illusion that he was getting to sleep later. It was a win-win situation.

In order to be a parent we must find individual ways that work for each child. It can be challenging! But, in the end, knowing you helped make a child's life a little easier and added some fun to the mix, makes it all worth it.

Susan, foster and adoptive parent, grandparent, and former foster family recruiter and trainer.

Five More Minutes

19 October

"Sit loosely in the saddle of life."
Robert Louis Stevenson

How many of us are really ready to get up when the alarm goes off in the morning? It is so nice to hit that snooze button and take a few minutes to get used to the idea that there is a whole new day waiting to be lived.

When we go to the park or other places, I always give the kids a "five more minutes" warning to let them know when it is almost time to go. This cuts down on arguments and tantrums—for all ages. This little five minute warning has saved hours, perhaps days of my life.

The kids respect it. It's kind of like hitting snooze on the alarm clock. Five more minutes of sleep, play, or moments to transition from one activity to the next. The truth is that the five minutes are as much for me as for the kids.

Dargie, mother and grandmother of many step, birth, foster, and adopted children.

October 20: Saying Good-Bye

*"There are two ways to live your life.
One is as though nothing is a miracle.
The other is as though everything is a miracle."*
— Albert Einstein

When I decided to end my short stint as a professional foster parent in a group home, I gave the children three months notice that I would be leaving in October. I was determined to give these children a positive good-bye experience and, without realizing what I was doing, I gave them a forum for expressing all their pent up emotions related to others who had left them in the past. It became nearly three months of torture as they vented and fumed their rage at me, another adult who was abandoning them.

One day while walking with my husky, no nonsense, sixteen-year-old foster son, he burst into tears saying, "Everyone leaves me in October." He then told me his mother had died in October when he was just three-years-old. He was not sure if she loved him or not and he had never been to the cemetery where she was buried. Over the next few weeks we explored his feelings, and we went for a drive to the cemetery where he lay on her grave and made some sort of peace.

I could never have engineered this; there was a bigger hand than mine at work in this coming together of emotions and events. I have learned through the years to simply accept that these things happen, play my part, and be incredibly grateful.

Susan, foster and adoptive parent, grandparent, and former foster family recruiter and trainer.

Surprises

21 October

*"If you jump to conclusions,
you are likely to hurt yourself in the fall."*
David Baird

One night I woke up (way past the kid's bedtimes) to the sound of kids running up and down the stairs. I got up and called them down, gave them a good talking to and sent them to bed—again. The next day I was grouchy, even a little mean. I couldn't believe how disobedient they had been. It really surprised me. They certainly knew better.

The next week, I found out what all the secrecy was about. The kids had been making pillow cases with hand prints on them and the statement: "Glad to have a hand in your twenty-one years of marriage."

On our anniversary, my girls proudly surprised me with the pillow cases, saying, "This is what we were working on when you got angry."

I almost cried because I felt so proud that they had given up precious sleep (they get up at 5:30 am) to make me such a wonderful gift, and I had yelled at them. Fortunately, they love me anyway, and I certainly love them.

Dargie, mother and grandmother of many step, birth, foster, and adopted children.

October 22 — Just One Kid

"The greatest good you can do for another is not just to share your riches but to reveal to him his own."
Benjamin Disraeli

I got a phone call the other day from one of my "old" kids. This kid was amazingly smart and charming, but he didn't like school and he certainly didn't believe he needed to listen to the adults in his life. He was emotionally draining, physically destructive, and many times showed no remorse for anything he did. During my work with him I spent many hours at his school and many more on the phone with his foster parents trying to console them for something he had done. I worried about him because underneath his hard, gruff exterior he was really a scared little boy. I lost track of him over the years.

He called to tell me he was living at home now, and he wanted to thank me. He thanked me for letting him work through his emotions, and for talking to him like a person and not just "a dumb kid." He also wanted me to contact a former foster father and give him a letter of appreciation he had written to him.

No matter what we think, they see what we do and hear what we say. This was just one kid, but there are many more that learn from the adults in their lives and never express it as well as he did. Please keep loving them and never give up. We workers need good parents to work with and the kids need you much more.

Liza, social worker.

Let Us Eat Cake

23 October

*"God does not ask anything else of you
except that you let yourself go and let God be God in you."*
Meister Eckhart

When I found out my cat was dying, I got concerned about how I could tell the six-year-old. Children have a very different way of understanding death than adults. This child had not had any direct experience with death, but I knew he was old enough now to have plenty of questions.

Our first discussion of death had occurred when he was two, and he and I were out for a walk. We came across a dead bird on the pavement and began to talk about what it meant to be "dead." Each time the subject of death came up after that, he has always referred to that bird and felt like he understood death because he had seen the bird.

This time however we brought in the discussion of funerals, and he became intrigued. His big question was, "When Maggie dies and we have a funeral, do we get to eat cake?" God, I love that kid! He grounds me and always makes me smile even through my tears. He reminds me we are all growing, leaving some things behind which may bring us sorrow; but also knowing there will be some gains that come along with losses. Maybe he and I could have cake at a funeral; after all, as long as it is my life, I guess I can make up the rules—well, some of them anyway.

Susan, foster and adoptive parent, grandparent, and former foster family recruiter and trainer.

October 24 — Weighing the Balance

"Life in itself is a strange mixture. We have to take it as it is, try to understand it and then better it."
— Rabindranath Tagore

Bonnie, birth parent, adoptive parent, foster parent of more than forty children over the last eight years.

Susan, foster and adoptive parent, grandparent, and former foster family recruiter and trainer.

One of the most common questions parents ask when they first consider fostering is, "How will this effect my family?" There is no question about it, the choice of fostering has a profound impact on the family system and that is why the decision must be considered carefully.

In reality though, there is no way to know exactly how a family will change by the addition of a foster child, or two, or more. This knowledge simply comes with time and experience; and it is natural from time-to-time to question the decision.

"I sometimes feel guilty when I look back over the last seven years, and I think about how things would have been with my own children if I had not fostered. I would have had time to enjoy them more and enjoy my husband if our paths had never crossed with foster care. And then I stop to wonder where these kids would be now if our paths had not crossed and I feel like the sacrifice has been worth it."

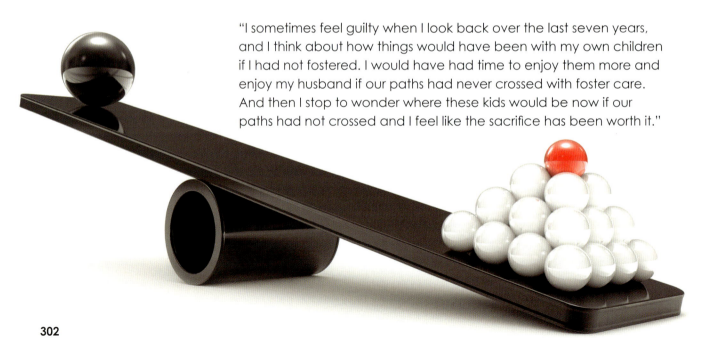

Through the Eyes of a Child

25 October

"Never put off until tomorrow what you can do today, because if you enjoy it today, you can do it again, tomorrow."
Unknown

My one-year-old was playing with a toy car when she decided to get up into the big wooden rocking chair in our living room. She placed the car in the chair and proceeded to climb onto the seat. Each time she put her weight on the chair it would rock forward and cause the car to roll off. She tried again and again, and again, never seeming to tire.

My husband and son watched her, admiring her perseverance. At some point, she probably didn't care anymore if she got into the chair to play with her car. She was just enjoying the new game she had invented.

There are many times when it wouldn't be as much fun to be where we think we want to be, as it is where we are. If we seek for the joys in life (as through the eyes of a child), we will find that the fun times are during our journey—not at the summit.

Dargie, mother and grandmother of many step, birth, foster, and adopted children.

October 26 — Loud & Clear

"The greatest happiness of life is the conviction that we are loved, loved for ourselves, or rather loved in spite of ourselves."
— Victor Hugo

I went to church on that day hoping for some inspiration, some clear thought to help me keep going; but, I got none. When the service was nearly over and the children had come in for the final prayer and song, I saw the boy I have brought here for several years now standing on the stage with the others. He has never shown evidence of being influenced by what he has heard there, but he goes without fussing. As he walked across the stage he was smiling, but he did not see me. When we linked hands and began the "Prayer for Protection" the minister lowered the microphone to the boy's mouth and I heard him say the words:

> The light of God surrounds me;
> The love of God enfolds me;
> The power of God protects me;
> The presence of God watches over me;
> Wherever I am, God is!

At least I heard the first few lines before I was overwhelmed with tears and the complete and total knowledge that the things I do have mattered to him. I didn't even know he knew the words to the prayer, but that day he was the messenger and the message, and I received it loud and clear.

Susan, foster and adoptive parent, grandparent, and former foster family recruiter and trainer.

Should Children Be Coddled?

27 October

"You gain strength, courage and confidence by every experience in which you really stop to look fear in the face… You must do the thing you cannot do."

Eleanor Roosevelt

One of the reasons I don't coddle my foster kids is that I've received wonderful advice from other foster parents. I've learned that my kids need me to be their parent. Friends they can make for themselves. And, although we may need to direct them a bit in the area of friendship, ultimately they are in control of that.

I know they all need to deal with their abuse, work through it, and move on. I also know it is hard to let go of childhood abuse and many people end up blaming every bad thing that ever happens to them on their childhood.

We need to be able to help these kids put their past in the right perspective and help them realize they can be and do anything they want to be or do. What service are we doing our kids if we do everything for them? Are we teaching them anything by protecting them from the real world? I don't think so; they need to know how to take care of themselves in healthy ways.

They need to know how to ask for help when things get overwhelming so they don't have to repeat the cycle of abuse they have experienced. We need to mean what we say, say what we mean, and do what we say we will do. And we need to teach them to do the same.

Deena, foster, birth, and adoptive mom to a great bunch of kids.

October 28 — Grief

> *"Even the most courageous warriors need to remember this simple wisdom: there is a time to take on the world and a time to rest, replenish and reflect."*
>
> Jilliam Klarl

During a banquet recently I sat by a couple who study foster care. They analyze statistics and talk to new moms hoping to find a way to make things better. I hope they find it soon.

As a foster parent I think I am in a constant state of grief. When I hear the stories of the children we serve, I grieve for their losses along with them. They have lost their family, friends, homes, and schools; indirectly, this affects me. Even in the best situation with all working together for reunification, we grieve the loss when they go home.

If you are a "good" foster parent, you will still be grieving the loss of your last child when another child needs to move in. After awhile the grief builds up and it can really weigh you down if you don't find ways to release it.

It is my wish that these researchers who are walking into hospital rooms and questioning new moms about their hopes, dreams, and fears will learn something that will make things change for the better. We all need a break from this cycle of grief and loss.

Dargie, mother and grandmother of many step, birth, foster, and adopted children.

Allegations of Abuse

*"There is always another chance…
This thing that we call 'failure' is not the falling down,
but the staying down."*

Mary Pickford

It is very painful to have someone accuse you of abusing a child. I have heard that foster parents, on average, will have an allegation and investigation about every two years.

Unfortunately for all of us, sometimes the allegation is true. If it is, then you should recognize that you are human and you made a mistake. Then seek counseling and take some parenting classes until you have the skills and self control to effectively foster parent without losing it.

Knowing the child's history, medical needs, learning disorders, and other issues helps foster parents decrease their risk level to allegations. It is important to ask questions before accepting a placement. It is perfectly fine to ask if this child has made any allegations in the past. Knowing this ahead of time can prepare you to set up a protective environment for yourself.

Joining your local foster parent association can be a great place to start for support and crisis intervention. No one can understand the feelings of such an investigation like an experienced foster parent. Reach out for the support you need, many of us have been there.

Cathy, foster parent to teen boys for 9 years.

October 30 — Adventure Walk

"We all live with the objective of being happy; our lives are all different and yet the same."
— Anne Frank

It was a cold day when I took a seven-year-old boy, full of energy, out of the house for an adventure walk. When we reached the railroad tracks he carefully explored the rocks he found there, picking them up and proclaiming them as gifts he wanted to give me. We finally settled on one very large rock with some shiny slivers on it that he found to be very beautiful. We walked along a creek bank, his brown eyes wide with wonder at all the treasures he saw there. He threw sticks into the water and watched them move in the icy current. He talked of a visit here when the weather was warmer as we followed the movement of the sticks he had launched into an adventure of their own.

When we rounded the next bend, he spied shells; just some little shells at the side of the creek and he was ecstatic! He chattered wildly about how he would give them to his brother and his mom. He gathered them until his pockets were full, his face red, his nose runny, and his heart about to burst with joy.

As we walked away, he said, "Don't you wish you were my size so you could get excited over stuff like this?" At first I started to agree, but then I changed my mind. At the moment I was happy to be just my age so that I could watch him being seven and enjoying his new-found relationship with the world.

Susan, foster and adoptive parent, grandparent, and former foster family recruiter and trainer.

The Halloween Costume

"It is one of the most beautiful compensations of this life that no man can sincerely try to help another without helping himself."
Ralph Waldo Emerson

Holidays can be difficult for foster children. They may be reminded of old traditions, memories, and how long they have been in care due to passing yet another milestone. One year my indecisive foster daughter was coming up with one dramatic choice of costume after another in anticipation of Halloween. She finally decided to be a queen. I altered an old wedding dress to fit her, powdered her hair and face and made her lips black.

For months after that she would come out of her room wearing the dress. She would watch television, talk, or just hang out in it. It made her feel important and special. When she went home, the dress went with her and we stayed in touch.

The following year she called excitedly to say she had won the costume contest at her local school as the bride of Frankenstein wearing the dress. She had worn it so much that it was frayed and had turned yellow from lack of washing, making a perfect costume.

It reminded me of one of the things she had left with me. In the back of her closet, along with strewn barrettes, empty nail polish bottles, and notes was her list of potential costumes for that Halloween. About number five on the list was my name; she had thought about going as me. It was both amusing and touching that she thought I would be as brilliant and entertaining as the bride of Frankenstein.

Robin, foster mom for 30 children in the last 5 years.

November 1 — Suggestions from a Foster Child

"Bless our family with peace and joy, let our words to each other be kind, and our actions gentle. May the love that we share be Your love, so that each of us can always say: Lord, it is good for us to be here!"

Anne Vogel

Listen to the stories of your foster children. Ask them what happened to them and listen if they are willing to talk.

Repeatedly let the children know that what happened to them was not their fault.

Give the children the time they need to come to trust you.

Help them discover their strengths and begin to build on them rather than always trying to fix what is wrong for them.

Make sure the kids know that there are former fosters out there who are successful, creative, loving adults.

Hang a picture of them in your house.

Marcy, successful, creative, loving adult, and former foster child.

Goal: Reunification

*"Life is about 1% what happens to you…
and about 99% what you do about it."*
  Allyson Arwood, age 14

We joke about instruction books and such, but how do we learn to parent? Most of us learn from our parents and role models. What if we didn't have any good role models? What if we came from an abusive family? What if we didn't have any family?

Very few birth parents have had their children removed because they don't want them. My guess is that the majority just don't know how to be parents.

I, personally, want the children to reunite with their birth parents if at all possible. This is generally the goal for every one of us as foster parents. What we can do to help that happen is to work with the birth parents as we would want someone to work with us if we were in their shoes.

I try to look at my time with children as a time to offer them hope—let them experience what a family can be. I try to let them be kids and have fun. We go to the park and have picnics; some children have never done that. We do a lot of activities, not expensive, but fun stuff—all in the hope that they will be able to break the cycle. Perhaps one day they will be able to become the sort of parents they so badly needed.

Dargie, mother and grandmother of many step, birth, foster, and adopted children.

November 3 — Nurturing Males

"All kids need is a little help, a little hope, and somebody who believes in them."

Earvin "Magic" Johnson

Many of the children I've worked with have been deprived of a positive male influence. So many of our nurturing adults are females and, while kids certainly need them too, I'm always so grateful to experience a nurturing male.

The Sunday School coordinators at our church work very hard to get both males and females in the classrooms. When my grandson attends with me he always develops an attachment to the men who are working there.

It is so important for him to see these men who can teach him the positive aspects of being a man. He lives with a female, his teachers are all female and even his physician is a woman. To walk into a room and interact with a man who loves children and is willing to spend time helping them grow is a wonderful gift.

So, just a reminder to all you male foster, adoptive, or birth parents, as well as all the male Scout leaders, Sunday School workers, teachers, and others: Thank You from a world which needs more positive nurturing men willing to share themselves with our kids.

Susan, foster and adoptive parent, grandparent, and former foster family recruiter and trainer.

Dress-Up Girl

4 November

"Every survival kit should include a sense of humor."
Unknown

After fostering some older boys, we decided we wanted to foster a little girl we could love and dote on. We picked her up and immediately fell in love with her. She was an intelligent, beautiful, brown-eyed, five-year-old and she was proud to tell you she was "white, black and Indian."

I loved dressing her in pretty dresses for church, but felt they were inappropriate for school because she was so active and played so hard. However, she loved wearing the dresses, and we had disagreements almost every morning. She would leave for school wearing pants, but very angry about it. On one of these days, we were shocked when we received a call from the school. It seems that our foster daughter had decided to make her own dress. She went to the restroom, removed her pants, rolled them up very neat and put them between her legs. She then took her jacket and using the arms, tied it around her waist to make a skirt. She would have been successful, but she had a very difficult time walking back to class and one of the teachers noticed!

Needless to say, I bought her some school dresses. She was with us for a year and a half. We loved her and still love her today. And although we hurt over our loss, we have to give thanks to God for her new home. She and her younger siblings were adopted by a minister and his wife, and we feel it is a miracle.

J. C. & Neva, foster parents.

November 5 — Visions & Dreams

*"To accomplish great things,
we must not only act, but also dream;
not only plan, but also believe."*

Anatole France

People who become foster or adoptive parents have a vision or a dream about how life can be better for the children they come to love. People who continue as foster and adoptive parents are those who can hold onto those visions and dreams even in the face of everyday realities that seem to be totally to the contrary.

Susan, foster and adoptive parent, grandparent, and former foster family recruiter and trainer.

Time for Yourself

"Your only safety is to be within the center of your kingdom, living from within out, not from without in."

Mary Strong

A trip to the grocery alone does not qualify as taking time for yourself! In this busy life that we lead, we all need to find a way to take time out for ourselves. When I do this, it helps me feel better about myself and more content with life in general. Even my kids sometimes insist that I take time for myself or to be alone with my husband.

In case you've forgotten what to do when you are alone try one of these suggestions:

- Take a bubble bath (with music).
- Go to a movie.
- Have lunch with a friend.
- Take a nap.
- Go for a walk or a swim.
- Take a drive.
- Take up writing, painting, knitting - a hobby of some kind.
- Go shopping (somewhere you would never take the kids).
- Go away for the weekend or stay home alone with your partner.

One more thing. DO NOT FEEL GUILTY! You deserve this time and besides, taking care of yourself will better prepare you to do all the other things in life you need to do.

Dargie, mother and grandmother of many step, birth, foster, and adopted children.

November 7 — The Best Interest of the Child

"God grant me the serenity to accept the things I cannot change, the courage to change the things I can and the wisdom to know the difference."

Reinhold Niebuhr

There is no phrase in child welfare that is thrown around more or understood less than "in the best interest of the child." All decisions are supposed to be made with that in mind, but how do we come to an agreement on what that means?

For me, it brings to mind the story of the women who came to King Solomon, both claiming to be the parent of an infant. Not being able to decide who was telling the truth, Solomon said the baby would be cut in half and each woman would receive a part of the child. At that point the "real" mother said NO. She was willing to let go of her child rather than destroy it.

Today I am grateful for all parents who have had the courage to relinquish their parental rights so that their child could live a better life. In my opinion, there is no act more deserving of the phrase "in the best interest of the child."

Susan, foster and adoptive parent, grandparent, and former foster family recruiter and trainer.

Owning the Road

8 November

"There is no such thing as a problem without a gift for you in its hands."
Richard Bach

Two brothers came to me one year while I was substituting at my son's high school. I had already agreed to finish out the school year for a teacher whose husband was ill.

The boys had been attending a preschool and the worker thought it best to continue with the familiar for them. This meant a long ride in the van every morning and evening.

We passed the time by "claiming landmarks;" like the big hill, the woods, the bump bridge, etc. With these landmarks, they were able to keep track of where we were on the ride to school (while munching Cheerios® and sipping milk) and the ride home (while singing and talking about our day).

What could have been the longest and most difficult part of our day became the most enjoyable. Even years since their departure, my kids and I remember the boys with a smile every time we go down the big hill, through the woods or over the bump bridge.

Dargie, mother and grandmother of many step, birth, foster, and adopted children.

November 9

Runaways

"Never regret. If it's good, it's wonderful. If it's bad, it's experience."

Victoria Holt

In fairy tales there are always happy endings, the heroine or hero rides away in glory. In foster care many of our stories don't end up so neatly. I had a wonderful 14-year-old girl I came to love so much. She was a little sprite, with blonde hair and blue eyes. She had a giggle and cute little sayings that made me laugh. Her mother's parental rights had been terminated, and she was to be adopted by her aunt. She came to visit me several times after going to live with her aunt.

One time she called and I couldn't let her come over. She ran away that weekend, and I haven't heard from them since. The aunt moved away and never finalized the adoption. I imagine my sprite is somewhere out there with her mother. I keep her in the back of my mind to remind me that a teen's need for independence and sense of urgency can cause them to run away from their problems. When I get a new placement, I remember her and take that extra minute to listen and understand.

I stay motivated by knowing that these children come from chaos and sometimes they perpetuate it despite our best efforts. If we can save even one, it is worth it—but you never forget the runaways. You never stop regretting some decisions. You just use it to motivate you to go that extra step the next time.

Robin, foster mom to 30 children over the last 5 years.

Teenagers

10 November

*"'Tis human touch in this world that counts,
the touch of your hand and mine."*
Spencer Michael Free

One day I realized that I had a 13-, 14-, 15-, 16-, 17-, and 18-year-old! I had always been afraid of the thought of taking teenage foster children. Sadly, many foster parents feel as I did—scared! Then I went to a workshop about teens to get help for myself as my children moved into their teen years. I learned that there were as many teens in need of homes as there were youngsters. Not long after that I got my first teen, then my second, and my third.

I believe the keys to working with teens are to LISTEN and talk to them, keep them busy, keep a camera and film ready, and pray a lot. And, according to my fifteen-year-old daughter, keeping some tissue on hand for sharing tears of joy, sorrow, hurts, and laughter is also a big plus.

While working with teens is a different sort of challenge, watching them mature has its own set of rewards.

Dargie, mother and grandmother of many step, birth, foster, and adopted children.

November 11 — Do You Work?

"I now realize that a large part of parenting is simple survival. I put on my combat gear each day and collapse each night in peace with the knowledge that my family has survived another day."

Patricia Robertson

When our three adopted kids first came to us I spent four days a week at the children's hospital for the therapy appointments for the older ones and the youngest was so sickly that I was at the pediatrician at least every other week. Then there was weekly parent visitation, visits with case workers, court appointments, going to school on almost a daily basis to get the oldest out from under a desk or out of a closet. And let's not forget the fact that I didn't get any sleep due to night terrors. Thank God life has settled down a lot.

Now it is just typical teacher meetings, room mothering, scouting, and a couple of phone calls a week from one of the teachers. I still get very little sleep. One of my sons woke me recently to tell me, "It is not morning yet," and that he had a loose tooth. They all three talk in their sleep. Kids—you gotta love 'em!

In the past two weeks I have been to the emergency room five times with cat bites, stitches, flu, and an ear infection; and we can't forget the trips to the pharmacies to pick up all the medications. When people ask me if I work, it makes me want to laugh out loud.

Linda, biological, adoptive, and foster parent.

Dress-Up

November

"The future belongs to those who believe in the beauty of their dreams."
Eleanor Roosevelt

When my daughter turned nine, we had a tea party for her birthday. I brought out a full length mirror, clothes, jewelry, a dab of make-up, but best of all my fine china and Grandma's teapot. The children had a wonderful time.

This party inspired me to make and collect a bunch of dress-up clothes. We have crowns, capes, hats, aprons, ties; all kinds of fun stuff. Every child that has been in my home has rummaged through that box. I've let some take it to school to share (great ice breaker when you're the new kid).

Girls and boys play for hours; even my fifteen-year-old daughter dresses up with them. The shyest child cannot resist delving into the box. It sparks conversation and imagination, putting me in mind of rummaging through Grandma's treasures.

Doctors, nurses, brides, mail carriers, kings, firemen, and ballerinas parade through my house at various times. And, I pray that they will be just that—every good thing that they dream they could be.

Dargie, mother and grandmother of many step, birth, foster, and adopted children.

November 13 Holidays

*"There are only two ways of meeting difficulties.
You alter the difficulties or you alter yourself to meet them."*
Phyliss Bottome

Jim, foster parent to teen boys.

Holidays can be a mixed bag. Foster kids can really have a hard time being away from home. Some are delighted just to receive a visit. Others are just angry. If you have three or four kids in your home on a holiday there can be a lot of mixed moods and emotions. It becomes a challenge to get the meaning of the holiday through to the kids and help them create meaningful memories. I try to get them to start seeing what the holidays can mean for them now, and stop basing them on past negative experiences at home. Holidays can be a wonderful time to teach.

Intermittent Reinforcement

14 November

"We may affirm absolutely that nothing great in the world has ever been accomplished without passion."
— Georg Hegel

It's like the desire to keep buying a lotto ticket or going out on blind dates—every once in awhile you strike pay dirt. Maybe that fifth person your friend sets you up with is a great person and you really have a wonderful time when you go out. Or, every few weeks you may win $5 in the lottery and it keeps you coming back. It is called intermittent reinforcement, and it is a very powerful motivator to repeat an action.

After you have fostered for awhile it will happen to you, too. One of your children turns around and says, "Thank you." A birth parent asks, "How do you get him to do that?" And then listens to the answer you give. That's it, you've been reinforced and it motivates you to try again. And again. And again.

"Today I received a call from a former foster daughter who stayed with us when she was fourteen. At twenty-eight, she has a daughter and a son by her first husband, is awaiting a promotion in a job that she trained for through a job placement program. And now she thinks she's found a man that will be there for her and her family. Although she was with us for only three months, fourteen years later she is still keeping in touch."

Trish, birth mom, foster mom to nearly 600 children in the last 20 years, and grandma to biological and foster grandchildren.

Susan, foster and adoptive parent, grandparent, and former foster family recruiter and trainer.

November 15 — Do It Your Way

"Don't impart the notion that your kids always have to be the best. Kids should be what they are."

D. Anthony Stark

At one time I worked in a college day care center. One day we were told to "cut out pictures of food" from magazines. There were four of us. The young hungry teenager tore out entire pages of cookies, cakes, and various goodies. The older, more mature teen meticulously trimmed an abundance of items from each food group. The mother and seasoned preschool worker chose pictures of goodies and foods from the various food groups, leaving enough excess for the children to test their skills at cutting with scissors.

This simple assignment spoke volumes to me. I saw three people do exactly as they were told, but they all did it differently. It showed me that nobody carries on even the most basic task in the same way, and that's okay. The important thing is getting the job done.

There are probably as many ways to do things as there are people to do it. Just because it isn't done our way doesn't mean it's the wrong way. I didn't know it at the time, but it was a perfect lesson for someone who wants to be a foster parent.

Dargie, mother and grandmother of many step, birth, foster, and adopted children.

Compassionate Understanding

"We arrive at truth not by reason alone, but also by the heart."
Blaise Pascal

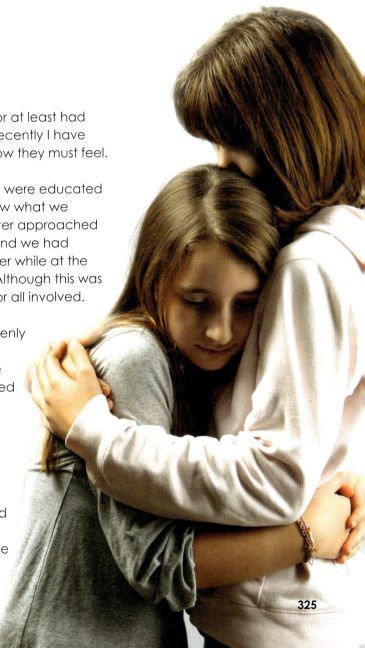

As a former foster parent I thought I understood, or at least had compassion for, the position of the birth parent. Recently I have come closer to an emotional understanding of how they must feel.

We adopted our daughter several years ago and were educated about attachment problems. We thought we knew what we might have to deal with as a result. As our daughter approached adulthood she chose to live with another family and we had no other choice but to try to keep in touch with her while at the same time letting go of her to a certain degree. Although this was awkward at times it felt like the right thing to do for all involved.

While I know there are obvious differences, I suddenly felt more like a parent with a child in foster care than I ever had before. This realization helped me see things in a different light. I now have a renewed vigor for keeping our daughter part of our family in whatever way she can tolerate. I also have a renewed respect for families who are willing to take on the task of caring for a child who is experiencing internal struggles.

This is not exactly how I had imagined things would work when we brought this child into our family. However, I believe that if we all practice some give and take, we can still be a strong family.

Steve, adoptive and birth parent, former foster parent.

November 17 — Letting Go

"The essence of being human is to love—first of all God, but never without the love of God transforming the way we love others."

Dan Allender

Even though you are nearly as tall as I am now, your hand still reaches for mine when we cross a road or go into unfamiliar territory. It is as if you unconsciously reach out to me for guidance in a quiet, trusting way. I treasure each time I feel your hand slip into my own where it feels so natural.

Very soon you will go home to your "real" mother who does not cut your toast into the little triangles that give you so much joy. I am trying to be happy.

When I got into this I knew it was temporary, that you would be going home. I knew that I had a part to play in your life and that your life would go on without me after awhile. I knew that you and your family needed me in this difficult time, and I was ready to help. I did not know that you would fill a place in my heart that I had forgotten was empty.

As I prepare myself to let you go, I draw on the strength of others who have done this many, many times before. One foster mom I know told me that "a heart that has been broken and goes on to heal is a strong heart and a foster mother's heart is one of the strongest hearts of all." After I live through this, I trust I will have a stronger heart to love the next child.

Susan, foster and adoptive parent, grandparent, and former foster family recruiter and trainer.

Landmarks

18 November

"The first rule of love is to listen."
Eric Maisel

There are certain places in our city I cannot pass without thinking of children who have passed through my home. I recall the very stretch of road we were traveling on the interstate when the eleven-year-old I kept for respite told me about the death of his father.

Each time I see the towers high on the mountain, I think of a teenager who remembered seeing those same towers out the window of his dad's hospital room right before he passed away when the boy was only five. I recall the spot in the street where one teen told me he rescued his drunken uncle from traffic when he was just a child.

I see a famous landmark in our town and recall a small boy thinking that his family lived near by because it was next to the DCS building where he had supervised visits. His father was so cruel to him that he will likely never know where their actual home is located.

Each of these sights, and many more, bring me memories of those children and I feel a little grief. I often wonder if their grief at seeing those sights is now a little bit less because they were able to share those memories with someone who cared enough to also remember. I certainly hope so.

Dargie, mother and grandmother of many step, birth, foster, and adopted children.

November 19 — Bunk Beds

"When we can begin to take our failures non-seriously, it means we are ceasing to be afraid of them. It is of immense importance to learn to laugh at ourselves."

Katherine Mansfield

There is a story about the adoptive parent who had newly placed twin boys, one who was a fire-setter and the other a bed-wetter. A mentor of this new family suggested they consider bunk beds. She called it a "trickle down" approach to the problem.

Most parents have been exposed to the kind of parenting that works in average situations. However, few parents have knowledge of the kind of parenting it takes to reach truly disturbed children. When you see yourself only as a parent, or worse yet, as a failing parent you undermine your ability to be creative, analytical, and flexible in your parenting of these difficult children. You also lose your ability to take advantage of times when a sense of humor and some laughter could lighten the situation.

It is important for you to know your value as a good and humane human being (beyond your successes and failures with the child) who also happens to be parenting a tough kid or two.

Rick, clinical psychologist, trainer, and consultant who has worked with foster, and adoptive children and their parents over the past 20 years.

The Fine Line

20 November

"The only way you can change is if you feel safe, and you can't feel safe if you feel criticized."
John Gottman

It can be very challenging for people who have raised their own children successfully to set aside the child rearing techniques that worked for them. What feels natural to us is what we tend to use, especially when we are stressed. With any sort of parenting, there will be times of great stress.

Every foster or adoptive child is different and requires a somewhat individualized plan for behavior management. This means some trial and error is inevitable until we find what motivates that particular child toward healthy, socially acceptable behavior. Soon after we discover the perfect path, something will most likely change, and we will need to adjust.

It is through this intricate dance of setting limits and making adjustment that we weave a web of unconditional love and security around the child. This act often allows him the freedom to release his "worst" self, his rage and bad manners, his fear and disgust with what life has dealt him. It may be the first time he has felt safe enough to do that. At this point it is important to remember how to walk that fine line of rejecting the inappropriate behavior without rejecting the child. In most cases, the parents who are able to do this will watch the behaviors subside, but it may take a long, long time.

Susan, foster and adoptive parent, grandparent, and former foster family recruiter and trainer.

November 21

Little Helper

"When you get to the end of your rope, tie a knot in it and hold on."

Eleanor Roosevelt

We were relaxing while watching television one evening when our sixteen-month-old foster daughter got really fussy. I rocked her for a while until she sat up and got sick all over both of us. I immediately headed for one bathroom to shower while my husband and the baby's mom (also in our care) bathed the baby in the hall bathroom.

My adopted six-year-old kept asking if he could help. We kept telling him, "No, thank you." Then he watched his Daddy wash out the baby's clothes in the sink and got an idea of how he could help.

When I came out of the shower he said, "I washed your clothes for you, Mommy." There they were, laying in a big wet puddle on the floor. Yes, it was a yucky mess. No, I didn't look forward to cleaning it up, but knowing he was willing to help that much blessed my heart.

My teenagers would have helped if I had insisted, but not with a happy heart. I am so proud of my young son. Of course, we later discussed the fact that he should NEVER put Mommy's clothes in the sink and run water on them again. I chose not to yell but to praise him for his efforts and tried to focus on the process and motivation of his actions more than the final results.

Dargie, mother and grandmother of many step, birth, foster, and adopted children.

What is Family?

22 November

"I can live for two months on a good compliment."
Mark Twain

One Mommy or two Daddies.
Two kids, four kids, six kids, a dollar!
No kids, just a dog.
Thirteen kids of all ages and backgrounds.

Families come in all shapes, sizes, colors, creeds, and religions. Some work fine and some don't. That is why foster care and adoption exist, for the ones that are not able to work in a healthy way.

I am not a foster parent, but I am drawn to foster care in the memory of someone I knew, someone I considered my sister. In her memory I'd like to say, "God bless you." Whether you are a family of three wearing Old Navy®, or a family of thirteen with warm hand-me-downs and lots of big brothers and sisters watching over you. Wherever you are in this spectrum of love and goodness, you have my thanks. I wish you all well.

Donna, birth parent, stepparent and former foster sister.

November 23 — "Thank You"

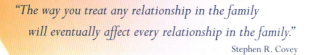

"The way you treat any relationship in the family will eventually affect every relationship in the family."
Stephen R. Covey

When our adopted son was a toddler, we would all sit on the floor in a circle and toss a basketball back and forth to each other. It made him laugh and soon the whole family became a circle of laughter. It was not only therapeutic for him, but for all of us.

His toddler stage lasted more than twice as long as any "normal" child. That gave our family time to enjoy him even more. We doted on every facial expression, every cute little thing he did, every stage of his progression. He isn't "normal," he is very special. We are so thankful to have been blessed with his influence in our family. As he grows up and reaches beyond any expectation that the doctors gave us hope for, I am overwhelmed again by what love can do.

To my family, I want to say thank you for… holding him… playing with him… praying for him… believing in him… encouraging him… being patient with him; and most of all, for loving him.

I believe God placed him in the perfect home to realize his potential, to be all that he can be.

Dargie, mother and grandmother of many step, birth, foster, and adopted children.

Impact

24 November

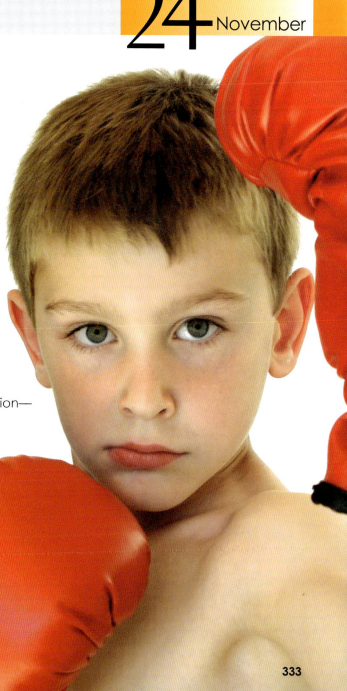

*"The second principle of magic:
…things which have once been in contact with each other continue to act on each other at a distance after the physical contact has been severed."*

Sir James G. Frazer

Don't ever think that the little time you were there for them didn't count or make a difference. You never fully know what impact you have made on a child until years later when they come knock on your door. This may happen even after you were the one who "kicked them out at eighteen," or sent them back to treatment, or sent them back to prison on a parole violation. Then after they have been gone awhile, they ask you to be their new baby's grandma! Knowing you have been able to break the chains of dysfunction to the next generation—that is a priceless treasure.

Cathy, foster parent for 8 years to teenage boys.

Magnificent Obsession

"Once the children were in the house the air became more vivid and more heated; every object in the house grew more alive."
Mary Gordon

When I was a teenager and prone to swooning over all things romantic, I saw a movie called *Magnificent Obsession*. Over the course of the movie a wealthy doctor becomes sorrowful about his self-indulgent behavior which caused an accident that critically injured someone. He eventually begins doing nice things for people without them knowing about it, and he finds great satisfaction in this new way of life.

At one point, when he does something for another character he explains that the only payment he wants is for this person to do something nice for someone else, to pass it on. He explains to the other person that in doing so he will discover that it will become a "magnificent obsession."

When I work with foster and adoptive parents I see this same trait. Even in the midst of all the difficulties and the stress and the strained finances, fostering and adopting children becomes a magnificent obsession. It moves into people's lives until they can't remember how they lived before, and it fills their hearts in ways they can't even describe.

Susan, foster and adoptive parent, grandparent, and former foster family recruiter and trainer.

Willing to Give

26 November

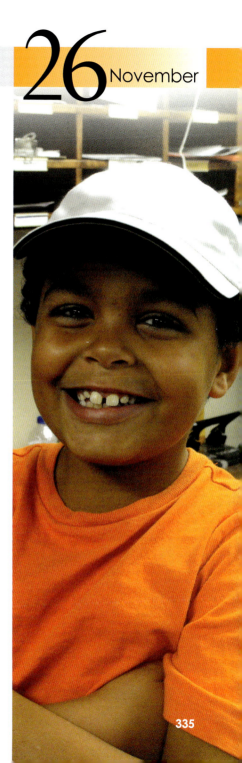

"How wonderful it is that nobody need wait a single moment before starting to improve the world."

Anne Frank

Lots of people say they respect the willingness it takes to give of yourself to be a foster or adoptive parent. Even though I have fostered for many years and I have adopted also, I learned about the joy of giving from my son.

When he was thirteen-years-old he had a kidney stone. It was a traumatic experience which involved a lot of tests and then surgery. During the tests we were told that he had a duplicated, or extra, kidney. Immediately, he became excited about having a kidney that he could donate to someone who needed one.

Then, another doctor explained that he didn't have a whole extra kidney. What he had was an extra tube coming from one kidney where usually there is only one tube on one end. He was disappointed that he couldn't share one of his kidneys.

We were proud that he was willing to give of himself (literally) to bring life to someone else. It is this kind of selfless outlook that makes our world a better place. And it is one of many situations where a child has shown the joy we can all experience through giving.

Dargie, mother and grandmother of many step, birth, foster, and adopted children.

November 27

Roots

"There is no place like home."
L. Frank Baum, *The Wonderful Wizard of Oz*

The young man in the passenger seat was in route to visit his biological parents who lived in a remote rural area. He had been living with a middle class family in a small town and was doing quite well with the adjustments that life had required of him. But there was a piece of him that was tied to his rural roots.

This was especially evident on this particular day. As we neared the area that he had called home, we came across a scene that was common in those parts. An older man, in spit-stained bib overalls, was parked on the side of the road with the hood up on his truck. Steam was spewing out of the radiator as the man worked furiously to keep something from exploding.

The young man next to me grinned from ear to ear as he visibly relaxed in the seat beside me. When asked what he was grinning about, he said, "It is so good to be back among the hicks again!"

S.I.

From Their Heart to Yours

28 November

"Each relationship you have with another person reflects the relationship you have with yourself."
Alice Deville

As a parent, professional, & mentor–I feel that there is no greater task than to impart a sense of personal values to the children in our charge. It is important for us to remember that we are not only raising our children, but also developing individuals to take charge of our future. It is essential that we understand as caregivers, that in order to be successful in our application of parenting skills, we must offer a view of the whole world and how these little people, with a good value system, can fit into it.

The following brief list includes thoughts shared by children. These ideas come from their heart to yours.

    Help them find something special they can call their own.
    Teach them to make healthy choices.
    Acknowledge their special talents.
    Teach them the value of spirituality.
    Volunteer with them in community projects.
    Watch a family movie with them.
    Give them words of encouragement daily.

Gina, counselor, mentor, mother, and author of "For the Kids."

November 29 — I Never Taught You to Breathe

"The greatest power that a person possesses is the power to choose."

Unknown

My sister is a wonderful mother! She comes up with great teaching examples for her children when they have something to learn. Her boys are six years old and they are deep into "…but you didn't tell me." You didn't tell me if I watched this movie we wouldn't have time to read a book tonight. You didn't tell me it was too cold to wear my sandals. You didn't tell me if I passed my turn my brother was going to play the game.

She responds to each of these laments with a calm, clear voice—well most of the time, she is human and subject to frustration like the rest of us. Anyway, she will say to her children, "You are very smart boys and this is one of those things I am sure you can know without me having to tell you. After all, you know enough to breathe don't you? I never taught you that."

Somehow that simple comment seems comforting to me. It affirms their innate ability to know what they need and gives them permission to use it. As she allows them to think things through on their own and experience the consequences of their choices, she teaches them the most important things of all. They are capable, competent individuals, and they can make choices and even self-correct when they dislike where their choices take them.

Susan, foster and adoptive parent, grandparent, and former foster family recruiter and trainer.

Believe the Impossible

30 November

"If we were really aware of our own powers, we would live in a continuous state of awe."
Earl Nightingale

The first time I saw her was in the hospital around Thanksgiving. She was less than five-months-old. They had asked if we would be willing to see her and think about bringing her into our home. She had multiple medical needs and was quite a sight with all the tubes sticking out of her body. They said her prognosis was grim because she would not eat.

When I went to the hospital the second time, I felt an instant bond. She drank some of her bottle, and in the next two days and nights she began to gain weight for the first time in a long time. When I went home she wouldn't eat for the hospital staff. Then, I found out that they weren't going to let me take her home. However, some kind nurses who understood that I was the one she needed, helped me to convince them that it would work. I took her home that day.

They never expected her to live, much less walk or talk. What a triumph it was when, five years later, she was walking, talking, learning, and most important of all, she was smiling when she went to her permanent adoptive home!

F.M.K.

Thinking of Fostering?

*"The service we render others
is really the rent we pay for our room on earth."*
Wilfred Grenfell

Do you need to have the last word on a subject?
Do you need to be in control of a situation?
Are you uncomfortable when things are out of place?
Do you expect family business to be private?
Do you require eight hours of sleep each night?
Is it a challenge for you to say "no"?
Are you easily shocked?
Can you adapt to change?

Not everyone is cut out to be a foster parent. It requires a great deal more than many people imagine. No matter how much love you have to share or how large your home is, the most crucial characteristic of a foster parent is tenacity.

The best foster parents are able to hang in there with the tantrums, the strange unexplainable behaviors, the intrusiveness and insensitivity of the system, and the challenges to one's personal parenting skills. It is quite a balancing act and not everyone measures up. Fortunately there are people who can set aside their own ego long enough to do what is best for the child. Foster parents need the ability to relax and release the ideas they were taught about "normal" parenting. They must open themselves to learning the practical parenting techniques necessary for doing this enormously important job.

Susan, foster and adoptive parent, grandparent, and former foster family recruiter and trainer.

A Good Christmas

1 December

"People cannot tell whether they are rich or poor by turning to their ledgers. It is the heart that makes them rich. They are rich or poor according to what they are, not according to what they have."

Henry Ward Beecher

As a foster parent in a group home setting, I became intimately familiar with the seasonal sense of responsibility felt by many residents of our community toward "those less fortunate" than themselves. In the Fall of the year, people would begin to call and offer to donate items: candy, bikes, clothes, and toys. And each year I had to struggle with how to be nice and find ways for those generous, well-meaning people to help without setting up a dynamic that taught the children they "deserved" these things simply because they had a hard life. How can you teach children that the measure of a good Christmas is not in the height of the stack of loot they get?

Most families struggle with this issue to some extent when parents want to buy everything for a cherished child, and the child begins to expect that those things just magically appear in life. With foster children it is even more crucial that they see balance because their lives have been so out of balance in the past. Creating situations where children are able to feel the joy of giving as well as the joy of receiving connect them to their world in a much more positive way. One day, if we are lucky, the measure of a good Christmas may be the number of smiles they put on other people's faces rather than the stack of loot they receive.

Susan, foster and adoptive parent, grandparent, and former foster family recruiter and trainer.

December 2 — School Meetings

"Don't find fault. Find a remedy."
Henry Ford

It seems that with foster care comes an assortment of meetings—counseling, doctors, and schools. I have come to know people well at about every school my children have attended. When I get a new child, I know exactly who to go to when I have needs to be met.

My family has had good favor with the school system, which is not to say that we haven't had problems. Fortunately we have been able to work through them to create a successful learning environment for the children. The important thing is to stay focused on that point.

Just keep this in mind:
Ask for help if you need it, and keep asking until you get it. Be kind, respectful and assertive. School/Faculty can provide great encouragement and resources for you and your children.

Dargie, mother and grandmother of many step, birth, foster, and adopted children.

The One We Kept

"We give thanks for unknown blessings already on their way."
Sacred chant

I am a true believer that everything happens for a reason. Never in my life had I intended to be a foster parent. I had worked too many years for the Department of Human Services and did not think I could handle the hurt and disappointment of the children, or the feelings that come with losing a child you love. But my sister informed me it was my "Christian duty," and far be it from me not to try just in case it really was.

We picked her up at the shelter. She was eleven-years-old, had pretty blue eyes and a blank, hurt look. We immediately found a place for her in our hearts. After a year and a half, all parental rights were terminated and she no longer had any chance of returning to her home. But there were plans for her that were yet to be revealed.

We have a daughter who had never married and had no children of her own. She loved our foster daughter and wanted to adopt her. It took a while, but eventually our daughter was able to adopt her and today she is our granddaughter.

J. C. & Neva, foster parents.

December 4

The Choice

*"I discovered I always had choices
and sometimes it's only a choice of attitude."*
Judith M. Knowlton

Most people come to fostering out of a desire to make life better for the children they serve. Along the way they discover many, many feelings about the birth families whose lives and choices affect the children they have come to love. It is sometimes hard to separate how they feel about the children from how they feel about the parents of those children.

One foster parent has come to understand her role in this way:

"I think our choice of fostering means that we stand in the gap. We are the dam that holds back the waters of despair and hopelessness in children's lives. We do not stand in judgement of the adults who, for whatever reason, have not been the parents we would have chosen for those children. We do our part, and we can only hope the parents do theirs also."

Wendy, foster and biological parent who has fostered off and on for 14 years.

Susan, foster and adoptive parent, grandparent, and former foster family recruiter and trainer.

Christmas Love

5 December

"If there is anything better than to be loved it is loving."
Unknown

After a four month struggle with a caseworker, we finally brought the sister of one of our other foster children into our home about a month before Christmas. Although she took to us immediately, it was clear she was in much need of love and attention.

We have a big family and lots of traditions, and we looked forward to sharing a big Christmas with this new child. However, she spent most of the time sitting there looking like a wounded bird, unsure of what she was allowed to do. With a household of five children at the time, the living room was filled to capacity with gifts, and only a small path led down the hallway and into the kitchen. All the children's faces were filled with awe at the pretty lights and breakfast cookies and juice that were for them, but mostly, they were dazzled by the wrapped packages all over the room.

When we handed our new foster daughter presents, she did not know what to do with them. By the time she opened her dolls and the new clothes she so desperately needed, she was the happiest little girl I had ever seen. My heart was so full I stood in the middle of my kitchen and had a good cry because this child made me realize just what is important in this world. Every child needs more than toys and clothes, but for those who have never had much, it is a good way to help the healing begin.

Wendy, birth mom of 3, adoptive mom to 1, and foster mom to 11 children in the last 5 years.

December 6 — All Kinds of Love

"We have what we seek. It is there all the time, and if we give it time, it will make itself known to us."
Thomas Merton

Once I heard a man say his family had fostered over thirty children, but only five of those had "gotten into his heart." It often comes as a surprise to foster parents that they love their foster children differently. Sometimes they feel badly about not being able to love one as deeply as they love the other. The role of a foster parent is to provide for the daily needs of a child as well as give them a loving experience of a healthy family. This does not mean you must be willing to adopt them if parental rights are terminated.

Most people who foster for any length of time will be asked if they want to adopt a child they have fostered. With some matches the answer will be a resounding "YES." With others it will be a "let me think about it and get back to you." There is much to consider when adopting a child and it is perfectly natural to be willing to adopt some and not others. It is a time when we learn there are all kinds of love.

"...You can love a child without it being the same kind of love that would lead you to being their 'forever' parent and there's nothing wrong with that. Sometimes it's that very love you have for the child that lets you let them go; you love them enough to want them to have something you can't give them."

Valerie, foster parent for medically fragile children for 10 years and an adoptive parent.

Susan, foster and adoptive parent, grandparent, and former foster family recruiter and trainer.

The Runaway

7 December

"God knows everything that you are thinking.
But you should talk to Him anyway."
Madison Gregory, age 10 as quoted by Dandi Daley Mackall in *Why I Believe in God*

Trouble at school… afraid to come home
Walking, thinking
Phone calls, police reports, prayer
Tired, scared, tossing, turning
Mind running wild.

Midnight call… Thank God!
Why? Who knows?
Silent ride home, sleep
A new day – home and safe.

Leave the door open
Don't say never or always
Life isn't like that
And, thank God, most of the time
We live to learn from our mistakes.

Dargie, mother and grandmother of many step, birth, foster, and adopted children.

December 8 — Foreign Worlds

"A mind that is stretched by a new experience can never go back to its old dimensions."
— Oliver Wendall Holmes

As we walked into the restaurant, all eyes were on us. It was my husband, myself, and the seven adolescents we were caring for at that time. It was the one night a month we took the kids out to eat and this month I had chosen a Chinese restaurant. One of the boys in particular had ranted and raved at how he didn't like Chinese food, only to later admit he had never really had any. I watched him as we entered this "foreign" world. He was amazed with the chopsticks and appalled that the won-ton soup only had one big noodle in it. We explained how to eat the soup, which utensils to use, and how to hold the chopsticks. It became a fun learning experience.

It also reminded me that many of these children come to our homes as if they were in a foreign land where baths come every night and food is eaten at the table. A land in which mothers and fathers don't hit one another and love is showered rather than held in reserve. It must be a terrifying experience to enter into a new existence, even when it is a more healthy one.

In my mind and heart, I hold the knowledge that this boy will never again be totally without the information of how to hold chopsticks. And, he will never again be without the information that there are families that operate in peace and with love for all their members.

Susan, foster and adoptive parent, grandparent, and former foster family recruiter and trainer.

Experience

9 December

"Right now my life is just one learning experience after another. By the end of the week I should be a genius."

Jeanette Osias

My husband and I are foster parents and we run a small trucking company from our house. He still drives, but it works for us. I believe we are closer than many families that are together everyday, and he is always a phone call away.

Several years ago, I went through an identity crisis. I went back to school thinking I wanted to be an accountant. If you knew me you would laugh. I did well, but I was drawn toward Elementary Education as I began a work study in the college day care. I learned as much in the day care as I did in my classes.

The bottom line is that no experience is wasted. I use all of it. The management/accounting helped me manage my home and our business. The Elementary Education opened doors for me to be a substitute teacher and enabled me to interact with my own children in more helpful ways. And, I am finally making use of my creative writing classes and that for me is the icing on the cake—another dream come true. I'd like to think that the example I set in living my life is a good one for the kids I love. I want them to know that, with patience, they can also turn their life experiences into something positive.

Dargie, mother and grandmother of many step, birth, foster, and adopted children.

December 10 — Power Struggles

"One day in retrospect the years of struggle will strike you as the most beautiful."

Sigmund Freud

When I teach classes for people who want to become foster parents I make one point over and over. If you get into a power struggle with a child, no matter what age, make sure you win. The second and most important part of that lesson is to pick those power struggles carefully. If you do not learn how to choose struggles you can win, life with the child will become one huge power struggle over everything.

I always tell my potential foster parents to "say what you mean, and mean what you say." That means you should not say, "I will think about it," or "Maybe," or, "We'll discuss it later." To a child all those answers mean, "Yes." You might forget the conversation, but they will not.

So, if the car horn is honking on Saturday night and you look out the window to see all your kids sitting in the car, it could be because, sometime on Tuesday, you mentioned that you "might take them to the movies over the weekend."

Carolyn, social worker & foster parent to teen boys.

Role Reversal

11 December

"Trouble is a part of your life, and if you don't share it, you don't give the person who loves you a chance to love you enough."
— Dinah Shore

One Sunday as I was trying to get ready for church, nothing felt right, nothing looked right. Usually, I have everything together for everyone else as well as myself; but it was time to leave, and I was still in my slip, almost in tears. My teenage daughter, who came in to use my curling iron, noticed my panic and became concerned.

We exchanged a few words and she began to take control. She pulled out a dress and said, "Put this on, it's going to be a long day and it will be comfortable." I obeyed. Then she said, "Now, put on your brown shoes and let's go." I was dressed, ready, and relieved. Sometimes even the best parents need a little parenting themselves. How fortunate I am to have a capable daughter willing to care for me when I need it most.

Dargie, mother and grandmother of many step, birth, foster, and adopted children.

December 12 — Coping with the System

"These are all our children.
We will all profit by, or pay for, whatever they become."
James Baldwin

According to the Child Welfare League of America (CWLA), one of the main reasons foster parents stop fostering is the stress of working with the foster care agency. It is important to understand here that we are talking about people who open their homes to care for abused and neglected children. We are talking about women and men who have felt the horrors of separating from a child who has lived with them, possibly for years. We are talking about single people and married couples who have rearranged their lives as well as their furniture to offer a home to children in need. We are talking about mothers and fathers who risk verbal and physical aggression, some who have lost personal property as a result of the child's rage. And one of the main reasons they leave fostering is because of the stress of working with the agency? There is something wrong with this picture.

I dream of a world where the people who lovingly care for children are honored and respected for the important job they do. Until we reach that place, we will just have to do it for one another. We know how important our role is and we know how much the children benefit from our love and guidance. We all need to find those groups and those friends who can support us in what we do and let us rage against the system if we have to, until we change it, even if we have to do it one worker at a time.

Susan, foster and adoptive parent, grandparent, and former foster family recruiter and trainer.

Learning

*"Parents teach in the toughest school in the world—
the school for making people."*

Virginia Satir

One of the unfair things about fostering is the transition time between coming into a new home and starting school. This is especially true knowing they probably won't stay for more than a few months. I worry that the children are not learning enough of the basic foundation that they must have to build on for the future.

By using computer games, workbooks from discount stores, flash cards, and old worksheets from school, I help the children keep learning. We also go to the library and read, read, read. Not all learning is done in books though!

It is amazing what can be taught on a trip through a museum, on a walk, or in a single conversation. Creating art or making crafts help children learn to cut and paste and also give them the joy of creating something.

Of course, as we work together to keep our home clean and our tummies full, we can teach life skills. We often overlook the importance of learning these skills as well as the everyday reading and math that are part of sorting laundry, measuring, and cooking. Not only do foster parents assume the parenting role for our charges, we become their teachers too.

Dargie, mother and grandmother of many step, birth, foster, and adopted children.

December 14 — Someday

"The only courage that matters is the kind that gets you from one moment to the next."
— Mignon McLaughlin

Children do not bounce back from difficulty as easily as many workers believe. My experience tells me it is not okay to move kids from home to home to home. It is not okay to keep giving biological parents endless chances regardless of what it does to the child. It's not okay to overlook bad foster families because they do not buck the system. It is not okay for workers to not consider every little aspect of what their decisions may do. It is also not okay for workers or parents to project their own past history onto families. We all need to work out our own personal "stuff" before we can hope to be of any help to anyone else.

We know too much to let these things continue. I don't have any sure fire answers; I wish I did. And I wish someone would listen to all of us who live the fostering life every day. We don't just do this as a job; we LIVE it. We breathe it; these kids are our lives. And this is why, even when we are tired, even when we feel we have no more tears to cry, we still fight for the rights of our kids. We continue to hope that someday someone will listen; that someday someone will hear the cries of the children and realize we have to stop doing wrong by these kids and those who love them.

Deena, foster, birth, & adoptive mom to a great bunch of kids.

The Mother & Child Necklace

15 December

*"In the depth of winter,
I finally learned that within me
there lay an invincible summer."*
                                Albert Camus

A teacher at our elementary school was in the process of adopting a beautiful baby boy when I met her. She proudly wore a mother and child necklace and would tell you about her son at any opportunity.

Near the end of the school year, they had the final court appearance for the adoption. The next time I saw her she looked deeply troubled, and I asked how she was doing. She explained that the birth father had come to the hearing and said he wanted his child back. I cannot imagine how devastating this must have been or how she could even begin to deal with the feelings of fear, grief, and anger that resulted from her loss.

I didn't see her again for a long while, but someone told me her son was returned to his birth father, and she was in the process of adopting another child. When I did see her again, she was wearing a different mother and child necklace.

Can you imagine the enormous amount of courage it took to remove that first necklace and to emotionally release her son into someone else's hands. I'm sure her first son will never lose the secure start in life she gave him. I applaud her ability to go on working with children each day in school; and I marvel at the strength she has to adopt another child.

Susan, foster and adoptive parent, grandparent, and former foster family recruiter and trainer.

December 16 — Leaving Too Soon

"A broken heart can be mended if you give God all the pieces."
Linda Allison-Lewis

A young girl was placed in my home two weeks before Christmas, and we instantly fell in love with her. She began giving us hugs a few days after her arrival that seemed to say, "I'm thankful for being part of this family."

We were at the grocery when I got the call she was to be moved immediately. I had to continue shopping even though tears filled my eyes. I had to tell her because she was right beside me, and I had to call home to make sure that her laundry got dry. We chose a turkey that she wouldn't be eating. I gathered ingredients for the dishes she had requested but would not be there to enjoy.

What do you do in this situation? I wanted to hug her, but I knew I would go to pieces and she needed my strength. We drove home talking of the unfairness of it all. When we got home, the kids said tearful good-byes, gave her small gifts of remembrance, and we loaded her few bags into the van and headed for the office. Another child delivered, another quiet ride home.

With all due respect to the authority and opinion of the powers that be, I hardly see how placing her with strangers less than a week before Christmas was in her best interest. I just keep hanging onto the words, "It is better to have loved and lost than never to have loved at all." Deep in my temporarily broken heart I know it's true.

Dargie, mother and grandmother of many step, birth, foster, and adopted children.

Unspoken Messages

17 December

"The best prayer of all is, 'Help me to help.'"
William Barclay

There is nothing quite like that look on a child's face who has waited patiently for a relative to pick them up only to be disappointed. It goes straight to your heart and cuts away a piece of it.

I overheard one boy calling a grandparent after waiting for him for several hours. His grandfather explained they would not be able to get him this week because he had some work-related event to attend. The boy simply said, "Okay" and hung up the phone. I cannot get the sound of that okay out of my mind. It was a sing-songy, sad sound. It said, "Oh, I understand work is more important than I am." It said, "I love you, and I can't tell you how angry it makes me that you pushed me aside once again." It said, "I have to stay in control of my feelings, I can't let anyone see this hurts me."

He went ahead and unpacked and had a good time that weekend with the rest of the kids. About the middle of the next week, as we approached the day his grandfather was supposed to get him, again he started acting out. He got extremely angry over every little thing that happened and he finally burst into tears and began repeating the litany of reasons people don't like him. All I could do was hold him, let him cry and assure him I saw lots of good in him. Oh yes, and pray that his grandfather didn't miss their time together again.

Susan, foster and adoptive parent, grandparent, and former foster family recruiter and trainer.

December 18 — Giving Back

"When we do the best we can, we never know what miracle is wrought in our own life, or in the life of another."
Helen Keller

When I was a teenager, our family took in a fourteen-year-old girl who had been emancipated from the system. She arrived with a paper bag that held all of her earthly belongings, but she would soon give back more than we thought she was able to give.

That first Christmas I explained it was a tradition to happily complain about the Christmas tree my dad would choose. He picked good trees but we always referred to them as "Charlie Brown trees" since we kids always wanted a bigger one. That year there was no complaining about the tree. My foster sister secretly took her hard earned allowance and went out and bought the biggest, most beautiful Christmas tree she could find. She surprised us by yelling, "Get the door!" as she valiantly attempted to drag it inside. I can still picture her face, flushed with excitement and pride as she looked at each one of us asking, "Do you really like it? Do you?" We did. We liked that tree, but we LOVED that girl.

Many people talk about what we can do for kids, but don't forget that often, what is good for them is to allow them a chance to do something for us.

Donna, birth parent, stepparent, and former foster sister.

Never Give Up

19 December

"In the game of life nothing is less important than the score at half time."
Unknown

When I looked into that seventeen-year-old's big blue eyes, I wondered again what in the world I had gotten myself into. This young woman had been with us for about a year, and it seemed that things were on a downward spiral. Her attitude and harsh tongue had about worn us out, and there were times when we felt that our best was not enough for her. We thought about giving up.

However, we can be stubborn too, and we wanted to give it all that we could. She had so much potential, and I wanted to see her through high school.

Now, nine years later, she is a very important part of our family. She worked hard to get her college degree and is working on her second one. She has a successful career, a stable marriage, her own home, and we believe that she can accomplish anything she sets her mind to.

F.M.K.

December 20 — Overwhelmed

"God holds the whole world in His hands, and about everybody knows that. But He also holds Pluto and the sun and everything else, too, and people forget that."

Brent Glover, age 8 as quoted in *Why I Believe in God* by Dandi Daley Mackall

Sometimes I get overwhelmed, we all do, I think. It still surprises me though, when I hear people that I see as being strong, successfully involved, and outgoing share about being drained or overwhelmed, even ready to give up.

People say that I am strong, and most of the time I would agree. However, when illness comes, finances waiver, the kids have problems, or sometimes for no obvious reason, I begin to wonder if I've blown it, misjudged a situation, or if it's all really worth it. I lose my confidence and my sense of humor.

No advice today - I just think it's important to remember that, occasionally, we all feel overwhelmed, but we'll get over it. At least, I hope we will.

Dargie, mother and grandmother of many step, birth, foster, and adopted children.

Winter

Up in the air I go flying again,
Up in the air and down!

December 21 — Finding One's Magic

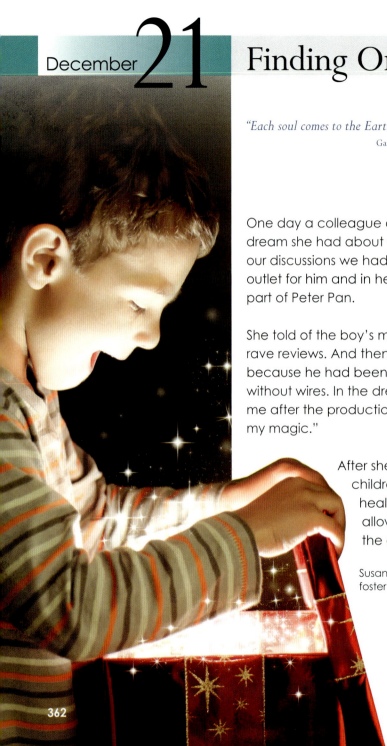

"Each soul comes to the Earth with special gifts."
Gary Zukav, *The Seat of the Soul*

One day a colleague of mine came into my office to describe a dream she had about a child we had recently been discussing. In our discussions we had pondered whether drama might be a good outlet for him and in her dream he was a child actor playing the part of Peter Pan.

She told of the boy's mastery of the role and of the audience's rave reviews. And then she told me all the people were amazed because he had been able to fly across the astounded crowd without wires. In the dream, she explained, he came running up to me after the production saying, "I found it. I found it. I finally found my magic."

After she left my office I realized that is my wish for all children - that they will find their magic and use it to heal their hurts. For it is their own magic which will allow them to fly toward the future untethered by the often painful wires of their past.

Susan, foster and adoptive parent, grandparent, and former foster family recruiter and trainer.

Christmas Memories

22 December

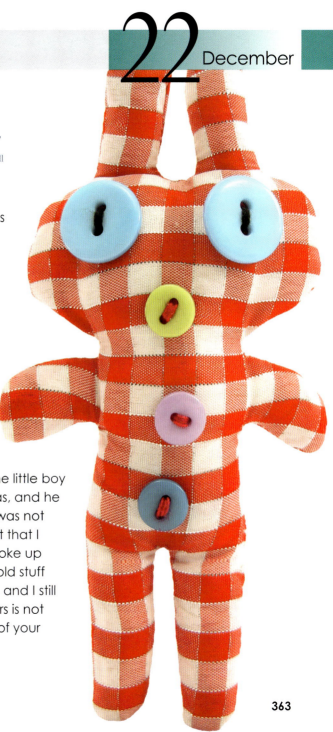

*"The past is our cradle, not our prison...
The past is for inspiration, not imitation, for continuation, not repetition."*
Israel Zangwill

One holiday that will always stand out in my mind was the Christmas when I was nine-years-old. I did not celebrate Christmas with my birth family so I did not really understand what the holiday was about. I thought it was just a time for people to get really crazy and kind of greedy; I was never really into the spirit of things.

In one former placement, we picked someone's name out of a hat. It was similar to a secret Santa gift exchange on Christmas Eve. We didn't have much money so we had to be creative, like making gifts instead of buying them.

The one present I had always wanted was this doll. The little boy who got my name was three years younger than I was, and he drew me a picture of a doll. I knew in my heart that was not what I really wanted, but he had worked so hard on it that I could not disappoint him. The next morning when I woke up there was this little tiny doll that he had made out of old stuff around the house. I just cried and cried. I am 24 now, and I still have that doll. It is a reminder to me that what matters is not how much of your money you spend but how much of your heart you give.

Stacey, former foster child who was in care for 14 years.

December 23 — Odd Lots

"I will not play at tug o' war. I'd rather play at hug o' war."
Shel Silverstein

People who foster and adopt must come to terms with how they will relate to the biological families of their chosen children. Whether we ever see these birth families or not, we deal with them through the thoughts, dreams, and memories of the children we nurture toward health.

"Last night I went to our local "odd lots" store and spent $60 on Christmas gifts for my foster daughter's mother, father, and two sisters. Did I do it because I'm a saint? Heck, no! No one has ever suggested that I fit that description. I did it because these are people she loves, and she is upset that they won't have a Christmas. I did it because I know that unless I am working with infants or toddlers, no matter how good a parent I am, I will never take the place of a birth parent. My child's relationship with her birth parents is critical to her well being. I can't get away from that, and I can't do anything to jeopardize their relationship. In fact, I believe that it is to my child's benefit that her relationship with her birth family improve while she is in foster care. It is hard though, these are not people I would spend time with under normal circumstances; but, fostering is not normal either, so I just grit my teeth and deal with it."

Pat, who has fostered almost 100 children over the past 30 year.

Susan, foster and adoptive parent, grandparent, and former foster family recruiter and trainer.

Wish List for Foster Parents

24 December

"Not merely what we do, but what we try to do and why, are the true interpreters of what we are."
— C. H. Woodward

Dear Santa, a few years ago we became foster parents and our understanding of the world changed. As we sit down this year to write out our Christmas list we find it is different from what it was in the past, because we are different now. If you could manage any of the following we would greatly appreciate it.

Thanks,
Foster Parents Everywhere

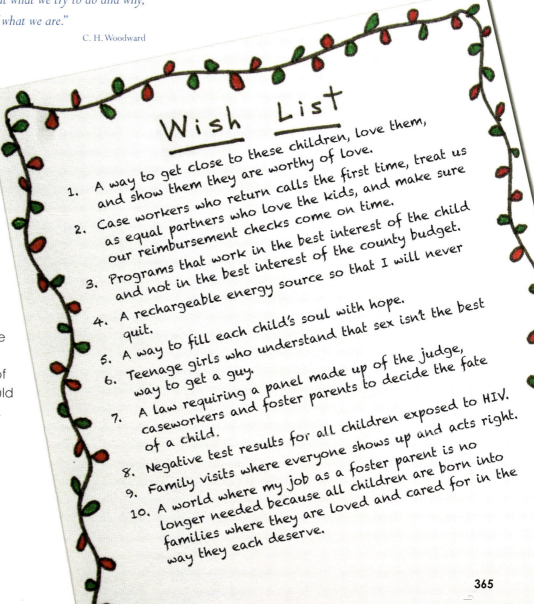

Wish List

1. A way to get close to these children, love them, and show them they are worthy of love.
2. Case workers who return calls the first time, treat us as equal partners who love the kids, and make sure our reimbursement checks come on time.
3. Programs that work in the best interest of the child and not in the best interest of the county budget.
4. A rechargeable energy source so that I will never quit.
5. A way to fill each child's soul with hope.
6. Teenage girls who understand that sex isn't the best way to get a guy.
7. A law requiring a panel made up of the judge, caseworkers and foster parents to decide the fate of a child.
8. Negative test results for all children exposed to HIV.
9. Family visits where everyone shows up and acts right.
10. A world where my job as a foster parent is no longer needed because all children are born into families where they are loved and cared for in the way they each deserve.

December 25 — The Joy of Christmas

"Happiness is a marvelous magnet to the human personality."
James Dobson

It's Christmas morning, there is an eight-foot tree in the living room and I am awaiting the pitter-patter of all my children's feet. The first and second child react with the anticipated "ooh's" and "aah's" at what they see. Slowly the third child, still in his blue sleeper, appears. He is four-years-old and has never had a Christmas tree and presents. His big, blue eyes grow with wonder and excitement as he turns toward the tree. The smile on his face is so bright I feel as if an angel is standing on my steps. I tell him Santa has left him lots of presents; he stands there not saying a word to any of us. I take several pictures so we can keep this memory forever.

Finally, he creeps down the steps toward the other kids who hold out his gifts. Then he puts his tiny arms around me and whispers in my ear, "Mama, Santa loves me just like you do, doesn't he?" I assure him that he does. My birth daughter hands him a train and tells him it is his. It takes him all day to open his gifts because he looks each gift over and holds it close to him and plays with each of his toys carefully.

My daughter was only five when this happened and today, at 23, she often shares how this moment affected her. That little boy gave us all a priceless gift that day and each Christmas morning, in my mind's eye, I see him on the staircase glowing with the love that he had never felt before. His presence truly enriched us all.

Tonya Jo, single foster parent who has fostered 120 kids over the last 21 years.

Heroes

26 December

"The world is round, and the place which may seem like the end may also be only the beginning."
— Ivy Baker Priest

With my first (now adopted) foster son, I attended every review board, staffing, visit, and so on at the social worker's invitation. I tried to work with his mother and encouraged her to feed, change, and burp him during visits. During the last review board, his mother looked at me and said, "He thinks you're his mom."

There had been a few months without visits due to transportation problems. I knew in my heart that she would never be able to care for him on her own. I said, "I feed, change, and bathe him everyday; he looks to me because I meet his daily needs. But, I will always tell him that you are his mother and that you love him very much."

The next afternoon, I received a call. The worker told me that the mother was ready to sign over rights, under the condition that we adopt him. She knew that we could meet his needs and she couldn't.

It was hard for me to imagine how she came to that conclusion. To me, she is a hero, unselfishly giving up her only son so that he might have a better life. It touched my heart. I thank God that I didn't have to prepare for that last meeting.

Dargie, mother and grandmother of many step, birth, foster, and adopted children.

December 27 — Courage

"Courage is the lovely virtue—the rib of Himself that God sent down to His children."

— James M. Barrie

I recognize something in you. It is the same thing I see in nearly everyone who provides a home for kids who were not born to them. Your friends may call it crazy, and others may call it "nice," but I know it's something different. I call it courage.

It's not the kind of courage that's needed for skydiving. Instead, it's that kind of courage that compels you to take on a seemingly impossible job, simply because you care for kids and wonder if you don't do it, who will?

This kind of courage makes you dance for joy because your child made it through the year with only two D's and one suspension. It helps you change the sheets one more time, knowing that you will have to do it again the next day and the day after that. It allows you to hear the words, "He will NEVER function normally," and allow them to pass through your understanding without ever becoming part of your vocabulary. It helps you to hang tough because yesterday she took your hand for the first time.

You have never met me, but I know you. I wish that the whole world could see you as I do—courageous, sacrificial people who take great risks every day, all for the sake of a child.

Anon

New Year's Eve Reflections

28 December

*"If a word of praise or thanks needs to be spoken,
it had better be spoken now—for life is an uncertain business
and you may never get the chance to speak it again."*

William Barclay

Each New Year's Eve the members of our church gather to reflect on the passing year and usher in the New Year with a prayer. It is a special, touching time as we all sit together in the beautiful and peaceful sanctuary sharing the things we are thankful for with our spiritual community.

One year, to our great surprise, one of our teenage foster sons raised his hand to speak. He told about the things he had experienced in past placements and how grateful he was to be with us. It was one of those times we cherish as parents, a genuine "you have made a difference in my life" moment.

I know it wasn't easy for him to speak those words, but his openness and appreciation was more precious than any gifts that had been under my tree that holiday season. It touched my heart to know that to him being in our home was one of his greatest gifts.

Dargie, mother and grandmother of many step, birth, foster, and adopted children.

December 29 — Prayer for Our Foster Children

"Before me, even as behind, God is, and all is well."
John Greenleaf Whittier

God, watch over these children,
We only have them in our care for a short time.

Let them see and feel You while they are with us
And I pray that You go with them as they leave.

Keep them safe in Your arms
When they must leave ours.

Amen

Dargie, mother and grandmother of many step, birth, foster, and adopted children.

Old Mommy

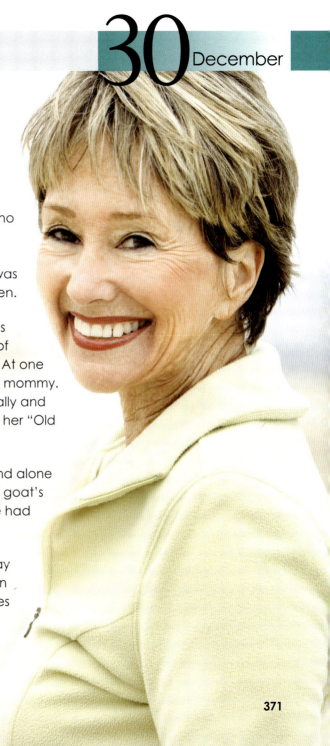

30 December

"For He orders His angels to protect you wherever you go."
Psalms 91:11

There are many foster/adoptive parents in the world who do incredibly courageous things day after day without credit or applause. One such woman came to my attention when, at seventy-eight, she became ill and was no longer able to foster her beloved HIV positive children.

She is a delightful, feisty lady who loves her kids and has devoted much of her adult years to assuring a quality of life for those children who will not have a quantity of it. At one point a kindergarten child said she was too old to be a mommy. She simply explained that all mommies get old eventually and she was just an old one. So, the children started calling her "Old Mommy" and the name stuck.

Old Mommy fostered with her husband until he died and alone after that. She bought two goats when she heard that goat's milk might help increase T cells to fight infection. All she had done was for the love of the children.

So, here's to Old Mommy and all the others like her. May your days be filled with as much love as you have given and may all your fostered angels smother you with kisses someday at Heaven's Gate.

Susan, foster and adoptive parent, grandparent, and former foster family recruiter and trainer.

December 31 — Endings

"There are lives I can imagine without children but none of them have the same laughter and noise."
Brian Andreas

As foster and adoptive parents we are often more dependent than birth parents on the stories of other families who have made it through the challenges and seen the beautiful rainbow on the other side. The stories in this book were written through the smiles and tears of parents just like you who are doing their best to accomplish the most important task of all—raise a healthy child.

It is my hope that these words honor all people who have chosen to share their life and their love in this special way. And for those of you who have moments of wondering if you can do it one more day, I hope you will find the encouragement and confidence to keep on going in these pages. The work we do is a matter of faith—keep it up and keep sharing your happy endings.

Susan, foster and adoptive parent, grandparent, and former foster family recruiter and trainer.

About Chaddock

Since 1853, Chaddock has been serving the needs of children and families. Our focus is serving children with developmental trauma and attachment issues. Many of the children in our care are foster children or have been adopted into loving families. We bring hope and healing to children and families through our residential treatment facility, on-campus school, foster care and adoption services, outpatient therapy, intensive in-home therapy program, Illinois statewide Caregiver Connections program, the Chaddock Trauma Initiative, and our worldwide training and consultation programs through The Knowledge Center at Chaddock. Chaddock has served children from more than 27 states, the District of Columbia and one tribal nation and has trained professionals from five continents. For more information, please visit our website at www.chaddock.org.

Index

Aging Out 2, 358

Animals 7, 13, 41, 94, 103, 170, 213

Attachment 3, 9, 10, 28, 29, 33, 58, 59, 66, 91, 214, 215, 325

Birth Children 9, 30, 58, 96, 106, 205, 221, 250, 336

BirthParent 5, 11, 37, 41, 49, 58, 59, 71, 94, 96, 106, 129, 141, 189, 204, 221, 225, 250, 264, 282, 316, 323, 325, 336, 344, 355, 367

Birth Family 82, 138, 186, 226, 250, 302, 311, 322, 336, 354, 357, 364

Change 44, 57, 64, 283, 329, 359, 365

Challenging Behaviors 21, 22, 32, 33, 34, 51, 53, 84, 86, 87, 91, 105, 107, 113, 116, 118, 119, 124, 137, 139, 156, 158, 161, 195, 200, 207, 210, 216, 220, 222, 239, 243, 255, 260, 263, 266, 267, 271, 274, 283, 287, 292, 294, 300, 318, 328, 329, 338, 347, 359

Confidentiality 67

Courage 11, 33, 112, 156, 259, 275, 331, 355, 368

Disruption 161, 260

Diversity 13, 23, 39, 123, 135, 149, 155, 224, 233, 283, 313, 324, 331

Endings/Beginnings 6, 10, 15, 19, 26, 45, 48, 64, 70, 74, 79, 82, 85, 89, 93, 94, 98, 100, 110, 113, 133, 143, 145, 150, 156, 165, 172, 183, 205, 226, 233, 257, 298, 327, 333, 367

Expectations 14, 17, 20, 23, 24, 28, 33, 34, 42, 43, 46, 57, 58, 95, 97, 114, 119, 129, 134, 140, 143, 146, 148, 151, 153, 160, 163, 164, 167, 169, 173, 177, 182, 209, 215, 232, 237, 247, 252, 262, 264, 265, 269, 271, 272, 278, 285, 299, 302, 325, 340, 348

Extended Family 19, 30, 52, 110, 126, 149, 226, 295

Faith 5, 6, 15, 27, 42, 45, 61, 82, 85, 94, 106, 120, 124, 134, 159, 164, 172, 184, 191, 193, 197, 202, 208, 238, 251, 257, 260, 279, 298, 304, 313, 332, 339, 343, 347, 370

Family Support 120, 126, 130, 162, 169, 196, 217, 223, 229, 234, 237, 239, 249, 268, 277, 332, 348, 351

Fears 18, 15, 27, 47, 66, 69, 75, 76, 78, 79, 90, 101, 104, 109, 112, 114, 145, 156, 167, 174, 197, 200, 209, 227, 228, 245, 256, 319

Financial 2, 54, 107, 129, 130, 151, 252, 276, 341, 360, 363

Gratitude 19, 22, 25, 26, 28, 34, 61, 70, 75, 85, 107, 114, 134, 136, 137, 138, 141, 166, 168, 180, 211, 214, 217, 219, 222, 226, 229, 239, 241, 256, 259, 283, 291, 299, 312, 313, 316, 331, 332, 367, 369, 371

Index

Grief/Loss 11, 14, 19, 37, 48, 58, 66, 85, 88, 94. 98, 110, 113, 120, 128, 133, 137, 145, 165, 183, 201, 204, 205, 210, 226, 233, 247, 248, 250, 259, 261, 269, 273, 275, 282, 293, 295, 298, 301, 306, 313, 318, 326, 327, 355, 356, 357

Holidays 96, 122, 129, 136, 137, 138, 139, 189, 196, 309, 322, 341, 345, 358, 363, 366, 369

Hope 55, 77, 130, 196, 279, 303, 339, 372

Humor 13, 16, 20, 32, 34, 36, 39, 40, 41, 44, 50, 56, 76, 84, 86, 89, 99, 104, 109, 111, 116, 122, 123, 125, 127, 131, 144, 152, 153, 169, 174, 182, 187, 191, 192, 203, 207, 212, 232, 240, 242, 253, 255, 268, 293, 301, 309, 313, 320, 330, 336

Infant 5, 74, 82, 106, 127, 339

Infertility 9, 55, 71, 88, 134, 138, 159, 214, 272

Just for Fun 8, 24, 26, 31, 38, 54, 65, 71, 80, 83, 121, 142, 187, 211, 212, 230, 235, 296, 308, 309, 311, 321, 348

Letting Go 14, 17, 37, 48, 53, 64, 97, 141, 143, 156, 165, 184, 190, 193, 195, 204, 220, 233, 243, 250, 257, 260, 264, 275, 284, 293, 298, 306, 325, 326

Males 15, 40, 52, 61, 87, 89, 96, 109, 119, 122, 126, 153, 159, 169, 171, 182, 195, 215, 224, 226, 267, 288, 312, 322, 325

Medical 42, 75, 77, 109, 114, 120, 124, 158, 197, 215, 256, 235, 339, 371

Parenting Teen 139, 164, 215, 221, 282

Perfection 4, 8, 60, 157, 208, 230, 351, 360

Planning/Scheduling 4, 56, 73, 102, 121, 127, 132, 142, 157, 178, 180, 297, 317, 320, 342

Prayer/Poetry/Metaphors 15, 28, 56, 66, 78, 90, 94, 98, 145, 146, 168, 170, 176, 183, 185, 198, 199, 220, 238, 246, 259, 266, 280, 281, 287, 303, 347, 370

Racism 39, 233

Relationships 147, 220, 346, 364

Resiliency 11, 72, 74, 139, 154, 161, 163, 200, 223, 224, 225, 229, 247, 248, 265, 281, 293, 294, 305, 326, 339, 355, 359, 362, 365

Respite 18, 178, 239, 315

Risk 7, 66, 115, 261, 307

Role Model 12, 16, 30, 31, 38, 43, 50, 59, 72, 87, 103, 163, 171, 178, 201, 203, 217, 224, 234, 244, 249, 267, 268, 271, 283, 300, 305, 311, 335, 349

Roots 9, 15, 44, 58, 59, 71, 138, 186, 201, 225, 245, 290, 310, 336

Index

School/Education 12, 30, 32, 40, 46, 77, 139, 140, 180, 203, 222, 231, 235, 237, 258, 277, 284, 300, 342, 349, 353

Seasons 82, 93, 99, 103, 131, 341

Sibling Groups 128, 248, 286

Single Parent 14, 110, 135, 149, 343

Solutions 4, 9, 12, 21, 32, 34, 36, 38, 44, 51, 54, 60, 63, 65, 71, 73, 79, 80, 83, 86, 87, 101, 102, 105, 107, 108, 118, 127, 129, 132, 140, 142, 144, 147, 148, 152, 154, 157, 161, 164, 173, 174, 180, 186, 188, 189, 195, 197, 198, 200, 203, 208, 210, 216, 222, 224, 228, 230, 238, 239, 248, 249, 256, 262, 264, 274, 290, 292, 296, 297, 310, 315, 317, 319, 337, 338, 365

Special Needs Children 21, 27, 29, 36, 42, 74, 77, 82, 87, 100, 117, 127, 135, 196, 200, 202, 222, 223, 229, 231, 236, 240, 247, 256, 267, 284, 332, 339, 345

Stress 102, 121, 132, 144, 238, 243, 265, 271, 285, 315, 320, 329, 352, 360

Support Systems 23, 35, 68, 75, 85, 112, 152, 160, 187, 194, 200, 207, 208, 209, 244, 262, 285, 300, 307, 352

Survival Skills 2, 34, 38, 57, 58, 90, 91, 105, 118, 119, 129, 161, 163, 164, 167, 174, 188, 194, 213, 216, 263, 266, 271, 278, 320, 362

The System 2, 6, 19, 49, 61, 113, 115, 150, 154, 159, 181, 186, 206, 218, 225, 231, 233, 248, 250, 252, 254, 257, 261, 269, 273, 276, 282, 285, 306, 307, 316, 320, 340, 345, 352, 354, 355, 356, 367

Teenagers 2, 7, 17, 22, 32, 43, 72, 104, 108, 112, 113, 118, 119, 131, 139, 146, 150, 151, 164, 168, 169, 172, 173, 176, 183, 215, 216, 219, 221, 232, 240, 242, 253, 255, 259, 263, 269, 277, 282, 294, 318, 319, 323, 324, 335, 348, 351, 358, 359, 369

Terminations of Parental Rights (TPR) 11, 128, 166, 343, 346, 367

Toddlers 49, 103

Traditions 8, 24, 44, 71, 99, 162, 169, 170, 180, 249, 267, 345, 358, 369

Transition 15, 37, 57, 64, 70, 76, 82, 93, 150, 162, 166, 168, 183, 215, 216, 250, 261, 297

Trust 22, 28, 40, 47, 58, 98, 164, 181, 200, 227, 263, 271, 326

Why We Do This 2, 10, 15, 24, 26, 27, 29, 30, 35, 45, 53, 55, 62, 64, 68, 70, 77, 85, 90, 92, 95, 100, 110, 113, 115, 116, 120, 133, 135, 136, 139, 141, 148, 158, 170, 171, 172, 177, 179, 181, 185, 206, 219, 227, 236, 250, 254, 272, 273, 275, 278, 280, 286, 287, 288, 289, 291, 302, 304, 308, 314, 323, 327, 333, 334, 340, 344, 346, 348, 354, 358, 366, 368, 369, 371